COGNITIVE APPROACHES TO CULTURE

Frederick Luis Aldama, Patrick Colm Hogan,
Lalita Pandit Hogan, and Sue J. Kim, Series Editors

SHAMING INTO BROWN

Somatic Transactions of Race in Latina/o Literature

STEPHANIE FETTA

THE OHIO STATE UNIVERSITY PRESS

COLUMBUS

Copyright © 2018 by The Ohio State University.
All rights reserved.

Library of Congress Cataloging-in-Publication Data is available online at https://catalog.loc.gov.

Cover design by Christian Fuenfhausen
Text design by Juliet Williams
Type set in Adobe Minion Pro

*To my tata, Luis Cota. I feel you with me.
Thank you for your guidance from beyond.*

CONTENTS

Acknowledgments		ix
Preface	Facing Shame	xiii
CHAPTER 1	Introduction to *Shaming into Brown: Somatic Transactions of Race in Latina/o Literature*	1
CHAPTER 2	Latin@/x Literature and the Human Sensorium	28
CHAPTER 3	Soma and Viscera in Oscar "Zeta" Acosta's *The Autobiography of a Brown Buffalo*	66
CHAPTER 4	The Ugly Soma Speaks Out in Octavio Solís's *Lydia*	90
CHAPTER 5	The Political Work of Sophia: The Blessed Soma, the Conversion Narrative, and Shame in Andrés Montoya's *The Ice Worker Sings and Other Poems*	124
CONCLUSION	The Soma and Transdisciplinary Beginnings	161
Notes		167
Bibliography		183
Index		201

ACKNOWLEDGMENTS

IS IT WEIRD to write of love in an academic book? I have loved so much these years—sometimes deeply, other times something like a meaningful exchange between eyes, and at other times, loving came for a season when I believed it would last for life. In all its varieties—even academic—maybe love is the mutual shine of two spirits. It is for me. And I am grateful for the way minds, hearts, smiles, and resources have honed my project and warmed my spirit with their generosity and collaboration. In return, I offer my sincere thanks.

This project began by gathering support for what felt like a bold and kind of scary endeavor—a transdisciplinary book that would take me into the hard sciences and other fields I would have never expected. Thanks to Chandra Talpade Mohanty for encouraging me to take a risk and write *this* book as opposed to a book on a much more conventional topic and treatment; and as I wrote and wrote, and revised and wrote, I am deeply grateful to Marshall Johnson for pushing me to take more and more risks and for believing in the value of this project indefatigably. To Frederick Luis Aldama, I admire you, and your work, which has been critical in developing awareness of the multifaceted nature of Latin@/x literature.

I thank Alberto Sandoval-Sánchez who, after reviewing my first inchoate book proposal, recognized the importance of the project of the opportunity more than the problem of the soma, shame, and the need to pin down the workings of intersectional racialization. Alberto, you warned me of the support I would need to carry out such a difficult project, and I have been fortunate enough to receive just that.

To Karen Mary Davalos for leading an incredibly helpful academic writing seminar sponsored by Mujeres Activas en Letras y Ciencias Sociales (MALCS), the professional association where I can breathe easily and laugh out loud while I learn. Karen Mary, you taught the group the business of writing and publishing, and you modeled for us how impactful a senior Latina scholar can be. I am grateful.

Who are better colleagues than Richard Delgado, Jean Stefancic, and Martín Camps, who read the entire manuscript, guiding me to think further on several points? I especially want to thank Richard and Jean for bringing to light the political valence of this project and its contribution to critical race studies. Thank you all for your enthusiasm for the possibilities for the project, a level of support matched only by Ignacio López Calvo, María Herrera-Sobek, and Alejandro Morales, whose professional development and friendship mean so much to me.

Thanks to Paula Moya, Rita Urquijo-Ruiz, Francisco Lomelí, Jorge Huerta, Sylvia Morin, and Carmen Serrano, to Daniel Weiskopf, Joyce Rupp, Bill Johnson González, William Demastes, and Patrick Riley, for reading chapters and providing instructive feedback and for their camaraderie. I appreciate the support and friendship of Daniel Chacón, Malaquías Montoya, Lezlie Montoya, Maceo Montoya, and Francisco Aragón and their appreciation of my passion for the poetry of the late, great Andrés Montoya, for sharing personal information about Andrés, and for giving me permission to cite Andrés's work broadly.

I thank the anonymous reviewers whose observations, opinions, critiques, and praise pushed me to write a far better book than I would have otherwise. To my editor, Kristen Elias Rowley, who has done a wonderful job shepherding this project when the series traveled from Nebraska to Ohio. Thank you, Kristen, for developing The Ohio State University Press into one of the foremost Latinx academic publishers. I am honored to join OSUP authors.

I want to acknowledge the Northeast Consortium of Latino Scholars (NECLS), a group I have met with twice a year for day-long retreats on scholarship, collegial development, and friendship for the past five years. I especially thank Alberto Sandoval-Sánchez, Mari Castañeda, and Mérida Rúa for founding the group, and Ginetta Candelario for her professional guidance.

I am grateful to the series editorial board: Frederick Luis Aldama, Patrick Colm Hogan, Lalita Pandit Hogan, and Sue J. Kim, for your support for my project throughout. I also acknowledge the College of Arts and Sciences at

Syracuse University for sponsoring my research and the production of this book and, in particular, for the constructive support of my Syracuse University colleagues, especially Silvio Torres-Saillant, Paula Johnson, Jackie Orr, Kal Alston, Alicia Ríos, Kathryn Everly, Harriet Brown, Richard Breyer, Philip Arnold, and the Democratizing Knowledge Collective, the latter, a space on campus where the complications of how I walk on this part of the planet are fully understood.

What would I do without my loyal, incredibly loving friends? I've been blessed by knowing Frances Douglas, José Guillermo Pastrano, Lisa Callahan, Bita Alaghband, Carla Weitkamp, Judy Cortés, Julie Brewer, Ron McDonald Jr., Mónica Rooney Riestra, Shannon Bidwell, and Melanie McCullough who believe in me, no matter what.

I express my deepest gratitude to my mom, Frances, who taught me to love the very things that made others believe we Brown people are socially inferior. To my dad, John, who is always there to lend an ear and who, since I was a teen, continues to tell me: "Stephanie, I am never too busy for you," and to my stepfather, Felix, for teaching me discipline, tenacity, and to stand tall in the face of blows. To my beloved sister, Gina, and brother, Brandon, who are both thoughtful and so funny. Again, to Marshall Johnson for having stood by my side when the chips were down, the days dark, and the nights cold. I also thank Emerson Johnson for those times when you patiently waited for the fun to begin. And some days, it never did. Finally, I recognize Farrokh Frank Alaghband—you are a generous, loving father to our children, but you are also my esteemed friend. I love you all.

Soul-shines abound but none more so than with the three of the most wonderful human beings I know: my children, Helena, Leo, and Max. You have watched your mama in all states—excited and encouraged, heartbroken and depressed, working around the clock for days and weeks (and then months and years), and sometimes, but not often enough, joyful and calm. Our move from SoCal and from the bosom of family and friends took a lot more out of you and me than I could have imagined. It was not your choice to accompany me on this wild but amazing and trying ride in Central New York and now, to Massachusetts. Thank you, mis queridos hijos, for your love, loyalty, faith, and cheer.

Lastly, I thank my Latin@/x students whose eyes shine fierce, wise, and bright in my classroom, sharing who they are and what they know with grace and sophistication. I thank my African American, Native American, Asian, and Asian American students who, in addition to contributing valuable insights, model the uncommon intelligence of knowing how to deeply listen. I thank my White students who are willing to grow more than curious about us so-called Brown people—they allow themselves to feel uncomfortable and sometimes bravely examine their social privilege. Together as a class, each semester, Latin@/x literature opens us up to one another, to understand that we have learned how to hold ourselves back and other's down. I notice sometimes we glow in each other's presence in deep acknowledgment of our common work, our mutual regard, and our openness to what I call love.

I am grateful to you all for your guidance and companionship on a wondrous and sometimes brutal project. I loved sharing the serendipities of my research and the excitement of the possibility of social impact. I appreciate the support in shouldering the resulting disequilibrium from spending years writing on the pain of racial shaming. Together, we grow courageous.

PREFACE

Facing Shame

I WRITE FROM my subject position as a Chicana woman born to a dark-skinned Chicana mother. Her circumstances and mine could help contextualize the importance of the present study, but I am not interested in defining who she is or justifying how I am. While stories and studies on migration, poverty, national unrest, bloodlines, and cultural affiliations are important and have uncovered many truths, I wrote this book because I want to understand the role of the soma—the intelligent, communicative body—in creative literature on racial discourse and in life. Building on the Greek etymology, I employ the term *soma* to chart how the gesture of the physical body evidences the internal response to external stimuli in a highly legible expression that is, some researchers argue, universally intelligible.[1] As I will argue in chapter 1 and throughout this book, the soma is a psychophysical and emotional register of our subjectivity, reflecting our response to our place in the world, and is also the unsuspected generative means by which we carry out political agendas. The soma is a powerful entity left out of hegemonic "method and theory [where] often we cannot recognize anything that is different from what the dominant discourse constructs" (Saldívar-Hull 2000, 46). Hidden in plain sight, the soma is a pervasive yet unexpected site of subjectivity, and pertinent to understanding racialization.

Although my mother's family has lived in the United States for over one hundred years, still we suffer varying degrees of political threat, economic hardship, and conditional social acceptance. The ways our bodies speak and listen in concert with, or in contrast to, how we might like to present ourselves socially, expose suffering intentionally caused. More than bloodlines or cultural ties, the pain I have suffered from somatic violence has led me, like my mother before me, to claim my Chicana identity.

In institutions where I have been relegated to a marginalized group and sometimes excluded from social goods, whether surmised Chicana on the basis of appearance or identified as such by virtue of ancestry or other reasons, I experience institutional racialization and racism much like a physical wall—a vertical force, erect, damning, impenetrable—but at least impersonal in its intersectional racism. More painful and stigmatizing are the interpersonal interactions that single me out for racial shaming.

These one-on-one and two-on-one scenes usually begin with a penetrating look—a look, too long and too deep, that betrays an agenda. More often, without approaching me physically, interlocutors use their somas to disturb my personal sphere with their glare, announced by their eyes, but soon communicated by their whole body posture. Beady eyes perch atop the neck, tense and extended, and a contemptuous half smile steadies on the authority of a tight jaw. Such racializers contravene conventions of polite physical and psychological distance, but their desire is not to know me, Stephanie. Their powerfully clear, imposing somas seek to expose what they consider my ethnic and racial secrets. An aping of intimacy, their incursion intends to pressure me to understand myself as different, inferior, apart from them and from majority culture. These experiences have emotionally carved me out of the imagined collective through a deep psychological whittling, setting me apart and away . . . and leaving me in a state I would later tenderly reframe and reclaim under the term Chicana, a politicized woman with Mexican roots and, in my case, U.S. citizenship. Contrary to what one might expect, these unwelcome encounters have occurred not only with strangers but even with people I know well.

In fact, friends have been among those who have most painfully shamed me into intersectional racialization. One of my earliest memories: I was a naive, eager eight-year-old, so fond of my best friend, Rebecca, a White, middle-class girl who had moved the year before from Texas to Southern California. We usually met up at the playground where we shared secrets, invented games, laughed. Then one day without warning, Rebecca refused to walk with me on our way back from the playground. Instead, she chose to accompany Mavorneen, our Irish-American friend. Confused, I ran up alongside Rebecca asking several times, and later imploring, "Walk with me! Why won't you walk with me?" She barely turned her head to address me, but the rigid arrogance of her back told me what she finally confirmed in words: "You're a dirty Mexican." Rebecca may have been the first, but she was not the last friend in my life to subject me to a *scene of racialization,* a stepped social practice I propose in chapter 1 in which, with or without words, bodies impose social asymmetries through somatic expression. This scene with Rebecca plays itself out again and again in the stories of intersectional racial shaming I am told by my mother, uncle, cousins, friends, and students—and maybe you, too, reader.

Childhood photos allow me to examine my own somatic expression before this scene of racialization, and as I stood afterward. Looking at my younger self, I see my being perceptibly changed by these denigrating encounters: after experiencing intersectional racialization and racist acts, I see my prior vital, energetic self had effectively shrunk. In photos around the period of Rebecca's rejection, I notice my neck stretches out far from my torso, a somatic attempt to quickly assess and hopefully head off the shame that I anticipated lay ahead. My torso appears somewhat retracted, shoulders slightly slouched, pelvis tucked, protecting my internal organs from further harm. In contrast, my eyes record deliberate happiness, a defiant counter expression against the sadness and fear into which I had been initiated. My body posture and facial expression—my soma—register how I was feeling during the time when I came to accept my life would be conditioned by the violence of intersectional racialization and racism. What these photos reveal in image, creative texts detail in words.

Initially, I was surprised to find what I am theorizing are scenes of racialization, a common narrative feature in many Latin@/x creative texts.[2] Regardless of genre, I came across scene after scene, usually appearing in the development of the protagonist's story, specifically indicating how physical postures and actions express feelings and intentions that shape racializing soma. And in text after text, I noticed how these scenes use the soma to accomplish the psychological pressure necessary to impose social marginalization. Specific social technologies of the soma emerged in these steps, shedding light on how human beings actually *transact* race where one comes to make another see herself in racial terms. I identify the soma, exemplified by Rebecca's hateful back, an efficacious, extra-juridical means of subjecting individuals to intersectional racialization where gender, sex, age, class, physical ability, religion, sexual orientation, and other factors dynamize the occasion of its expression.

Similar to the accounts of family and friends as well as my own story, literary characters often describe a time before they understood themselves as Chican@/x or Latin@/x, a time in which they see, in retrospect, they held impressions of social discord but did not see themselves clearly demarcated as social inferiors. Writers posit particular events as the catalyst for this transition, revealing the theoretical importance of an *evolving cognition* in which characters learn and practice how to racialize and how to manage the experience of being racialized. In my study of these narratives, I trace specific social transactions in which corporeal gesticulations of the soma interpersonally cathect racial shame onto the other. This volley, receipt, and response to shame demonstrates first, how feelings power social paradigms (Ioanide 2015), and secondly, how racialization specifically employs shame to give affective materiality to the physical notion of race. How one negotiates this oppressive, largely unspoken, stigmatizing social imposition charges my investigation of the resonances between these literary depictions and lived experience.

In their careful and compelling exposition of these experiences, Latin@/x creative texts are my "unexpected source," to use Saldívar-Hull's words (46), for my theory, providing a literary roadmap of the soma as a primary tool for racial shaming and for expressing the social investment, codification, and successful implementation of the soma in intersectional racialization. This theory helped me appreciate what confused me as a young person about my Brown mother. After a lifetime of subjection to such scenes, I now understand the pained and frustrated look in my mother's nevertheless smiling eyes; the crooked, angry resistant corner of her mouth when she grins. With a twist of her neck and head held back, her eyes can blaze her retort at the whiff of disparagement, while moments later she may display a slightly collapsed torso and pelvis, eyes wide but slightly self-loathing as she crumbles into self-deprecation, railing against a sociopsychological landscape that acts as if she is just *naturally* wrong for some unspecified reason. My mother's contrasting somatic countenance and responses reveal the mark and conditioning wrought by numerous formative scenes of racialization where she resists being made to feel Other and lesser than herself.

No paradox here: somatic expression is ephemeral, changing moment by moment in its environs at the same time, in its resting state, it reveals longstanding hurts and joys. Its temporalities do not confound the soma's succinct register and record of its experience. Is somatic expression any less reliable and real than the fleeting, varying machinations of our minds and spirits? Indeed, as René Descartes elaborated his *cogito*, Princess Elisabeth of Bohemia, his epistolary friend and intellectual peer, challenged his disregard for the experience of the body as an integral source of human subjectivity.[3]

Sometimes I am asked, why study this problem of the soma and shame through Latin@/x literature? Such questions are typical of hegemonic thinking and leave me uneasy and agitated. They attempt to compel nonhegemonic subjects to produce theories in symbolic, rhetorical, and physical forms with which hegemonic forces feel comfortable and, therefore, authoritative. These forces impose practices in an effort to contain others in what they suppose are neutral terms, somehow magically outside the machinations of racializing social agendas. Underlying such questions is a demand to essentialize Latin@/xs in certain forms of academic discourse or compel Latin@/xs to disappear as subjects of study.

As subtle as this effort at co-optation may be, the question is ultimately misdirected. Had I studied the soma in Shakespeare's work, nary a critic would believe justification necessary. I have no desire to quantify or qualify Latin@/xs along any rubric: the dynamic I study has nothing to do with Latin@/xs in terms of who or what they are or are supposed to be. I study racial shaming as a disturbing and powerful phenomenon inflicted both institutionally and interpersonally on individuals some refer to as Hispanic or maybe, as a concession, Latina/o and more recently, Latinx. The use of these terms by certain parties gentrifies the contempt that lies behind the hegemonic discourse that attaches the stigma of Brown through the generic "Mexican" or "Spanish," just as it does in the more overtly derogatory terms: *beaner, spic, greaser, brown nigger, mongrel, illegal, wetback,* etc. In line with Linda Martín Alcoff's recent work on Whiteness, so-called race is not a problem of the Latin@/xs or other communities of color: the notion of race and subsequent racism is a manufactured problem of White interest and culture (2015). For those interested in race as a term or category, there are excellent studies specifically addressing *latinidad,* many of which make the case for its viability as a political construct, while others highlight the unassimilable contradictions and differences that such a pan-ethnic term connotes. I refer my reader to those studies because I am not interested here in race per se but in racialization, a study of social practices that conduct hegemonic interests and normalize interpersonal and institutional interactions that coerce certain people to feel "Brown."[4]

Inspired by my experiences in learning about racialization from a transdisciplinary approach, I leave it to readers to decide how, where, and whether my work will be of use to them.[5] I offer the soma as a dynamic entity to study racial shaming in particular, but I propose that somatic analysis may be useful as a general method to unpack the body as a register of subjectivity in various disciplines. Scholars of some disciplines, and particularly literary scholars, may feel discomfort with taking something as ephemeral as somatic expression—a feeling, an attitude, a complex physical gesture—seriously. Is a fleeting corporeal expression worthy of scholarly attention? I counter this stance throughout *Shaming into Brown: Somatic Transactions of Race in Latina/o Literature,* but here I assert that our bodies are fundamental to how we live and how we make meaning. Our everyday self-perception as mind-dominated individuals denies that our human condition is thoroughly interpolated by the intelligence of our material organism and simultaneously influenced as "beings amongst" in a social field. We bring the soma—this physical, emotive, and social register of our subjectivity—to the text as we do to our lives. This more complex conception of what it means to be human has been widely accepted by scholars in several fields in the social sciences, and by researchers of cognitive science, biology, and neuroscience.

Other fields and social practices employ, or conversely, interrogate narrative. As an example, as legal scholar Gerald Torres often says, court cases are about storytelling. They seek to determine the truth through a process of contrasting the facticity of narratives, but narrative also shapes how facts can be known and who can be known. Critical race theorists have shown how the reliance of the law on hegemonic legal narratives has unearthed the cultural incompetence of judges and juries. These theorists advocate counter-storytelling, using narrative to make the complex situation of raced people legible to hegemonic judges and juries (Delgado and Stefancic 1993). Similarly, scientists formulate hypotheses in narratives, the form of discourse they deem appropriate to present a problem for research. Later, conclusions are drawn in relation to whether and how the hypothesis told in the original narrative proved true or untrue. Yet, despite the use of narrative across nonliterary fields, and despite the work on the embodied mind in cognitive literary studies, feelings in affect theory, and body studies, many literary studies continue to look askance at the body's patent role in the act of reading, in connecting the role of narrative to our lived experience, and, specific to my interests, the importance of the soma in social practices in literature as in life.

Despite self-professed progressive political leanings in practice, many literary scholars seem protective to any threat to the Cartesian self, employing modes of analysis that sustain the notion of a mind-dominated, individualistic literary subject, and its reader. This oddly conservative practice stands in contrast to the facility with which other disciplines engage our disciplinary subject, in general terms, narrative. We literary scholars should consider our disciplinary sublimation (if not rejection) of the material body in our work. We simply cannot ignore society's reliance on many forms of reading that impact the material functioning of the body. Nor can we isolate the experience of and by the flesh in some incommunicable realm such as the abject. Much work has been done on reading bodies as social surfaces, in gender performance, as inscription sites, but rarely do we consider the actual workings of the body, especially in relation to the expressive soma. Why do other fields claim the authority to challenge issues of ontology while many literary scholars remain so bound to Cartesian norms?

Let me alert the reader that throughout *Shaming into Brown*, I use "we" frequently, rather than write in an authoritative phantom voice typically ensconced in scholarly declaratives. I do so because the social practices studied are so culturally embedded that, like it or not, whether as racializers, subjects of racialization, or witnesses to scenes of racialization, I contend we all participate in racialization in some way. I make this claim based on what I have learned by analyzing somas in Latin@/x literature. Racialization and racism are vividly portrayed as moment-by-moment exertions of social power expressed and imposed by the soma. The power to racialize and to commit acts of racism is not exclusively held in the hands of hegemonic subjects to be wielded against given other(s). Power shifts across space and time.

The same actors in another place can occupy a different position of power, and the racialized can assume the position of the racializer. The contextual nature of power does not mean that all harms are equal, nor does it negate historical legacies that continue to legitimate institutional and interpersonal oppressions of Latin@/xs and other groups. However, as with many forms of oppression, we all, when the occasion arises, may take advantage of our temporal ability to subjugate another. Allow me to point to my own experience again. It pains me to recall how, in middle school, I ignored the migrant farmworker kids who stood out so starkly against the blindingly intolerant 1980s White culture of Irvine, California. And perhaps like you, admitting to my abuse of my relative social power against others did not come easily. I turned my back on these first-generation migrant classmates; defiantly, and in my situational hegemony, I was baldly dismissive. Many of us have internalized shaming racist attitudes and thus frequently commit racism against ourselves or our kin as well as against those we consider out-group members.

This focus on the process of racializing does not obviate responsibility or in any way equalize grievances. Racializing by a member of the dominant group stands apart from other acts of racializing and racism committed by the racialized, most notably because of the support the culturally dominant racializer receives from peers and from institutions of the State. By pointing to racialization and racism as processes, we may come to understand why we are (in)variably victims of a retrograde human sociality, impeding ourselves and others from fully appreciating our respective humanity. Accordingly, I entreat the reader to have the willingness to deeply consider their own role in these entrenched practices of U.S. culture. I humbly invite you to accompany me on a read that may expose your biases with respect both to literary interpretation and to people. Racializing behaviors and racist attitudes may surface, and with them, perhaps you will acknowledge the pain you've suffered—and perhaps the pain you have caused.

CHAPTER 1

Introduction to *Shaming into Brown: Somatic Transactions of Race in Latina/o Literature*

YEARS AGO, I sat down on my couch, coffee close at hand, to read for a second time Piri Thomas's 1967 autobiography *Down These Mean Streets*. I anticipated Thomas's prescient analysis of intersectional racism, and of the social imperative to accept assignment in U.S. and transnational racial schemas, glossed in historical circumstance—New York metropolitan area circa 1930–50s—of Piri's life. The son of a Cuban father and a Puerto Rican mother, Piri eventually ventures to other regions of the United States and beyond where he continues to encounter the intersectional racism he suffered as a young person, the narrative argues, a global phenomenon. Like most Latin@/x[1] texts, through the prism of Piri's life, his autobiography clearly establishes a "most rudimentary examination of the history of the Americas making it clear that Latina/os and Latin Americans have been racialized—both within their national boundaries and vis-a-vis the United States" (Jiménez Román 2007, 326). But I am not reading *Down These Mean Streets* to study the impact of Latin American racial hierarchies on U.S. Latin@/xs or his personal subjection to global racism against Blackness.

I am rereading this first-person account to see how Piri sorts out his racial identity, how he negotiates his ethnic identification as a New York "Porty-Ree-can" amid U.S. nationalistic conceptions of identity that so deeply affect him, they condition his familial relations (Thomas [1967] 1997, 121).[2] In this second read, I want to closely study how Piri puts cultural and national affiliations in tension with the implicit and strident cultural demand to make him see himself Black. Curiously, I find myself deep in *feeling* rather than thought while reading the following passage:

> "Say, *paisan*," one guy said, "you even buying from us *paisans*, eh? Man, you must wantta be Italian."
>
> Before I could bite that dopey tongue of mine, I said, "I wouldn't be a guinea on a motherfucking bet."
>
> "Wha-at?" said Rocky, really surprised. I didn't blame him; I was surprised myself. His finger began digging a hole in his ear, like he hadn't heard me right. "Wha-at? Say that again?"
>
> I could feel a thin hot wetness cutting itself down my leg. I had been so ashamed of being so damned scared that I had peed on myself. And then I wasn't scared any more; I felt a fuck-it-all attitude. I looked real bad at Rocky and said, "Ya heard me. I wouldn't be a guinea on a bet." (31)

While there are scenes that characterize Piri's resisting, negotiating, and begrudging acceptance of his social location as a Black Latino man,[3] I offer this long passage from *Down These Mean Streets* because when I read of Piri's sudden urination, I realize that what I've understood has been most compellingly expressed by Piri's soma—the perceptive and expressive body—a key register of Piri's subjectivity throughout his autobiography.

Despite Piri's bravado in rejecting the Italian-Americans' assertion of ethnic and racial and thus social superiority, he pees, and I suddenly grasp the degree of threat he feels. While his face and words say one thing, embarrassingly, his body overrides his social presentation to express deep fear about the physical and psychological pain to which he will be subjected. Hurtful language and the threat of ensuing physical harm course through his body; its unmediated response of unwilled urination compels Piri to face how he truly feels—afraid, alone, vulnerable, and shamed. This recognition is somatic, giving Piri physical information of threat. Piri acknowledges his soma's communication but soldiers on with the fight and accepts the beating he will take as a matter of racialized pride.

I wince as I hear, through Piri's description, the expletives "nigger" and "spic" (24) and imagine myself in his place, in the emergency room with an eye filled with gravel. Disturbed, I put down the book, and I open an online video where I witness Seattle police officers beating a man who they believe is Latino. The youth contorted on the ground looks dazed and withdrawn, perhaps a protective physiological reaction of his somatic body to make psychological space to comprehend why he is being beaten, or to disassociate from the abuse. The police receive a call; they have detained the wrong man. One of the officers helps the young man to his feet, directs him to regain his balance on the hood of an automobile, and sends the man on his way without apology (Helgadottir 2010).

As the video ends, the eyewitness filming the brutality asks the man: "Do you know why they beat you?" Still coming to, the man responds smiling: "I don't know, they just knocked me down and kicked me in the head" (Helgadottir 00:49). The police have thrashed this man, yet he kneejerks a perfunctory smile. My eyes wide and startled, I notice my breathing has become shallow, my heartbeat quickens—my body's response to the shock of such deliberately senseless violence. I use the word "senseless" but the unjustified infliction of pain is ironically *sense-making*—the experiential conduit through which the notion of race acquires sense, giving the term *race* social weight but also the aura of physical materiality. Inflicting psychological and physical pain on those deemed intersectionally Brown has become a somatic semiotic communicating the shameful wrongness of difference, a process that creates the social power of *race*, laid out for careful examination in Latin@/x creative literature.

Throughout *Shaming into Brown*, I focus on the soma as the critical apparatus to study the role of shame in a stepped process that transacts intersectional racialization and racism. Because *race* cloaks ideology as empirical fact, I will resist employing the term. I use the term *racialization* to indicate an entrenched U.S. cultural practice of using phenotype and performative markers to designate a subcategory of people as separate and inferior. I employ the term *racism* to indicate a politic that seeks subordination of sectors of the population as out-groups based on the *perception* of human variation.[4]

I make these distinctions in line with other scholars who critically engage racialization and racism in empirical studies while disavowing the claim that *race* has biological legitimacy (Bonilla-Silva [2006] 2013; Flores and Rosaldo 2007; Gracia 2007; Hurtado 1996; Jiménez Román and Flores 2010; Lima 2007; Menchaca 2010). Research on implicit racial cognition, unlike that on gender recognition, dispels the notion that we are hardwired to identify race. To date, there are no points in the brain that reliably illuminate in fMRI scans to support the notion of perceiving phenotypic difference by natural design, leading researchers to argue that, unlike gender or age, we are *socially* scripted to perceive race. Regardless, studies show that what we qualify as race is one of the first assessments we make of another.

I return to my computer screen where the police beat this supposedly Latino man, but who knows where the man is from? The man is beaten for

Brown in accordance with centuries of such abuses against *Mexicans* of the United States, where *Mexican* is often used as a derogatory that summarily signifies Latin@/x Otherness despite different cultures, ethnicities, and physical appearances that such diverse populations encompass. The police punctuate the beating with some racially coded expletives such as, "I am going to beat the fucking Mexican piss out of you, homey!" (Helgadottir 2010, 00:14), but most of the emotional tone of the footage comes from *how* the police officers kick the man's torso, head, and legs.[5]

This innocent man could have been any of my cousins, who probably have had similar experiences. (If so, are they too ashamed to tell the family?) As a viewer, I locate these feelings in a physical sensation in my chest, now thrust forward and tense, a posture defending against another feeling that I locate in my burning cheeks, and I realize I am feeling shame. Combining what I have just read in *Down These Mean Streets* with the video footage, the shame I feel arises because it is as if it was me being beaten for Brown, as if it was my body suddenly betraying me with urine. The shame Piri feels, like that of the unnamed man who ashamedly smiles after the beating, somatically registers their torment in me, my body recognizes the power others have over my being too. Racial shaming morally excuses such treatment. I brace myself to defend against the psychosocial and physical pain engendered by the hateful encounter I am reading about, another I am viewing, and those I have personally experienced growing up Chicana in Orange County, California. I am safe in my home at the moment, but shame and fear arise because of the somatic relationship we share with one another, where the notion of the separateness of my body does not completely disconnect their experiences from my own.

While the video can be replayed for analysis, the inner thoughts, insider information kept between the officers, and particular social arrangements are visually palpable but left unspecified, whereas the passage cited from *Down These Mean Streets* narrates specifically how racialization works. An unflinching rendering of the pain caused by racializing, Thomas's narrative elaborates a cognitive practice of contentious negotiations between who Piri is in his own eyes, and who and how Piri socially registers in the eyes of others. Perhaps this is a reason *Down These Mean Streets* has been banned in different states throughout the years. Below, I describe scenes of racialization in which Piri navigates his life through a collective fiction where he is a social inferior.

The shame *of* race has been compellingly argued in critical ethnic studies by Frances Negrón-Muntaner (2007a and b), Ginetta Candelario (2007), and José A. Cobas, Jorge Duany, and Joe R. Feagin (2009) as a heterogenous but nevertheless hemispheric discourse. Like Thomas's project, these studies explicate colonialist projects in analytical terms where we learn that in order to socially navigate, we must understand ourselves through the lens of intersectional racialization.

The eloquence of Negrón-Muntaner's theorization of shame in the term *boricua* and Candelario's reveal of Dominican Blackness "behind the ears" are supported by the findings in studies by Cobas, Duany, and Feagin. Shame becomes a central enterprise in some of the work of writer, scholar, and filmmaker Frances Negrón-Muntaner, who argues the term *boricua* resounds pride at the same time it marks shame as an affective colonial legacy (Gonzalez 2004, 1352). She argues the term *boricua* captures an historic sense of self before colonialism, which she qualifies specifically in affective terms, a time before racial shame.[6] From a national sense of shame, in "Looking Good" (2007a), Negrón-Muntaner identifies shame as a somatically conveyed affectivity that transpires in "the interplay of glances—and the relationships made flesh in them—that produce us as worthy or undesirable bodies, unacceptable or permissible objects of violence, and as wanted or undesirable subjects of any given polis" (428). While Negrón-Muntaner signals the soma in racial shaming, Muñoz specifically addresses body posture and *latinidad,* arguing that racialization leads Latin@/xs to "feeling brown, feeling down" (2006), a depressive (in my terms) somatic countenance, whereas literary scholar Laura Halperin focuses on the burden of racial shaming as a physical, psychological, and geopolitical harm (2015). Literary scholar Suzanne Bost connects Chicana writer feminists, illness, and disability to argue that, although we may feel down, constellations of oppression have also given rise to cutting-edge aesthetics and theory (2010) to the experience of nineteen academic women in testimonials in Elisa Facio and Irene Lara's edited collection *Fleshing the Spirit: Spirituality and Activism in Chicana, Latina, and Indigenous Women's Lives* (2014).

These formative thinkers do not express the promise of equanimity and good health in the face of the burden of intersectional racial shame but argue that, despite its nontranscendental nature, intersectional racialization can nevertheless motivate spiritual practices that are also intellectual critiques, motivate community activism, and provide other paradigms for living. Implicitly, these projects articulate somatic processes and practices through which we learn, name, and expose intersectional racialization in a daily collective craft of shaming, harming, hurting, and gaining a sense of superiority over another, and more often than we would like to admit, we physically and psychologically debilitate one another. Whereas these theoretical and creative texts focus on Latin@/xs lives thus conditioned, I focus on the affective social practice of racialization itself.

Unnamed but underlying these critical texts is a cognitive schema powerfully infiltrating our relations with others that, forty years earlier, Thomas laid out in creative terms: "Pops, why we always on the outs? Is it somethin' I done or somethin' I am?" reads the opening epigraph (1). The epigraph situates the text's central question: the breadth and depth of racializing Latino Blackness infiltrating his sense of self and conditioning his social relations. Later, his light-skinned brothers will admit to prejudice and shame over Piri's Blackness among neighbors, where outside the neighborhood, Piri's Blackness and latinidad more poignantly influence the fate of his relationships with friends and lovers. Similarly, his rapport with strangers and institutionally-identified characters such as teachers, police, judges and juries, and employers is tainted for Black over the course of his life and travels. Familial prejudice implicates the Thomas family to the extent of intimacies with endemic psychosocial and physical violence of multiple colonialisms (i.e., Puerto Rican, Cuban, and U.S.). An early contemporary employment of a trans-American imaginary (Moya and Saldívar 2003), Thomas's autobiography delivers the shamed soma as key to unpacking the pernicious centrality of U.S. racialization and racism in multiple realms of social relations. Thus, what initially appears to be unfortunate familial prejudice reiterates in concentric circles of racializing interaction.

Racialization uses the soma to unleash its will-to-power over another through shaming with the intention of making the other feel inherently flawed. An emotional assault emitted and received largely through somatic expression, shame drives through the malice perceptible in the scowl on the policeman's face while he kicks; through the dumbstruck expression of the supine, abused Latino; and in Piri's uncontrollable body function in contrast to his battle stance. All emote the volley of shame under the made-up rubric of biological difference. Reading, watching, and recalling in this moment, I become aware of the intensity of shame marking this succession of interactions, and I feel slightly nauseous.

More than the study of individual experiences, in *Shaming into Brown*, I look at literary renderings of the cultural practice of racial shaming, a common lived experience for Latin@/xs that occurs in interpersonal exchanges but also is deeply embedded in laws, legal interactions, hiring practices, loan policies, marketing strategies, and more. As I will present, creative texts powerfully illustrate scientific findings of the harm inflicted by intense and/or repetitive acts of shaming. I argue racialization uses the pain of shame as a psychosocial strategy to generate the material experience of socially confected categorical inferiority, an ontology threatening the life conditions and well-being of Latin@/xs and other marginalized peoples. As a social and psychological assault on another, racial shaming seeks social submission and emotional internalization.

From this optic, we can discern the potency of the soma that underlies social discourse on race where, in the case of legal theory for example, debates generally focus on racist language and overt physical violence—the effects of these processes—but seldom study mechanisms through which racialization and racism transact. The important work on hate speech by critical race theorists Richard Delgado and Jean Stefancic (2004) identifies the impact of racist speech and the need for legal address while sociologists Joe R. Feagin and Karyn D. McKinney's *The Many Costs of Racism* (2003) presents evidence of the physical and psychological harms incurred when we are subjected to racist speech. The latter note the frequency and qualitative subjection that materially affects the body with elevated blood pressure, hypertension, depression, and other ailments. In the face of gross racist acts, popular discussion generally does not move beyond whether racialization or racism has truly occurred. Long-standing social practices are instead treated as isolated events, episodic, and studied after the fact—after the job has been denied, the innocent has been beaten or killed—beyond the everyday, where we so often employ our somatic bodies to oppress. Studies on the cumulative effect of life under intersectional racialization are critically important to track these harms; however, the paucity of knowledge on the semiotics of racialization and racism is so marked, it seems almost intentional.

Literary texts illustrate that racialization operates through habituated, socially cued behaviors that are not readily subject to intentional control. Because the soma works at the organismic level—at the level of musculature, organs (such as the stomach and the bladder), sudden corporeal sounds and actions (e.g., burping, stomach rumbles, crying, gasping)—the soma expresses what one believes and feels in an unmitigated fashion. Thus, when the police officers racialize the "Mexican" over the course of a beating, their posture, facial expressions, and the tone of the sounds they make (whether in semantic or sonorous vocalizations) communicate their fear, desire, and contempt for him as much as do the blows themselves. These scenes raise questions I seek to address: Could the police officers beat the man without the attendant somatic expression of contempt and rage? How does their somatic expression confer their racialization of the man?

Creative texts illustrate shame, a critical tool in many Latin@/x texts across literary genres, and inculcate "race" onto others through *scenes of racialization*, key narrative events presenting an interaction in which one party assumes the position of racializer who shames the other into believing him or herself different and unworthy. Thus confronted, the person-cum-Latin@/x responds variably, but scenes of racialization conclude with the acknowledgment that he or she will now be seen as Brown (a catch-all name for terms like "Hispanic," "beaner," "Mexican," "Spanish," "wetback," "illegals"), thus pressured into an "identity-in-difference" as Chicana studies scholar Norma Alarcón theorizes (1990) and a social problem as performance studies scholar José Esteban Muñoz argues (2007). Being treated as a problem (Muñoz 2007) is a process that uses shame to impose an internal notion of self as inferior, a member of a socially constructed and stigmatized race. My study of scenes of racialization shows this process to be a social technology discernable in lived experience and qualitatively rendered in literature.

We must recall that we readers and writers are also social beings who are subject to these processes to which we also subject others. We carry the cultural prism of racialization and racism from our lives to the text, and from the text to our lives, affecting how we cognitively make sense of it, draw conclusions, form opinions, and ultimately how we decide to act. In fact, before we open a book, we are alerted to how the subject matter of the book has been scripted within the U.S. publishing market. As Manuel M. Martín-Rodríguez (2003) argues, from book cover design to back cover reviews, books are codified as Latin@/x and marketed as Latin American-esque, sometimes in derogation of the author's preferences. Often employing a childlike naïf aesthetic and pastel color palette in cover art, publishers extra-diegetically conspire to racially codify these texts, suggesting they are less-than-serious literature and not quite *American* before we even begin reading (131).

The research I cite in this study will show that reading, like all cognitive tasks, *is* also a corporeal process. The task of reading employs our minds in an embodied way, beginning with the most obvious—yet overlooked and underanalyzed—fact that we use our eyes to read words, but we also use our senses and other somatic faculties to process actions and images, a topic explored in chapter 2. A process driven not *by* but *through* sense data, our corporeal engagement in the act of reading allows us to flesh out characters' voices, smells, and touch that are perhaps intimated rather than detailed, such that reading comprehension entails that we fill in the textual nuance and gap with rich sensory detail (Margolin 2003) that I argue we provide through an imagined community of somas. Perhaps less in our mind's eye than in our embodied minds, we conceive of fictionalized others through somatic resonance.[7]

The multidisciplinary sources I employ illustrate racialization as a problem of the social real, firmly centered on the sociality of our physiology, but uniquely elaborated in creative literature. I draw support for my thesis from the social and natural sciences to argue that the soma is an effective primary social actor. Specifically, I propose *somatic analysis,* the semiotic study of somas as method. Here in *Shaming into Brown,* somatic analysis sheds light on how the body conducts intersectional racialization and racism. In addition to providing reading pleasure, I argue creative literature cogently identifies social problems, often providing valuable qualitative insights well in advance of other disciplines. I hope readers will find somatic analysis a productive nexus between creative texts and these fields.

THE PAIN OF SHAME

Racial shaming, like other forms of shame, seeks to convey an intractable condition of self. Psychological studies show that shame, evident in infancy, is one of the most painful feelings humans experience (Tomkins [1962–92] 2008, vols. 1–4). In addition to physical ailments, many psychological theorists, practitioners, and researchers have concluded that repeated experiences of shame result in lowered self-esteem, social withdrawal, depression, substance abuse, deviant behavior, and suicide (Jacoby [1994] 2015; Johnson and Moran 2013; Kaufman [1989] 1996; Hunte, Haslyn E. R., Kathryn King, Margaret Hicken, Hedwig Lee, and Tene T. Lewis 2013; H. B. Lewis 1971, 1987a, 1987b, 1987c; M. Lewis [1992] 1995; Nathansan 1987, [1989] 2004, 1994; Tomkins [1962–92] 2008; Wurmser 1981, 1987). A globalizing assessment, shame generates "humiliated fury [that] has very little place to go except back down on the self, when one has been seduced, to become a component of one's humiliation," explains psychoanalytic shame theorist Helen Block Lewis (1987b, 100). Shame threatens marginal belonging and marks the shamed despicable, unworthy of society's respect or respect for the self, a situation where one becomes Other to oneself. To this point, clinical psychology professors Gershen Kaufman and Lev Raphael state, "Shame is the most disturbing experience individuals ever have about themselves; no other emotion feels more deeply disturbing because in the moment of shame the self feels wounded from within" ([1983] 1991, xiii–xiv). The social and moral efficacy of the pain of shame follows a logic that may claim origin in the Bible: "Blows that wound cleanse away evil" (Proverbs 20:30). Kaufman and Raphael further note that shame leads to social exclusion and often to self-exclusion that psychological theorists Silvan Tomkins (1911–91), and Alexander Lowen (1910–2008) discern in one's body posture.

The psychological state of shame has postural manifestations that shield the self from others. When one is ashamed, the soma almost unconsciously takes the form of a slouched upper body, eyes downcast, chin toward chest, and sometimes face flushed. In the case of racial shaming which, rather than being an isolated event, burdens one's life to varying degrees, the soma develops a habituated stance. I will elaborate on the soma argued in postural descriptions in Tomkins and Lowen's theories in chapter 2's discussion of the human sensorium and scenes of racialization, but here I note that their work on bodily positions cues specific beliefs, personal histories, and goals, which, despite individual experience, typically stay within an identifiable range (Tomkins [1962–92] 2008, 123–33; Lowen [1958] 2006, 145–351).

The soma actively responds to shame, whether it is momentary or longstanding, but the pattern of pain can differ in intensity, depending on the incident. Humiliation, the more intense expression of shame, is generally limited to the duration of the humiliating experience, but humiliation can have an affective afterlife and become a contributing factor in the psychopathology of the shamed self-evident in the soma. Timidity and shyness are also somatically expressed where the torso, neck, and head retracts downward and inward, avoiding or limiting engagement with the world. This soma can be read as a preemptive tactic to ward off shaming and humiliation by making oneself less perceptible to others and thus less susceptible to shaming.[8] Erica L. Johnson and Patricia Moran paraphrase clinical psychiatry professor Léon Wurmser, who noted shaming can become so severe and/or chronic that "the shamed person feels his/her own perceptions to be flawed and dirty," and thus concludes that shame "blocks engagement with the world altogether" (Johnson and Moran 2013, 6).

The specifics of what triggers racial shaming and how Latin@/xs respond are compendious subjects with much local variation. A *flux* of perceptions rather than a finite set of traits, racializing Brownness as a shameful form of being is a staple practice in many parts of the United States. We see the collusion of racial shaming in generating the specter of a near-future Brown United States. Brownness is treated as a social virus currently expanding, as Richard Rodriguez argues, to include East Indians and Middle Easterners (2003).[9] Alongside the government's preferred term, *Hispanic*,[10] the terms *Latino/a*, *Latin@*, and most recently, *Latinx* have gained popularity as pan-ethnic determinations for people across gender identifications who affiliate or are otherwise tied to Latin America. Muñoz argues *latinidad* arises from the common feeling of "'apartness together' through sharing the status of being a problem"[11] against an imagined national whole (Flores and Rosaldo 2007, 444). I argue that such terms are premised on a social practice of shaming that makes heterogeneous people into a political and cultural collective against this stance.

At the level of national culture, the Latin@/x literary texts and research findings I have gathered lead me to question American anthropologist Ruth Benedict's ([1946] 1954) well-known assessment of guilt as the dominant emotional method for compelling conformity in the United States. In her cross-cultural study of the U.S. and Japan, Benedict notes that guilt motivates nations to make amends for wrong deeds (e.g., reparations paid to the interned during WWII), and, in so doing, supports the dominant culture's self-view as humble, earnest, and capable of regret. Shame, on the other hand, naturalizes subordination through steady condemnation, both subtle and overt. Benedict's argument casts the United States as a guilt culture, and while this may be true for hegemonic subjects, my research challenges the universality across U.S. populations of Benedict's claim.

My analysis of Latin@/x literature and my reflections on lived experience show it is not guilt but shame that structures and maintains U.S. race relations. Taking the position of racial shamer has become constitutive of hegemonic identity. To tease this distinction out a bit, racists may recognize that they are guilty of racism, and so elect to change. The racialized, on the other hand, are irrevocably shamed into social stigma and cannot simply choose to change. The racialized can only hope for alterations in the color line that will bring them into the fold (as in the case of Germans, Jews, Irish, and Italians).[12] By ignoring the nationalist politics of guilt versus shame, hegemonic forces tend to naturalize racial shaming as a sensitivity of particular individuals of color, thus attributing the cause of marginalization to personal weakness. Normalizing shame as an experience internal to the individual rather than an oppressive social practice relieves hegemonic subjects from the responsibility of examining shame as a socially inflicted harm.

I agree with Muñoz, who argues that considering some people Brown is a "capitalist ethic that attempts to 'manage' groups through socially toxic and racist protocols" (2007, 444), and further contend that this social management takes place through racial shaming—a systemic paradigm carried out interpersonally by racializers in situational hegemony. What I want to make clear is that racial shaming is not limited to Whites. That is, Latin@/xs sometimes racially shame los *morenos* [African Americans], los *chinos* [Asians and Asian-Americans], los *arabes* [Arabs or Middle Easterners], and out-group Latin@/xs such as los *mojados* [undocumented Mexicans]. Pressures redouble for Latin@/xs in their ancestral country, reflected in shaming terms such as *agringado* y *pocha*. Latin@/xs also inflict in-group shame through political expressions such as "coconut," "Tío Tomás," and "vendido" (variations on the notion of the political sell-out).[13]

Different than these racializing words, in-group racializing or intraracializing cannot attribute social stigma except at the most local of levels. Publicly discernable, affective shaming expresses social rejection of an individual, elucidating sociologist Erving Goffman's observation on racialized stigma where "an individual who might have been received easily in normal social intercourse possesses a trait that can obtrude itself upon attention and turn those of us whom he meets away from him, breaking the claim that his other attributes have on us" ("us" refers to what Goffman calls "normal" or the nonstigmatized; [1963] 2009, 5). Consequently, disgust, contempt, anger, and fear become affective capital used by racializers to claim harm done by the mere existence of another punishable by shaming. In a scripted reaction, the racializer assumes Whiteness by simultaneously taking up the stance of social victim.

In fact, the racializer's offended affect *shamelessly* justifies deauthorizing and constraining claims of foul by those it targets.[14] Irving Thalburg (1972) long ago argued that racists—who coincidently he codified as suffering from "visceral" racism—do not necessarily feel forms of hatred while carrying out racializing and racist acts. He argues racists have so thoroughly adopted a habituated attitude toward Blacks (Thalburg's subject of inquiry), they do not need to necessarily feel hate or disgust in order to harm. Latin@/x literature shows similar treatment when describing racist behavior of White liberals, who much like the racist, may feel no overt adversity. I agree with Thalburg that this habituated attitude may obviate racializers from recognizing their disdain at the moment of racializing, but it also indicates an overall cultural attitude that daily impregnates our social sphere with latent and potent contempt and disgust for Latin@/xs and other marginalized populations. These feelings normalize into an affective backdrop that conceals one's awareness of how or how much negativity one is feeling or practicing against a person they consider Latin@/x.

Racial shaming efficaciously maintains the psychosocial bonds of racialization and racism on those colored Brown while materializing the racializer's claim to superiority with or without conscious feeling. The racialized may experience a range of feelings in response to racial shaming, but the range of their expression is bounded by the shamer's tolerance. In this system, the racializer usually does not abet shaming until or unless the racialized responds in a way sanctioned by the racializer (per larger cultural scripts). We have discussed the postures of the racialized's shamed somatic expression, which, in some cases, is the only response the racializer will accept. Goffman offers a list of socially nonpenalized responses that can be summarized as ignoring or feigning agreement with racist comments, humor, and deference; a list designed so that the racializer can feel comfortable with his or her racism. Latent promises of provisional acceptance of the well-behaved racialized include honorary and temporary status as "normals" (Goffman's term; 12).[15]

Similarly, Alison M. Jaggar (1989) argues that women are pressured to stay within a range of responses to oppressive behavior. I extend Jaggar's critique to the case of intersectional racialization and racism where responses of anger are "considered wrong and denied to marginalized groups precisely because these emotions challenge cultural hegemony" (Diaz-Strong, Luna-Duarte, Gómez, and Meiners 2014, 9), thus protecting racializers from confronting how they racialize and the effects of racialization on their interlocutors (Goffman 114–25). These responses sideline the natural reactions of anger, resentment, and outrage, variations on feeling that Audre Lorde argues thwart their productive use to birth change ([1984] 2007, 124, 131). These scholars theorize what Latin@/x texts narratively illustrate: tiers of mutually informed but separate repertoires of affect,[16] emotion (a mental elaboration of affect), and the soma in racializing in this study of corporeal gesture.

The soma's role in enacting and maintaining intersectional racialization is a fundamental expression of social asymmetries. Racializers deploy contempt, "dissmell" (Tomkins' term; [1962–92] 2008),[17] anger, rage, and disgust at will, but selectively tolerate shame, humiliation, depression, self-contempt, startle, joy, or affection from the racialized and then, only to a degree, depending on the context deemed appropriate or useful to the racializer. Affect and emotion are innate human capacities lived out in the United States in a highly prejudicial fashion, in that a full range of display of human emotion is conditioned by one's social position. The more social power one has, the bigger the range of emotion s/he can display. The color line is strong and unforgiving in this regard. Some intrepid racialized interlocutors who freely respond to racial shaming do so at their peril, and too often, risk their lives.

To this point, Piri's account of words and somatic expression that landed him in the hospital provides a template to understand the social logic operating in lived experience. Somatic and verbal assumptions of peer-to-peer relations with a Texas state trooper set off a chain of events that found Sandra Bland dead. The central issue in the Bland death was that on July 13, 2015, she challenged a police officer's right to arrest her for failing to use her turn signal. That challenge was met with the officer's increased hostility and derision to which Bland affectively responded with normal irritation, an expected degree of anger, and an overall empowered stance, refusing to comply with the officer's bogus demand for her to step out of her vehicle without cause. Bland errored in expressing a typical measure of feelings and emotions in this situation; she crossed an unspoken line of racialized tolerances for verbal and somatic expression, which the officer did not accept. He took umbrage, brutally pulled her out of her car, after which he handcuffed her, and took her to jail where she died three days later.

In an interview with retired New York Police Detective Harry Houck, Houk confirms my argument when he characterizes Bland as "very arrogant from the beginning," (CNN News report, July 22, 2015, 1:14). He refers to her nondeferential somatic expression accompanied by her objectively reasonable words. For Houck, the officer in question, Bland fell outside of that unspoken range of accepted feelings for the racialized and the consequences were deadly.[18] Whether by murder or suicide, Bland was deeply and unequivocally punished for daring to show frustration, upset, and self-respect. Bland was called arrogant simply because she refused to somatically and verbally communicate submission to intersectional racial shame.[19]

Whether we openly express dissent or cloak our feelings of injustice in a deferential attitude, we perennially defend against racial shaming, sometimes resisting showing acceptance of the harm done to us, and at other times, displaying our anger and resentment, in spite of the consequences. Either way, our soma reveals the defense we choose. Over time, in Lowen's frame, the habituated defense manifests in our somas and, especially, in our resting expressions ([1958] 2006, 1967, 2005). The jutted chin, narrow eyes, thrown-back shoulders, and a rigid torso contrast with tucked in buttocks, and thick, rigid thighs, are signs which, according to Lowen, reveal a masochistic character, a soma accustomed to defending against shaming the once-child experienced likely at the hands of sadistic family members, to which Latin@/x literature adds, sadistic racializers. A second body posture that Lowen calls the oral character, the head and torso take a spoon-like form, the head reaching forward of the neck, lips parted, eyes wide in a gesture evocative of seeking to fulfill an infantile disconnection, and revealing the shame of the neglected child.

In addition to the face, the oral character's arms hang somewhat lifeless alongside a slumped torso, a somatic disassociation from the adult subject's inherent relative power and agency, where the character's buttocks attempt to disappear under the hip girdle while the legs, typically underdeveloped and weak, lead to outturned feet, in the waddle stance of the disempowered. The interested reader can find descriptions of the psychopathic, schizoid, and rigid character types in Lowen's published work, but I describe the masochistic and the oral characters to give the reader an idea of the way our musculature adopts a defense (or, for the oral, a solicitation) to protect us from further maltreatment. Sapping vitality better used for other endeavors, these postures at one time defended against a threatening environment in Lowen's model but developed into a resting somatic expression in the adult's everyday countenance. To dissuade further disparagement and/or to seek healing (explored further in chapters 3, 4, and 5),[20] we can purposefully attempt to override our somatic expression and sublimate our true feelings by adopting a body posture, facial expression, as well as a tone and a pitch of voice to minimize (or, depending on the context, maximize) our presence.

Like Jungian archetypes, Lowen's characters allow us to read trauma and defense to trauma from such corporeal topographies. Tomkins's and Lowen's theories are not formulas I apply directly in my analysis, but they provide rubrics to unpack the somatic semiotics of racial shaming. Certainly, what triggers affect is historically and culturally situated as is our conscious reaction to such triggers. However, our body's somatic responses appear to be a human universal.

THE STEPS IN SCENES OF RACIALIZATION

In scenes of racialization, literary texts present the ways bodies interact as the primary means of racializing. To describe the somatic sequences of how the notion of race is interpersonally transacted, I propose scenes of racialization consist of four steps: *step one*, withdrawal of rapport; *step two*, deanimation; *step three*, confirmation; and *step four*, foreclosure. Scenes of racialization can vary in sequence and sometimes one or more of the four steps are consolidated in a very brief passage. Others draw out one step, but rarely are all four steps treated similarly in length. Scenes do not necessarily include dialogue as bodies in these texts are the entities that impute power asymmetries in somatic portrayal. In these scenes, the racializer takes race—something that is actually not real—and by shaming the other, creates meaning between phenotype and other communicative data in making color a social reality with concomitant social inferiority. Scenes of racialization radically depart from the psychosocial norms that drive human contact.

When we meet, social cognition normally guides us to mirror a significant amount of input from our interlocutor to ourselves to which we respond in a feedback loop. Neurocognitive studies show that "we activate similar brain regions both when we observe a bodily state in others, and when we experience that bodily state ourselves" (Keysers and Gazzola 2009) such that in normal relations, by *somatically* mirroring our interlocutor, we build interpersonal rapport (Miles, Nind, and Macrae 2009; Vacharkulksemsuk and Fredrickson 2012). This mirroring includes emulating facial expressions, adopting the posture of the other's torso and limbs, and/or employing characteristic words or verbal sounds.

Apart from building rapport, cognition studies argue a kind of perceptual bodily overlap, finding that we understand and respond to our interlocutor by responding to what we ascertain from the other's somatic cues (Gallese,

Keysers, and Rizzolatti 2004; Keysers and Gazzola 2009). One party tends to dominate the exchange, and so the other follows her cues. She may learn of her dominance in a situation by noting how the other somatically imitates her. Somatic resonance communicates how each party assesses herself in interpersonal power hierarchies that, in turn, informs her self-view. Albeit limited to mental imagining, a version of this somatic mirroring occurs when we read. Neurologically speaking, we clearly distinguish reading from our lived experience, but fMRI studies also show that we read and program our bodies as if the literary events were, with a critical level of remove, happening to us. This somatic pull toward each other stands in contrast to the somatic semiotics of intersectional racializing in scenes of racialization.

Neurocognitive studies evidence the role of racial categories in somatic mirroring that "modulat[es] . . . whether the other being observed is a member of a racial ingroup or outgroup" (Désy and Théoret 2007), where an out-group member stymies somatic resonance (Gutsell and Inzlicht 2010), even blocking empathy for out-group members' physical pain (Avenanti, Sirigu, and Aglioti 2010). These studies show that test subjects notably alienate out-group members, making racialized perception an important factor in rapport and social acceptance. Furthermore, somatic dissonance is an effective source of shame.[21] When the racializer shifts from this normal, healthy flow of somatic mirroring, the racializer still pays close attention to the racialized somatic cues and words. However, the racializer somatically withdraws into a nonmutual perceiving state evidenced in a rigid and physically retracted bodily expression, a hostile or cold facial expression, and often intimidating vocal tone. In *step one*, racially motivated discernment thwarts somatic resonance, a mainstay of human relations. The racialized perceives the shame communicated in the clear social distance as the racializer somatically withdraws.

In scenes of racialization, this flow is abruptly compromised in *step one*, the withdrawal of rapport. As we read Piri's situation, we may feel as if we are Piri, the racialized Other, but depending on how a character is drawn, our empathy in this form of somatic mirroring can be uneven. In some texts, especially in cases of phenotypic ambiguity, or in plots where a hegemonic character is either sadistic or, conversely, wrangles with a desire to connect with the racialized, the description tends to be longer and more detailed, perhaps in an effort to arouse neural empathy for either the racializer or the racialized. Intersectional difference instigates *step one*'s withdrawal, creating the somatic dissonance to then deanimate the other in *step two*.

Philosopher Dan Zahavi proposes that deanimation is a matter of cognition. Zahavi, elaborating on Max Scheler's early twentieth-century phenomenology, argues: "it is not the case that we first see inanimate objects and then animate them through a subsequent addition of mental components. Rather, at first, we see everything as expressive, and then we go through a process of de-animation" (2014, 122). This cognitive practice of deliberate devitalization is critical in transacting the assignment of race onto another. In this specific ideological use, deanimating leads with the affect of contempt that Tomkins describes somatizes in a curled upper lip, narrowed eyes, and chin jutting forward. Tomkins explains that contempt focuses one on a loathsome object, to such a degree, contempt requires self-vacating, maximizing the distance between self and the despised object (2008, 2:356).

There is a relationship between contempt and threat underlying this cognitive script. As Allen J. Hart, scholar of neuropsychology, argues, "Anyone perceived to be different from those my brain (the amygdala) perceives as 'friends' or belonging to my 'in-group' automatically triggers a threat response,"[22] such that the social scripting of Latin@/x difference becomes just such a threat (Hart et al. 2000). This response, in turn, fuels the process of making some*one* into some*thing*. Piri and the victimized man, like us, have become screens onto which the racializer ascribes "thingness." In the first two steps, we are perceived as intersectionally Brown, withdrawn from, and become an object of contempt for our racializing interlocutor. We are still vital beings; in fact, it is our vitality from which the racializer willfully distances herself in fashioning us into an object of threat cast as suspicion in *step three*.

In *step three*, the racializer approaches the deanimated source of threat with the need to confirm suspicion of the interlocutor's so-called race. Whereas deanimation works through contempt, racial suspicion works through disgust. Disgust, for Tomkins, underlies the expression of contempt, but has its own somatic expression where "the nose is raised and the head is drawn away from the apparent source" that when too close "will produce nausea" (2008, 356). On a continuum with what Tomkins names dissmell, the affect of disgust arises by the desire for contact with something or someone, as we move toward the object/person. Entering into the other's physical proximity, the object/person reveals itself as radically different than how we believed it would be. Disgust becomes the affective response to desiring something that one then comes to find inherently flawed and unfit for contact (Tomkins 2008, 357). Dissmell works on the same affective logic as disgust, but specifically engages the olfactory sense instead of taste to inspire disgust. Where dissmell biologically protects humans from ingesting noxious fumes, disgust acts to stop us from eating rotten or harmful food. We use the somatic protocol of socially thwarted desire for interpersonal connection, expressing contempt, disgust, and dissmell to isolate and then marginalize the offending source, the one shamed Brown (362).

These affects are socially scripted to look for and qualify difference as indigestible, a threat to the organism, and by shaming, they instantiate the physical and social distance that effectuates and maintains hierarchical relationships among individuals, social classes, and nations. Cultural critic and essayist Richard Rodriguez ties Brown, in his work, a racial symbol of the history and influence of Latin@/xs, to the color brown, a source of desire and disgust of dirt, feces that later connotes historic racialized disgust for miscegenation that portends a repulsive future Brown United States. Perceiving Brown through sense data bears the material sign of our biological tie to an "erotic tunnel . . . the color of consort . . . of illicit passion . . . brown, the stench of rape and of shame, sin, slippage, birth" in the making of the United States and its future (Rodriguez 2003, 133). Underlying disgust is the issue of proximity, desire, and connectedness that sociologist Thomas J. Scheff explains leads to shame: "Shame is the emotion that occurs when we feel too close or too far from others. When too close, we feel exposed or violated; when too far, we feel invisible or rejected" (in Hage, 2009, 40), a state of shame that for Rodriguez is endemic to Brown. *Step three*'s need to confirm racial suspicion leads with disgust of erotic inappropriateness, to orifices, and to dirt, all using proximity as affective excuses to justify (neo)colonial violence, oppression, and atrocities, and normalizes the move in *step four* to socially foreclose upon Latin@/xs.

Once the racializer's suspicion has been confirmed, in *step four* the affects conducted through somatic expression in previous steps make social foreclosure—the assignment of Latin@/xs to an inferior and intractable social position—a reasonable social necessity. In literary scenes of racialization, the racializer uses the steps to establish his Whiteness, and thus authority, and in this final step, he consolidates his social power by completing the scene in the final adjudication of shame: he affixes the other with social stigma—a permanent, socially definitive attribute used to racialize a subject as an Other into social asymmetry. This foreclosure instantiates permanent withdrawal of rapport. We marginalize by ignoring the presence of the racialized, intentionally withholding somatic mirroring, and, instead, engage the racialized with somatic indifference, contempt, and disgust, or, conversely, feigned social cheer and acceptance in a managed bodily appearance (studied in chapter 4). Our bodies speak somatic hate that pressures complicity of bystanders in marginalizing the racialized in generating a pervasive shaming cultural ambiance. A shaming soma-scape affectively paves the way for organizing larger formal practices such as racially motivated and unfair detention, sentencing, incarceration, redlining practices, and physical abuse, all forms of social foreclosure. Literary scenes of racialization elaborate on racial shaming, coursing through the soma where "bodies tell stories that people cannot or will not tell, either because they are unable, forbidden, or choose not to tell," as social epidemiologist Nancy Krieger argues (2005, 350), making "race" appear a socially material reality. Thomas's autobiography's opening epigraph situates the text in the intimate suffering of intraracialization at the hands of his father, but a second scene illustrates the way Latin@/x authors aesthetically articulate the steps in somatic expression. This scene begins with *step three*, suspicious confirmation when Piri challenges his fair-skinned brother José on the question of whether José sees Piri as inferior to his light-skinned brothers. In a confrontation between the two, Piri and José reveal how much each has suffered racialization, a harm against their phenotypically varied family that has created a fissure in the way the Thomases relate to one but broadens to their neighborhood dynamic, the catalyst for their ensuing fight. José gives voice to how he has defended Piri against the racial suspicion and accompanying shaming contempt of neighbors by suggesting Piri may not be White, but he could be Indian, and therefore, not Black (145). Piri will not refuse his Blackness or default into the Whiter category of Indian (common in Caribbean racializing projects) to which José responds:

> "Like I said, man, you can be a nigger if you want to," he said, as though he were talking with a ten-ton rock on his chest. "I don't know how you come to be my brother, but I love you like one. I've busted my ass, both me and James, trying to explain to people how come you so dark and how come your hair is so curly, an'—." (146)

The somatic resonance ends with the words "you can be a nigger if you want to," somatically authenticated by describing the tone and cadence of José's voice "as though he were talking with a ten-ton weight on his chest" (*steps one* and *two*), later confirmed with words of racial suspicion: "I don't know how you come to be my brother" (*step three*) that threaten to foreclose on their relationship as blood brothers (*step four*). Because of Piri's appearance, José loves him *as if* he were Piri's brother.

José, along with their sibling James, has responded to the racial suspicion (*step three*) of the people from the neighborhood and attempted to maintain Piri's social inclusion through racialized terms. Unable to override phenotypical information, the brothers rely on relative Whiteness of José, James, and their White mother that they believe should lend honorary Whiteness to Piri. Meanwhile, the perception of Piri's body to employers, girlfriends, police, friends, and his father tells a different story. Thomas's autobiography shows the shaky ground on which such an argument rests for the racialized. Layered scenes of racialization from the neighborhood to the family home and beyond deanimate Piri into the unaccepted racial category of Blackness, physically and emotionally punished for his dark-skinned father and for which his brothers have been racially shamed by association to him.

In response to racial shaming, Piri expresses suspicious disgust for his brothers' complicity, as the reader will recall, an unacceptable affect for the racialized in *step three*:

> I said, "You and James hadda make excuses for *me*? Like for me being *un Negrito*?" I looked at the paddy in front of me. "Who to?" I said. "Paddies?" (146, emphasis in original)

Thomas writes the exchange as a first step toward foreclosing on Piri's relationship with his brother, José. Piri authenticates in his somatic experience of being socially marginalized by his brother by responding in kind, deanimating José into "the paddy" in front of him, a pejorative term referring to the Irish, which in this instance, connotes an odious, unrelatable White person of indeterminate ethnic background. Piri's shame turns into righteous rage as:

> Lights began to jump into my head and tears blurred out that this was my brother before me. The burning came up out of me and I felt the shock run up my arm as my fist went up the side of his head. I felt one fist hit his mouth. I wondered if I had broken any of his white teeth. . . . I saw an unknown face spitting blood at me. I hated it. I wanted to stay on top of this what-was-it and beat him and beat him and beat him and *beat beat beat beat beat*. . . . As the hurting began to leave me, I slowly became a part of my naked body. I felt weak with inside pain. I wondered why. (146–47, emphasis in original)

Seeing lights, shedding tears, and the sensation of irate burning are somatic reactions of contemptuous deanimation of *step two*, in reaction to José's unwillingness to accept Piri's Blackness. Note the change in order of the steps: this violent response to a scene of racialization is made possible by Piri's situational power as José's older brother. Piri is taken over by his soma and he notices in hindsight, his shock of seeing his fist punching his brother. His soma has become the primary actor in expressing Piri's shamed subjectivity.

In lockstep with his somatic rage, Piri gives us a deanimating series of distancing nouns where José becomes an "unknown face." There is a blow, then an "it," another blow, and then a "what-was-it," to the point where he no longer sees his brother; he sees a White racist that he *"beats beats beats beats beats."* Piri's disgust and infliction of pain forecloses on José as White and, thereby, an Other to Piri. His response is reactive but nevertheless uses the social technology of pain and shame to attempt to denigrate José. The materialization of race between the brothers complete, Piri is momentarily relieved from active self-contempt, manifesting a relational distance from the disgusting object that, for Piri, his brother has revealed himself to be. In effect, Piri confronts the divisiveness of José's social privilege and the way intersectional racialization mitigates their relationship. U.S. commitments to racializing has erected a barrier between the brothers—one that both brothers painfully had tried to deny.

SOMA AS STRATEGY IN SCENES OF RACIALIZATION

> Words in themselves have no meaning; their meaning is given to them by the particular context in which they are used. So to study verbal context without a thorough knowledge of performance context is a futile exercise indeed.
> —Américo Paredes

More than words, the performance of everyday affect generates the texture of our lives (Cvetkovich 2003). In the case I make here, shaming leads with disgust as the "ugliest of ugly feelings" (Ngai 2005, 335), generating the performative context Paredes speaks of in our social relations and our experience of ourselves. As shame uglifies rooms and spaces in intimate spheres (Brennan 2004), it also permeates institutions, ripening the potential for qualitative analysis of our social environments that normally lies almost outside of awareness.

Such a lived experience is described well by Latin@/x literary and queer studies scholar Larry La Fountain-Stokes in "Gay Shame, Latina- and Latino-Style: A Critique of White Queer Performativity" (2011). A phenotypically White-looking Puerto Rican, La Fountain-Stokes suddenly comes to know himself as ethnically unacceptable, if not almost disgusting, to his gay peers, through somatic repudiation at a cocktail party in New York City. La Fountain-Stokes is shamed simply for wearing a brightly colored tropical print shirt which, in this milieu, reads non-White and therefore embarrassingly wrong in a crowd of hushed grays, cool black/Black, and classy white/White.[23] Skin color does not immediately out La Fountain-Stokes as non-White. His Brownness cues in clothing and is perhaps additionally signaled in non-White gestures, speech patterns, and other bodily output, a deliberate sensorial assessment confirming Paul Gilroy's argument, "How we see 'race,' how the signs and symbols of racial difference become apparent to our senses . . . [and] does not admit the integrity of any avowedly natural perceptual scheme" (2005, 251). These sense data mete out racializing shame without words.[24]

As I will argue in chapter 2, racialization works within a rich social affective fabric of concerted sensory data breeding contempt, shame, and disgust, affects at the heart of many intersectional microaggressions. This affective practice overrides other affiliations in situations where we might expect to feel acceptable and accepted despite our so-called racial difference. And while Lawrence La Fountain-Stokes's sense of marginalization in this instance may be critiqued as relatively minor, as Scheff suggests, the deep human need for social inclusion reveals the impact of differing levels of shaming:

> Since [shame] involves even a slight threat to the [social] bond, [it] is pervasive in virtually all social interaction. . . . All human beings are extremely sensitive to the exact amount of deference they are accorded. Even slight discrepancies generate shame or embarrassment. (2006, 266)[25]

Furthering its impact, the shame we experience by somatic racializing and racism is more difficult to denounce than verbal insult or physical impropriety. La Fountain-Stokes's gay peers racialize and socially marginalize him via the communicative power of the soma; no one verbally criticizes him for there is no need—the social efficacy of somatic racialization marginalizes its target surreptitiously. Meanwhile, the daily quiet yet cutting harm of somatic shaming remains largely impervious to the charge of racism and, thus, is seldom researched.[26] More than actions or bodily comportment, as Richard Delgado and Jean Stefancic argue (2004), U.S. culture focuses instead on certain words to identify harmful actions as racist, yet *how* we racialize in harmful yet non-criminalized ways is left in the cognitive penumbra.[27]

METHODOLOGY AND ORGANIZATION

Because racial violence continues to galvanize the American public into confronting the prevalence of racialization and racism in the United States, I find it somewhat hollow to speak of or analyze Latin@/x literature without considering the socially pressured relation between Latin@/xs and the pain of shame that is in evidence in studies from relevant disciplines. I began researching one field and then another in the hope of coming across theories and studies to analyze the soma and to concretize these processes intricately described in literature for lived experience. I found fascinating, helpful studies from Latin@/x studies, literary and critical theories, social psychology, sociology, and critical race studies, but was surprised by the relevant data I found in studies from cognitive science, neuroscience, and social epidemiology, among other fields. The critical need for focus and assembly of this data and theory on these crippling social issues motivated what became a transdisciplinary analysis where, as presented earlier, I identify scenes of racialization in creative texts to draw out the role of the soma in social manufacture of Brown. Scientific theories and empirical data substantiate my literary analyses and concretize the value of my thesis of the relevance of literary depictions to explain and theorize lived experience.[28] My research was inductive—findings from one field held insights into another aspect of the problem studied. I beg my reader's openness to my inductive presentation, a method that may have a heuristic value and was difficult to avoid when marrying somatic analysis of literature to this breadth of research.

Inspired by the transdisciplinary manifesto written by de Freitas, Morin, and Nicolescu (1994),[29] my analysis uses scientific as well as literary sources to arrive at a more global assessment of racialization and racism that I hope will suggest more avenues for integrated understanding and effective address of these issues and others. Building on the narrative turn in social science research, I loosely borrow the term *qualitative data* to propose looking at texts as sources of deep exposition, adding layers of meaning to social negotiation not usually present in data collecting tools such as surveys or interviews. Specifically, I demarcate scenes of racialization as a specific social phenomenon driven by racial shaming, the hard-to-elucidate inner workings of which are portrayed in rich context and detail in literary examples. These scenes indicate the soma as the key medium through which to understand this social practice as it often functions in our lived experience. Furthermore, the chapters that follow point to the somatic body as a core constituent of subjectivity and interpersonal relations.

While the fields I draw on may seem odd bedfellows, statistical studies often treat race as an ontological fact, a position often interrogated in literary and critical theories, cultural studies, Latin@/x studies, feminist theory, and critical race theory (and especially Latin@/x critical race theory). I concur with literary studies scholar Frederick L. Aldama's assertion that "the separation [between the humanities and the sciences] itself was a line drawn in the sand—specious and artificial" (2010, 1). What seems to many an irreparable disciplinary rift, I see as complementary engagement: the latter disciplines deconstruct the terms of racialization and racism, while the former empiricizes their materialized ideations.

A transdisciplinary project such as the present one presupposes that most readers will not be thoroughly versed in all of the methods and disciplines brought to bear. While many academics regularly read outside their field, that knowledge may not enter their scholarship. Even if a literary scholar reads scientific accounts of a medical condition appearing in a literary work, her engagement with science research may be shallow compared with her employ of literary theory. Likewise, the cognitive scientist may read fiction for leisure without considering the implications of fiction for her study of perception. Transdisciplinary studies dispense with the notion of an ideal reader, calling on readers to keep an open mind to fields they know less well and a willingness to engage in an inductive argumentation that presents various types of data and analysis to more fully appreciate the scope of the problem in life and literature. In the chapters that follow, I studys Latin@/x literature, attending to the role of the soma in formal features of characterization, voice, dialogue, and structure in resonance with lived experience per varied disciplinary studies toward understanding the practice of racial shaming.

CHAPTER OVERVIEW

Somatic analysis, the breakdown of how racialization and racism are socially transacted, and the primary role of shame are the three primary contributions I seek to make in *Shaming into Brown*. Each of the four remaining chapters argues a specific social technology of the soma in relation to racialization and racism of Latin@/xs.

Chapter 2 presents a critical approach to the soma from the vantage point of three faculties: vision, audition, and smell. "Latin@/x Literature and the Human Sensorium" traces sense perception as key to the stepped process of *scenes of racialization* in transacting intersectional race onto another. Passages from five Latin@/x texts decentralize the importance of mental machinations and reveal culturally crafted sensory scripts where we selectively perceive for Otherness. These sensory scripts are an integral political strategy naturalizing hostility, contempt, shame, and disgust in affective materialization of difference. This discussion begins as a visual practice similar to the way Fanon speaks of the trepidation of a young girl who shudders at his intersectional Blackness but differs from the project of phenomenology per se to study scenes of racialization from the perspective between both the racializer and the racialized. These scenes utilize sight but also the damning senses of smell and sound. Research exposits how data like scent, the tone of speech, and gait as much as (and sometimes more than) visual assessment of phenotype are used to racially shame in an internalization of hegemonic practices. Although I treat them as single sources in chapter 2, these three senses are often copresent in racial shaming, deepening the somatic experience for the character(s) and, in turn, the reader. I present focused analyses to argue the co-optation of the human sensorium in racializing Latin@/xs. I demonstrate that scenes of racialization begin and end with multisensorial cognition as the medium through which we shame.

Building on the somatics of multisensory output in chapter 3, I look at racializing shame and the soma in racism from the perspective of the *interior* of the body. In *The Autobiography of a Brown Buffalo* ([1972] 1989), the first of two of Oscar "Zeta" Acosta's germinal texts, Oscar journeys across the country in an extended experience of *step three*, where he negotiates a sense of self through suspicious disgust. He has internalized intersectional shaming to such a degree, he has become ill. This chapter examines the soma as an interiority—the subject expression of his gut—to narrate the deleterious physical and psychological effects of racialization and racism in his bleeding ulcers, vomit, constipation, depression, addiction, and sense of powerlessness that contradicts Oscar's public presentation of arrogance, callousness, recklessness, self-aggrandizement but also self-pity. However far he travels, Oscar cannot get away from his troubled viscera as the world relentlessly racially shames him. Accepting the inescapability of his subjection to intersectional racialization, Oscar declares himself Chicano and a brown buffalo. The disparity between Oscar's socio- and psychological perceptions of himself as an estimable U.S. citizen with the right to express his full humanity, set against the reality of how he is actually treated by friend and foe finds form in a secondary but definitive character, his soma. This intelligent subjectivity expressed in his entrails ultimately leads Acosta to face and finally accept the impact of his social circumstances.

Whereas Oscar attempts to outsmart or one-up oppressive forces of social rejection, in chapter 4, Ceci and Lydia, the two protagonists in Octavio Solís's Pulitzer Prize–nominated play *Lydia*, expose the stakes of the disabled and the undocumented when socially acting out of turn. *Lydia* presents the situations of Ceci Flores, a seventeen-year-old in a persistent vegetative state, and of Lydia, a young Mexican woman who has crossed the border and into the United States without permission to work for Ceci's family. In this chapter, I analyze the May 9, 2009, performance as well as the 2010 published script to study the role of the soma for actors. Depending on one's social position in life, the play exposes how we pressure the soma into hiding as a mode of survival. Lydia's circumspect behavior elaborates her social vulnerability in relation to Ceci, her doppelganger, who delivers her story of intersectional racialization in fantastic soliloquies, as she convulses her way through the play. These two characters are very differently situated, but the women's extralinguistic recognition of their shared shame and pain stages their deep connection. Importantly, *Lydia* proposes an archetype of the female racialized Latina domestic worker, a magic*o* nanny, who in conjunction with the severely disabled coprotagonist, Ceci, illustrates the tension between the freedom to portray authentic expression of oppression and the managed self as a method of self-protection. In a dramatic, somatic subterfuge and conversely, abandon, Solís illuminates the social power we unfairly wield when perceiving people socially inferior.

Lastly, in chapter 5, I study shame as a legacy script in American culture interpolating racial shaming, moral shame, and the soma in two genres: poetry and the conversion narrative. In the American Book Award–winning *The Ice Worker Sings and Other Poems* ([1999] 2017), Andrés Montoya writes a conversion narrative in verse, an unusual endeavor in Latin@/x poetry and in U.S. poetry in general. The collection reveals the psychosocial fallout of social asymmetry at the same time the speaker searches and encounters spiritual deliverance. The collection expounds on the ills of racial shaming while the poem "the ice worker in love" marks the collection as a spiritual conversion. The poem employs structure and rhetoric of the Puritan conversion narrative, a paradigmatic American genre of social acceptance through religious redemption (Caldwell [1983] 1985) that today continues to operate in meaningful ways. A politically savvy injunctive, the conversion narrative instantiates the speaker as fully American, positioning him to stand, like regenerate Puritans before, on equal social footing. Emotionally, the conversion narrative is unique in its demand that shame be spoken and, most importantly, empathically received. Rather than admitting to feeling ashamed and reifying racialized inferiority in obeisance to the conversion narrative, in my analysis, his strife and terrific sin lead him to Sophia, the divine presence who interpolates the speaker's life with meaning and beauty in the midst of untenable life conditions. One of the contributions in this chapter is (re)introducing Sophia, the second figure in certain Christian trinities, to literary analysis. Sophia is not only a figure but, I argue, offers a powerful analytic of the divine soma.

Shaming into Brown argues racial shaming is a social technology that uses the soma to materialize Brown into social fact. Scientific research affirms my thesis, drawn from Latin@/x literature, that racial shaming is a continual, pervasive, and deep harm from which we should investigate literature as a source for research problems and perhaps solutions across disciplines. My final hope for this book is to open somatic analysis as a line of inquiry that should be useful to various fields. In Latin@/x literature, the soma exposes the commanding role of the expressive body in crushing cultural practices that darken our days.

CHAPTER 2

Latin@/x Literature and the Human Sensorium

THE SOMA, our communicative precognitive corporeal self, tells many stories, among them, the story of how we racialize and diminish one another. Taken from the Greek, *soma* is an expressive intelligence of the physical body that I argue challenges our delimiting conception of the dominance of the mind. While René Descartes advocated for mental reason in arbitrating how and what we know, his argument falls short on the issue of racism as Chicana poet Lorna Dee Cervantes counters, "Racism is not intellectual" (1981, 37, line 38). Studies show race lacks a rational origin, but it lacks a neurological one too. Yet, race is often one of the first categories of discernment we make of one another (Cosmides, Tooby, and Kurzban 2001, 2003; Hugenberg and Bodenhausen 2003; McConnell and Leibold 2001; Phelps et al. 2000; Richeson et al. 2003).[1] We immediately perceive what we call race, an intersectional enterprise where we also determine the other's gender, sexual orientation, biological sex, social class, physical ability, and more. Within a matter of seconds, we use this information to interpret the social power of the other. And we transmit these perceptions, knowingly or not, through our somas. Lying largely beyond conscious or rational intention, the soma physically broadcasts its interpretation of the world and of the self.

Using the soma as a register of subjectivity, *somatic analysis* contrasts in aim with Maurice Merleau-Ponty's phenomenology of *the lived body* ([1945] 2014). The latter, designates sense perception in environs as the basis for our mental subjectivity. Michel Serres makes the following declaration: "The era of the linguistic animal has come to a close.... The body, or more particularly the senses, is never a mere object, but itself a kind of work" (Serres in Abbas 2005, 166).[2] The soma does not exclude these theories or others but moves the focus to *somatic expression* as the relational currency that shows what we feel in relation to the other and to ourselves, whether love or hate or something in between. As a social dynamic, *somatic exchange* has gone underacknowledged as a primary source of knowing and being as well as an important site of social discipline, and particular to my project here, the study of racialization and racism.

Somatic analysis bridges human understanding of our lived experience with written expression. Close readings of Latin@/x texts illustrate that we infer race through our senses. Although made up of words, Latin@/x literature nevertheless invokes the soma as a medium for reading character and deepening our understanding of plot and intention, as well as social practices in lived experience. Literary scholar Paula M. L. Moya argues close readings of literary texts "serve as an excavation of, and a meditation on, the pervasive sociocultural ideas—such as race, ethnicity, gender, and sexuality—of the social worlds, as well as the worlds of sense, within both authors and readers live" (2016, 9), which becomes more acute when considering sense data in somatic analysis.

Somatic analysis traces affects in these immediate perceptions. Whereas emotions are mentally deliberated and tend to require more processing time, affects are the feelings our somas register. The impact of feelings is considerable for they "give people's psychic realities and ideological convictions (however fictional or unfounded) their sense of realness" (Ioanide 2015, 2), a process that situates the soma in a key position in transacting racialization and racism. Racial shaming writ large entrains affective relations between hegemonic subjects and Latin@/xs, and other people so colored, in a widespread, multisensory cognition that engenders cultural phobia where "affect has a priority that defies all rational thinking" (Fanon [1952] 2008, 133). In this chapter, I closely read passages from Luis Valdez's *No saco nada de la escuela*, Américo Paredes's *George Washington Gómez: A Mexicotexan Novel*, Xyta Maya Murrya's *Locas*, Nelly Rosario's *Song of the Water Saints*, and Angelo Parra's *Song of the Coquí*, and illustrate how the senses enact ideologies and selective prejudices.

SENSE PERCEPTION AND SOCIAL INTELLIGENCE

Our sensory perceptions key how we read our environment and each other, and yet our senses are underappreciated as sources of social intelligence and even more, ignored as mediums of oppression. But each of these categories of identification is itself informally assessed through sense data. It is not so much what we see, hear, or smell, but *how* we do so that flows into socially constructed scripts of feeling that are used to further oppressive political agendas. What hegemony instructs us to see is discursively naturalized *simply* as *sight*. We treat vision as if it is an all-encompassing capacity while scientific studies reveal that sight is actually quite discriminating. As an organ and nerve system, the eye selects what it chooses to focus on, discarding the majority of images in its purview in any given moment. Scientists argue the particularities of selective visual data as "change blindness," to refer to the lack of recognition of changes in a visual field, and "inattentional blindness" to account for the large number of items present in a given moment that we claim *not to see* (Luck and Ford 1998; Mack and Rock 1998, respectively). Less studied, however, is the cultural impetus for that selection.

Not if, but when we believe we are seeing another's race, we are following a racializing script where we give visual dominance to phenotype, ascribing it with faux biological finitude, to which we add a socially scripted perception of threat. This combination of biosocial sense perception creates a somatic platform with our sense of threat we unknowingly serve to naturalize the categorization of humans. In fact, the social scripting of race is so entrenched and teachable, studies show sight is not necessary to racialize. A study by Osagie Obasogie showed the legally blind understand socially constructed categories of race and employ them in social interactions (Obasogie 2013). With or without actual sight, Obasogie's study inadvertently underscores my premise that senses regularly work as an ensemble.[3] Rarely, we do only see: while we are seeing, we are hearing, smelling, and touching (or deciding not to touch), as well. And while we cannot necessarily control the sense data we are receiving in a given moment, as philosopher of psychology Alva Noë argues, we do not receive the world via our sensations, but rather actively *move to select* both what we perceive and *how* we will perceive it (2006). The deliberateness of these moves is especially notable in stigmatization and social foreclosure where we believe we are merely responding to sense input in categorizing human variation, when in reality, per the steps in scenes of racialization, we actively select sense data in determining social status.

When we refer to race as a social construct, we might ask what role the four steps—again, *step one*, withdrawal of rapport; *step two*, deanimation; *step three*, confirmation; and *step four*, social foreclosure—I proposed in chapter 1 play in scenes of racialization. As elaborated in chapter 1, in *step one*, withdrawal of rapport, we look to assess phenotype and then somatically express startle over another's Brownness. We register this startle as a form of dissent as we begin executing a racializing script where we arbitrate how much or how little social esteem we will confer onto our interlocutor. The startle cues our alert that something is fundamentally wrong with our interlocutor, and we withdraw somatic resonance, stymieing the peer-to-peer interaction we might have desired. When interacting with another without prejudice, we often mirror the other, imitating his or her somatic expression that may include paralinguistic verbal sounds and/or body postures, which tells our interlocutor we are present with them, a somatic way of conveying that we accept and appreciate our interlocutor. We are usually unaware that we are mirroring the other; we simply tend to feel that, to varying degrees, we understand the other and/or like him or her.

In effect, we are sympathetically mirroring the other's soma in accord with their favorable social standing relative to our own. This mirroring is a socially validating process conferring the respect that is withdrawn in *step one*. As the racializer proceeds to deanimate the other into an object in *step two*, instead of somatically mirroring him, the racializer plays out a culturally sanctioned and habituated social script of contempt for the person now deanimated into an object. Contempt registers in angry disapproval (beaded eyes, curled upper lip, upright neck holding inclined head) in response to his fabricated threat. Although these affects are not monolithic in temporal terms, I parse out each affect for the purpose of distilling its somatic charge that materializes the notion of race. For this purpose, I argue the physical expression of contempt as the first affect in generating the 'thingness' of the person society seeks to marginalize. In a similar circular, socially-cued, affective logic, in *step three*, suspicions of out-group status are expressed in the racializer's somatic disgust, the feeling of aversion is culled to verify out-group status, and race becomes a social fact.

Scenes of racialization illustrate that even when parties have already asserted the other as racialized, racializers enact a compulsive desire to reaffirm somatic power over the other, instantiating over and over again the other as elementarily despicable. In Butlerian fashion, this reiteration helps concretize, naturalize, and disseminate this scripted soma, developed into a national script operating at many levels in U.S. society. The sensory data selected to racialize is given such social weight, the script has us override contrary information that could disrupt the racialized's assignment to social illegitimacy (i.e., the other is an upstanding person, is educated, performs honest work or may seem more phenotypically White than of color). Deanimation is key here because it thwarts the human value of the person so colored. Even when we personally value ourselves and others as Latin@/xs, we do so against this social backdrop in which we live daily. Each step racially shames and the scene is complete when the other somatically assumes his/her inferior social position.

Literature stakes out this process in texts useful in deciphering our lived experience. Donald Trump's 2017 presidential call for a travel ban on Muslims makes this point well. He simply but consistently refers to Muslims as "Mooslims," and this pronunciation may pretend to respectfully adhere to Arab diction, but Trump's somatic expression contradicts this intention. His exaggerated protrusion of his lips, his narrowed eyes, and stiffened neck intends to shame Muslims. Trump proctors support for his political position by cueing racial shaming through this acoustic dissonance. In fact, Trump's "Mooslims" shows contempt per *step two* and suspicious disgust per *step three* toward social foreclosure in *step four*: his call to ban Muslims from entering the United States. "Mooslims" easily contorts into an acoustic datum of social difference and, therefore, inferiority associated as the term is with people largely phenotypically imagined as Brown. Hence, "Mooslims" plays so well into a generalized threat of Brownness, the threat of the latter generating support for the wall Trump proposes to build between the United States and Mexico. Much like the proposed border wall seeks to keep *Mexicans* out of the United States,[4] his rejoinder, "We have no choice!" makes visceral the Muslim ban without the need to appeal to reason.[5] The acoustic affects of contempt and disgust in the *steps* develop an affective environment that legitimates the need for social foreclosure of both groups in *step four,* ipso facto.

From the Oval Office, Trump socially crafts sensory data to flesh out the threat of the other. We should not underestimate the social power of this process. As described in creative literature, even when counterarguments, facts, and statistics demonstrate the hollowness of such claims, the interpersonal resonance of somatic expression authenticates the need to racialize, strengthening the practice of and the power taken in scenes of racialization. The politicization of sensory input, particularly sight, smell, and audition, combine in bodily postures, gestures, and paralinguistic sounds (e.g., crying, laughing, hiccupping, snorting, moaning) that transact race onto another and, in turn, create the affective logic for racist acts. "Hostility does not stem from rational thought but from deep prejudices that are somatically marked" (Shusterman 2012, 189) and aestheticized in creative literature through the soma.

THE SENSES IN COGNITION AND KNOWLEDGE

In the passages I analyze, I am less interested in emphasizing the individuality of a character's soma, than in discerning the psychosocial influence of the soma: a biologically led and affective biosocial membrane that reacts, interprets, and responds to one's experience in the world. First, I differentiate the soma from other notions of the body in an outline of the ways the West has trained sense perceptions. And second, I note the role of three primary senses—sight, smell, and audition—in scenes of racialization.

While we might give variable credence to somatic knowledge in statements that describe, for example, "a feeling in my gut" indicating a lie or ascertaining guilt "written all over your face," as a society, we attribute a significant truth value to how our bodies publicly project how we internally feel. Many institutions such as courts of law, parole boards, and, increasingly, businesses,[6] run somatic tests to distinguish truth from lies. Skin temperature tests, penile plethysmography (PPG), polygraph tests, and the like premise the body's somatic capacities as a more reliable communicator of truth than our words.[7] As previously stated, we often manage the image of how our bodies are perceived to the best of our ability, but somatic expression often escapes such efforts to control. Test administrators look to the soma in the penal system for inconsistencies with one's words, while in business, marketing researchers study the soma to determine customer preferences, and where in interpersonal relationships the soma speaks volumes on how our partner really feels. The soma is an unwieldy entity, a kind of holographic form of subjectivity, materially present, but generally outside of conscious awareness. These tests and perceptions rely on the unwieldiness of the soma in the face of our individual will to control what we share with others. This data, in turn, informs criminal justice matters, public opinion, medical science, and increasingly, capitalistic endeavors, as well as an important subjective register in our relationships.

Related but different from the soma, body image and body language are ways we *consciously* manage how others perceive us. Driven by concern for how we socially appear, we often think of body image as the visual corporeal sense we attempt to craft of ourselves with the help of marketers who sell us products and services. Body language, on the other hand, looks at how we somatically portray ourselves in gestures, a register of the body expression we often alter to achieve particular social goals. Body language may or may not register somatic data, but acquires a spectral quality often broken down in body parts. The job interview is a commonplace event where observers can appreciate the differences between body image, body language, and the soma.

In this scenario, an interviewee prepares for the interview with a concerted effort to manage his body image. He wants to look suitable for the job so he attends to his personal grooming and carefully selects his apparel. His body image comes into play with an appraisal of his normal body language. He may practice his interview countenance, including a decisive gait and a firm, calm handshake. During the interview, the interviewee makes sure he looks directly but not forcibly into the interviewer's eyes in the hopes of appearing confident and capable, but not overbearing or intrusive.

When caught without an answer to a tough question, the soma appears. The interviewee suddenly loses his composure, stammering a weak response to a question, his face tinges red with embarrassment, his voice cracks and becomes increasingly less audible. He looks downward, avoiding eye contact with the interviewer. He begins to perspire. His hands tremble slightly. *These are the elements of somatic expression.* Should he become aware of his nervous somatic expression, he may shift to a more composed posture of feigned relaxed hands clasped lightly in his lap, casually crossing his legs. In a feedback loop, the interviewee may become aware of how his soma is displaying, in light of which he adjusts his self-presentation—body image and body language management. Regardless, he has much less control of his soma underlying these confections of countenance.[8] His soma continues to spill out in rapid speech, traces of sweat, a racing heart. And though people often accept our deliberate mien as if unaware of our soma's competing account, the soma continues to provide its response.

Despite important theoretical differences, the soma could be argued an unspoken premise in the respective theories of Edmund Husserl, Maurice Merleau-Ponty, and Jean-Paul Sartre. Whereas the focus of phenomenologies often lies in the subject/object relationship acquired through perception, in a sense, these theories rely on an intelligent, sensorially cohesive human organism that qualifies what it experiences in recognition of its aliveness. I leave the debate to others,[9] but I note the soma in these philosophies, a figure in relief. Guided by multiple senses, communication research terms similarly describe human nonverbal communication where "several bodily 'channels' are coordinated in social interaction to show how environmental sources of meaning are drawn into the production of intersubjective understanding and how interaction, in turn, structures its own semiotic and material environment" (Streeck, Goodwin, and LeBaron 2011, 9). I argue that unless we consider the confluence of gestures, poses, affect, and energies—in fact, the whole bodily emanation that includes interior corporeal feelings and paralinguistic sounds—we are underappreciating the role of the soma informing so much of what we understand of one another. The soma, often the cognitive premise underlying research and theory, is the entity with which we daily influence, pressure, and compel each other.

As Moya argues, we individually hold ideologies in mental schemas of which we are generally unaware and, therefore, effectuate little to no agency over how we construct notions of reality (2016). This willed ignorance of how we racialize one another forms schemas, rote cognitive practices that have led to the popular and false notion that we, as a culture, have moved beyond so-called race and operate in a postracial, colorblind society (Bonilla-Silva [2006] 2013). These schemas inform policy, protocol, and behavior despite political parties. The Obama administration, like presidents before, ordered massive deportations of undocumented people, the majority of whom were of Mexican descent, that set some of the groundwork for Donald Trump's unabashed vilification of undocumented Mexicans as rapists, criminals, and drug runners (Trump 2015). I argue mental schemas lead to behavioral scripts from ideologies that co-opt sense perception in somatic racializing. Latin@/x literature, and other marginalized literatures, allows us a unique opportunity to expose ourselves to the life experience of someone we often cannot perceive without narrow mental schemas and discriminatory scripts.

Excellent work has been done in narratology scholarship and in cognitive literary studies, examining the application of cognitive science in literature and, especially, to the question of reader empathy in processual cognitive studies signaling brain reactivity when reading visual imagery, cues for sound, and depictions of emotions (Bal and Veltkamp 2013; Kidd and Castano 2013; Mar, Oatley, and Peterson 2009). This scholarship, however, has not addressed thornier questions of how ideology factors into reading cognition, effectuating a kind of cultural blindness in what we comprehend.

When we ignore or refuse to appreciate the imbrication of racialization as a key script in how we organize and participate in U.S. culture, we defend our self-view that we *ourselves* do not racially discriminate. We partake in the hegemonic myth that we no longer think or act against others or ourselves in racialized terms. It is convenient to believe racism is what other people do, not us. As the data mount from narratology, cognitive literary studies, cognitive science, social science, neuroscience, and communication studies, it is somewhat curious why so much attention is paid to spoken communication when so much is happening *between* bodies.

Though the soma figures into many disciplines and theories, the occlusion of the soma results from what we hold as our "natural attitude" based on "pre-understanding and prejudices which very seldom come to light" (Bullington 2013, 19). The current spate of studies of the body, emotions, and the brain synthesizes the connections among cognitive processes, bodily feeling reactions, and evaluative perceptions. Studies in neurology, cognitive literary studies, behavioral studies, theories of mind (ToM), philosophy of mind (PoM), body studies, and affect theory do not employ the term *soma*; however, their work positions the soma as psychobiological agent and social actor.

In the field of neuroscience for example, the amygdala is the physical location in the brain usually identified as the site that registers fear, but how do we know fear, in order to track it in the brain, if not what we observed as somatic signs of fear? In fact, neuroscientist Joseph E. LeDoux has found that what we name fear emanates from our observation of sudden sweat, the release of adrenals in the system, a rise in heart rate—the *embodied* amygdala's commands producing an internal and external somatic response to threat is what we call fear (2014). Likewise, studies of reading and empathy regularly indicate the neural rehearsal of narrative events as necessary for reading comprehension, but these studies fail to acknowledge that these rehearsals imagine somatic body postures of the characters as a means of basic understanding (see chapter 1). Similarly, psychological and ethnographic descriptions of behaviors, events, individual actions, and apparent responses to these often consider somatic expression without naming it as such. Similarly, in philosophical arguments over the relationship of the mind to the body in ToM and PoM, shouldn't the soma—a multisensorial entity that is both material and also intelligent—figure more squarely in the debate? Somatic expression is often implicit across disciplines and theories but rarely is it made an explicit point of inquiry.

Scholarship specified as body studies are too diverse to generalize their investment in the soma while some affect theories, outside of Silvan Tomkins and Alexander Lowen, theorize *motivations* for somatic expression but rarely address the whole body as a subjective register. As it concerns racialization and racism, these fields and others liminally engage the soma as a nexus between what we believe the body evidences about so-called race and the soma's role in the materialization of social asymmetries.

Carefully crafted by the author, literary renderings of the soma mediate the immediacy of the whole body in lived experience, but the literary soma also elicits the mentally mimetic soma of the reader. Reading comprehension depends on the reader programming the character's experience as if his own. While the brain clearly delineates the character from the reader, like my experience rereading Piri Thomas's *Down These Mean Streets* discussed in chapter 1, I understand Piri most fully by somatically empathizing with him: I program his sudden bladder release by, at some level, feeling as if afraid myself and imagining urine running down my legs. Styles of neural programming vary as "neural structures make possible a range of aesthetic experiences" (Otis 2015, 520); however, the mind's "complex of embodied structures, processes, and contents . . . to a great extent . . . are universal" (Hogan 2015, 330–31). While each person has a different experience of affects, we are generally designed to mimetically replicate characters' experiences. Cognitive narratology positions texts in an aesthetic nexus of embodied mind, the body, and the environment (Zunshine 2006, 115–33)[10] while many Latin@/x texts specifically engender a semiotics of the soma, providing a deep account of characters' understanding, intentions, and response.

Tests of involuntary body function verify how somatic intelligence significantly motivates how we physically feel, regardless of what we would like to express or, for that matter, feel. In our day-to-day lives, we are quite competent at what Serres refers to as "the work of transforming mere sensitiveness into sense and sensibility both" (Connor 2005, 331), for we read somatic expression through the senses without being told explicitly how to do so. Culturally informed, as children, we imitate how elders read and respond to the somatic expression of others (Van den Stock, Righart, and de Gelder 2007). While the ability to somatically respond is a feature of being human, what motivates somatic expression is socially embedded in historically contingent cultural paradigms and customs. Whereas one culture may find homoerotic conduct a rite of passage, another culture finds it shameful, for example. Accordingly, what causes shame depends on cultural mores, although the human feeling and expression of shame will likely appear very similar.

HISTORICAL ANTECEDENTS

Racializing uses physical attributes as grounds for understanding an affective countenance—hardly a new endeavor. Ancient Egyptian and Indo-European studies of the humors offered somatic expression as a critical element in the assessment of an individual's health. Predecessors to humoralism, ancient Egyptian and Ayurvedic medicines assessed one's expressive face and overall somatic posture as an indicator of one's quality (and quantity) of blood but also of one's character. Countenance as medical diagnostic data dominated European, South Asian, and Middle Eastern medicine for nearly two thousand years (Porter [2002] 2003). Through the early 1900s, popular and scientifically respected medical assessments of phrenology predicted character and health by the shape, features, bumps, lumps, and size of the head but also indicated intellectual ability, generating a material connection between one's physical structure and one's character (Sorisio 2002, 21–24).

This historical practice of linking the material body to personality and social capabilities evolved into their further medicalization via "somatotypes" argued by twentieth-century American psychologist William Herbert Sheldon (1942) and later adopted by constitutional psychologists, criminologists, and eugenicists, and, particularly, Francis Galton (Hartl, Monnelley, and Elderkin

1982). Sheldon's taxonomy of ectomorphic, mesomorphic, and endomorphic bodies predicting one's character was later adopted per the Heath-Carter formula still used today (Norton and Olds 1996). This linkage between physical form and/or somatic expression as predictors of intelligence, health, and disposition were and continue to be a fertile ground for legitimating rationales in which physical features of a person denote faulty character—a useful logic in racializing and racism justifying social asymmetries in perpetuum. The racialization of Latin@/xs, mestizo and indigenous Latin Americans, and Native Americans across the American continents has been built on the extensive corpus of European and U.S. literatures on racist science, an example of which I offer the influential and popular *Crania Americana* by Samuel Morton (1839). In addition to the race science at the forefront of Morton's tome, historian Ann Fabian contextualizes the consolidation of Whiteness but also class for its readership. Fabian describes the world-making layout of the book that sold for today's equivalent of $500 a copy:

> The book would be large, a folio, printed with "new and beautiful type," on fine paper. It would include a map of the world, with continents color-coded by race, and sixty or seventy lithographs of skulls, near life-size and done with "great fidelity and elegance" by professional artists . . . [and] should appeal to "everyone whose attention has been directed to the study of physical man" and to everyone interested in owning a sample of American bookmaking at its finest. In the words of a supporter: "We can conscientiously and strongly recommend it to everyone who takes the slightest interest in anthropological or ethnographical investigations, and who is there that does not?" (Fabian 2010, 81)

Crania Americana and books like it mediated the violence of settler colonialism and eugenicist thinking against indigenous peoples across the Americas, attributing sophistication to the reader who had access to such exquisite and costly bookmaking. While we may find the findings and premises laughable or pathetic, we less often recognize their continued legacy in racializing cognition, an unchecked critical practice of consolidating socialized social superiority in the formation of the armchair racializer, one social script in a constellation of scripts, operating and underlying today's abysmal social relations in the United States. This cursory history supports a genealogy of racializing that combines physical attributes with and disposition as a pedagogy developed from an early systemic use of the human sensorium to fake empirical fact. As if it were a question of ontology, these disciplines elide the recognition of the employ of epistemic methods where physicality predicts character, legitimating one's social position. Thus, in addition to producing politically motivated truths, phrenology, eugenics, and other disciplines generate *deliberate* sense planning and interpretation, schema and scripts, promoting racializing as a cognition of affluent and cultured Whites.

Centuries of racist social training of our senses and judgement may explain results from cognitive neurological studies that show, as previously stated, that we almost instantaneously assess someone as an in- or out-group member. Given most of these studies test a subject's immediate response, results show we immediately racialize, assign sex and gender, determine the observed subject's age group, physical capacity, and often, sexual orientation. Our brains are structured to recognize some of these categories, but our brains do not show evidence of a site dedicated to racial identification in fMRI studies.[11] This immediacy suggests the extent to which our epistemological practice of "seeing race" relies on learned scripts of sense perception. The cultural dominance of the visual is duly noted, but how often do we identify someone as Latin@/x by what we hear? What ethnic and/or racial associations do we make based on the way a person moves or gesticulates while talking? And we are especially reactive to smell. In the sections that follow, I argue many Latin@/x texts rely on somatic data of sight, smell, and hearing to racially shame.

INTRODUCING SOMATIC ANALYSIS AND SHAMING THROUGH THE PROPER NAME

Humans commonly gather more sound than what appears externally present. To this seemingly odd statement, I add that while we listen, we simultaneously assemble other types of sense data affecting what and how we codify what we have heard. The auditory modality gathers sounds from the exterior world (e.g., voices, car horns, motors) while we speak, or smell, touch, and taste. Although we may physically filter sounds out or psychologically focus on something else, when we speak, we are also registering the sound of our own voice speaking. In addition to content, we might catch the pitch and cadence of our speaking and consider their effect in recognition of our somatic expression. In addition to these sounds, we simultaneously catch ourselves speaking internally—physically, a verbal vibration, simultaneously accompanied by our verbal mental chatter. Though "we integrate [these multiple data] unconsciously without effort," such hearing requires a sense of subjectivity capable of isolating each source of sound—mental chatter, organ function—from external environmental sound that effectively "puts one apart from oneself" (Miller 2005, 335), a capability we find elaborated in examples of Latin@/x literature when exposing how we effectuate racialization and racism. The soma situates the subject as always in relation to a given context, making the multiple registers of sound one of several categories of sense data relaying the quality of feeling in words. Inside and outside, audition inputs co-constitute what is possible to hear at a given moment. In chapter 3, I argue the inner rumblings of the innards are meaningful, but here, I point out the aspects of speech that communicate qualities of racist feelings in somatic expression.

To introduce this concept, I excerpt a scene from Luis Valdez's *No saco nada de la escuela* ([1971] 1990), a play exposing U.S. schooling as a site of institutional racial shaming and the role of the somatic audition in that process. In *No saco,* students are confronted with racial shaming in a dramatic piece that draws out their struggle, negotiation, and sometimes internalization of institutional and interpersonal racial shaming. While the children take different avenues in efforts to assuage the social threat of marginalization that racial shaming presents, I focus my remarks on the formative experience of young Moctezuma, marking the steps in this *aural* scene of racialization in the passage below. Teacher takes a role and struggles with the pronunciation of the boy's name, shaming him so he eventually surrenders to "Monty," an Anglicized sign with an English sound:

> TEACHER: ... Who's next. Moc ... Moc ... (*She can't pronounce his name.*) Ramirez!

Here, the stage directions indicating her cultural incompetency ends the struggle in an exclamation point as she withdraws social mutuality per *step one* in this scene of racialization. Her "Moc ... Moc ..." followed by the exclamative, "Ramirez!" in what I imagine an anglicized pronunciation of the boy's surname racializes somewhat like Trump's "Mooslims" discussed earlier. I imagine as a reader "Moc ... Moc ..." leads to frustration, anger, and some contempt. The child has been clearly singled out as problematically different than the other students:

> MONTY: Yes, teacher?
> TEACHER: How do you pronounce your name?
> MONTY: Moctezuma.
> TEACHER: What?
> MONTY: Moctezuma.
> TEACHER: Oh! What a funny name! (*She laughs and class joins her.* TEACHER *stomps foot and shuts them up.*) Class!

Teacher moves to *step two* where she ridicules the boy with classmates following suit. While she enjoys the stretch of her authority using the boy as fodder for communal derision, her need for control over the affective environment motivates her somatic stomp of the foot indicating her command for silence. The boy continues to act as obstruction, an objectionable object in the lines that follow. From this affective somatic place of contemptuous deanimation, Teacher moves to *step three,* suspicious disgust:

> (*To* MOCTEZUMA.) And whatever does it mean?
> MONTY: He was an emperor in the times of the Indians. He was a Mexican like me.
> TEACHER: Oh! You mean Montezuma.
> MONTY: No, Moctezuma.
> TEACHER: Montezuma.
> MONTY: Moctezuma.
> TEACHER: Montezuma! (70)

Moctezuma's attempt to maintain the Spanish spelling and the pronunciation of his name in a U.S. classroom is the primary tension in this exchange. Ultimately, Teacher wrests control of Moctezuma's name, insisting on her knowledge of the Aztec king named "Montezuma." In addition to stage directions, we imagine how bodies would deliver the exchange on stage. I envision the back and forth between an adult character playing a young boy in this scene forging the strength to assert himself in the face of being racially shamed by his teacher and by his classmates, peers who on the playground he probably considers friends. Racial shaming efficiently marginalizes while simultaneously consolidating the power of the racializer and provoking complicity from nontargeted witnesses. After several exchanges, she insists on calling him "Monty," effectively demeaning the boy into a degree of ethnic erasure rendered symbolically in the spelling change, but also through the aural register pressuring the child and his classmates to sound his name and thus resignify him as if culturally assimilated, a form of social marginalization scripted in *step four.* Eventually, Moctezuma gives up the fight with Teacher and adopts "Monty," avoiding further shaming and perhaps hoping to gain institutional favor (79–86). The degree of harm becomes evident when "Monty" mocks himself as a "bright, Mexican-American *comprado*" (a sell-out) later, as a college student (86). Shame internalized, Monty cows to Teacher's acoustic shaming, and because cognition of dramatic scripts requires us to fill in the actor's moving, gestural, feeling body with meaning amid typically sparse words

(McCarroll 2016, 142), Teacher's somatic intimidation completes this scene of Monty's racialization.

Latin@/x writers often trope naming as a fundamental site of hegemonic attempts to control.[12] A combination of a Mexican name, accented English, and native pronunciation of the Mexican name make the name a potent sense sign. Because "U.S. language stigmas are so deeply embedded that monolingualism is treated as a sign of class privilege, and bi- or multilingualism can be viewed as evidence of insufficient patriotism and lower-class social positions" (Miller 2011, 6), the purported undecipherability of Spanish for English monolinguals obfuscates the sonic charge of an ethnic accent as auditory sense data with which racializers shame. According to the dramatic argument, the purportedly unknowable becomes knowable to Teacher by a single consonant change, from Moctezuma to Montezuma. Hardly unpronounceable, his namesake is actually a known historical personage to Teacher—of course, on her terms, not the student's. Teacher ignores the student's explanation of Moctezuma as the Aztec emperor of Mexico, and instead, recontextualizes this historic ruler into a figure of vanquish, analogized in the Marine hymn "The Halls of Montezuma" that she hums, memorializing the 1847 U.S. military operation of Chapultepec Castle in Mexico City during the Mexican-U.S. War. The boy proceeds to address himself as Monty instead of Moctezuma. He has become other to himself, internalizing this harm in compliance with performing racial shame that concludes this scene of racialization.

An aural contest with sociopolitical stakeholders gives credence to Serres's assertion that hearing is a sense "no more located in one place than [is] the skin" (Abbas 2005, 159),[13] demonstrating the politics of sense perception in the practices of racialization and racism. The name designated ethnic audibly intrudes into the public sphere in need of regulation and branches out to other sense realms in the struggle for control of the Othered self. Two examples further indicate the specific symbolic power of the proper name in lived experience and presented in Chican@/x texts. In Américo Paredes's *George Washington Gómez* (1990), a father names his borderland Chicano son after the U.S. president. "A Gringo name he shall have!" Mr. Gómez exclaims, reflecting the father's desire to see his son as part of the national whole (16). However, this desired level of social acceptance was unlikely for Chicano and Mexican families in South Texas during the twentieth century. Gumersindo aspires that his son, nicknamed "Gualinto" by the boy's grandmother (16–17), link himself to the American Dream through his name "George Washington Gómez," but the narrative delivers the tonal rendering of the boy's name as "Jorge Wachinton" (15). Paredes gives us "Jorge Wachinton" in the manner of gestalt. The Spanish phonetics of the quintessential historic figure challenges what the reader expects to read—a narrative exclusively written in English with maybe a few italicized (signaling foreign) Spanish or Chicano words. For the hegemonic reader, referring to George Washington Gómez as "Jorge Wachinton" could task the unfamiliar reader with sounding out the letters in order to hear and thus recognize this Spanish aural production in what might seem a parodic cultural appropriation of a U.S. icon. "Gualinto" nor "Washington" will afford him the social fluidity hoped for by his father; however, Paredes's phonetic transcription of these names and their bound social aspirations creates a compelling aesthetic that confronts readers' expectations. Thus begins an aesthetic rendering of the disjunction between the desire for social inclusion and an aural tie to familial Spanish in production of his "gringo" name. Interestingly, despite knowledge of the family's cultural heritage and daily life among principally Chican@/x families, readers may be surprised by their sudden prejudice exposing their monolingual and middle-class reading expectations in a standard American English accent, regardless of character or context.

The Spanish phonetic spelling of the protagonist's name marks the oppressive assumption of reading and, in one's mind, hearing U.S. middle-class English. Had the author maintained the English spelling only of the boy's name, we would have continued our carefully scripted blindness to produce White middle-class sensory output in writing, as many of us do in our lives. Where George Washington becomes Jorge Wachinton and Gualinto, each name acknowledges and simultaneously negates the social position imposed by the name, the body it signals, and the subject position of the person calling the boy, evidencing the productivity of "double negations" in the "unstable grounds" of borderlands argued by Ramón Saldívar (2006, 188). I add the sonic variations of George Washington Gómez as aural aspirations for "redemption of the hopes of the past" (Saldívar 2006, 188), but later they become a sensory source of biting irony, a somatic venue for racializing shame. By naming his son George Washington Gómez, Gumersindo seeks to bypass the a priori social marginalization his son will suffer in *step four* in the many scenes of racialization that plot of the novel. George Washington Gómez foretells Gualinto's assimilation and eventual spiritual demise.

The "tensions between U.S. Anglo-centrism and increasingly audible multilingual populations" that have given "rise to powerful, unpredictable social and cultural conflicts," suggested by Joshua Miller (2011, 16), are succinctly drawn in the battle over the power to name and the social politics played out in uttering one's name. The semiotic content of names becomes an important symbolic site for people in most cultures, but in the context of the strength and specificity of intersectionally racializing in the U.S., the name is a deictic site that aurally *sounds* a body, signifying a relation to phenotypic appearances and the nation in a locutionary scene. Like Valdez and Paredes, many Latin@/x authors focus on how naming is aesthetically efficacious in presenting the immediacy, complexity, contention, and harm of everyday racialization practiced through conferring race. Sociological research on naming in Sweden points to the substantial material and social benefits of taking a culturally assimilated first name, even more evident by adopting a Swedish surname (Arai and Thoursie 2009). This research joins research by U.S. scholars over the past forty years that identify name change for economic and social gain (Bertrand and Mullainathan 2004; Doleac and Stein 2013; Oreopoulous 2009), suggesting levels of assimilation are cued by sense data to read and hear levels of social belonging in the assimilated name.

These studies tend to focus on the artifact nature of the name as sign rather than the discernment and processing of signs, but the multisensory nature of somatic discernment underlies what we cognitively structure as "race" by organizing sense perceptions into social scripts. The human sensorium—touch, taste, sight, smell, and audition—is the primary locus for the somatic expression evident in human interactions, concepts, ideologies, and social practices coalescing in literary scenes of racialization, which in my analysis, is shaped by the work of Silvan Tomkins and Alexander Lowen, two key thinkers who made somatic expression primary to their psychotherapy work and research.

THE DECIPHERABILITY OF THE SOMA

The soma responds internally to our life circumstances through a rumbling in the stomach, a pain in the neck and shoulders (the subject of chapter 3), but in narrative, the soma more often externally broadcasts how we visually consider others, the way we smell, and how we sound, conveying how racialization and racism are conducted. This chapter explores the sense emanations of somatic expression, giving a text a particular "cognitive flavor" (Rabinowitz 2015, 87) that tools negative value to bodies browned Latin@/x. Building on the theory argued in chapter 1, shaming is at once a serious psychological harm and also a sociological and a biological harm that, in literary treatments, exposit shame, transacted through the senses, as a primary strain on well-being transacted through the senses. I begin by analyzing the complexity of audition to address seeing, then smelling, and return to hearing in this study of the impact of the senses in their somatic work of racializing.

The soma is a psychologically—and physiologically—layered entity responding to the body and society, simultaneously and continuously. Its expression is clear and decipherable; in fact, it is readily, and most often instantaneously, understood. I am indebted to the psychotherapy practitioner, scholar, and theorist, Silvan Tomkins, and practitioner and theorist, Alexander Lowen, who treated somatic expression as an essential interlocutor in diagnosing psychological issues. Silvan Tomkins considered temporally cued affect a spontaneous embodied communication, while the work of Alexander Lowen assessed and treated long-standing shame in the soma. Tomkins and Lowen[14] developed useful typologies to unpack the suffering expressed in the physical body; bioemotional and psychological topographies provide me a somatic context to argue sense perception in scenes of racialization in Latin@/x texts.

Professor and researcher at Princeton University, City University of New York, and Rutgers University, Tomkins conducted a study of children to determine the biological capacity of humans to display nine affects on a continuum of interest-excitement, enjoyment-joy, surprise-startle, distress-anguish, anger-rage, fear-terror, shame-humiliation, contempt-disgust, and dissmell-disgust ([1962–92] 2008).[15] Tomkins's background in theater was surely influential in developing his subject of analysis of the precognitive, innate felt response that most tellingly registers in facial expressions. His work has most famously been disseminated by Paul Ekman's facial analysis, used in institutions such as the Central Intelligence Agency, the Federal Bureau of Investigation, and other governmental entities, and to which I extend Jan Van den Stock, Ruthger Righart, and Beatrice de Gelder's challenge: "Considering the emotional value of bodily expressions, it is somewhat surprising that the study of perception of whole-body expressions lags so far behind that of facial expressions" (2007, 487).

While Tomkins focused mostly on research, the therapeutic approach of Alexander Lowen has been influential around the world. The Alexander Lowen Foundation sponsors national and international conferences where practitioners from a variety of fields broaden and deepen the application of Lowen's work. Lowen, the author of nine books translated in over a dozen languages, both in his private practice and in his leadership roles in prominent psychological organizations, systematized some of his mentor Wilhelm Reich's theories to read body posture, musculature, and facial expression in relation to the therapy client's verbal description of presenting problems. Lowen found quite a contrast between the client's self-disclosure and her somatic expression. Finding clients often defensive and otherwise limited in what they would verbally reveal about themselves or what they knew of themselves, Lowen developed *bioenergetic analysis,* a protocol to appreciate the soma's full expression of underlying hurts, traumas, and frustrations. His curative protocol sought to put aside verbal expression and unleash the harm trapped in the somatic body through physical activities like bending backward over a bench or ball, stretching open the torso to physically surface pains it hides and guards against. The client was often able to bring hidden or forgotten issues to the fore where, together with talk therapy, Lowen's clients relieved themselves of many long-stored defenses against shame and other feelings (1958–2005).[16] With some specificity, Lowen argues particular kinds of early childhood shaming, decipherable in somatic reactions, are so ingrained that they build expression into one's musculature apparent in posture and legible whole-body expression, even when in a resting state.

In *character analysis,* Lowen identifies long-standing postures defending against earlier, repetitive trauma. The trauma conditions the body in the figure of the psychopathic, the schizoid, the rigid, the oral, and the masochistic. Lowen's somatic map is more conceptually helpful to me than applicable as an analytical tool for my study. Taking as its premise, in my terms, somatic manifestation, I present his theory as one of the few available to evaluate somatic human response to cumulative life experience and, particularly, shaming. I do not directly employ his theory in the texts I examine in this chapter nor elsewhere; however, his extensive clinical engagement supports my analysis of the soma in studying how we transact racialization and racism through shame. While the work of Tomkins depends on sensory input for facial output, Lowen maps lifelong stifling and protective reactions to emotional harm. Both models utilize the expressive body—the soma—as an interlocutor of experience and social interaction. With these thinkers' paradigms in mind, I lead with the visual legibility of shame to appreciate how the soma materializes intersectional intraracialization in multisensory fashions through the character Cecilia in Xyta Maya Murray's *Locas* in the next section. In the remaining sections, I exposit the faculties of smell and conclude with the aural in the specific literary context of the soma and intraracialization.

SIGHT

I know I'm no beauty. They call me Muñeca because I'm short but that doesn't make me dainty. I got these square hips and shoulders, like a little fat box, and I'm Aztec looking with a flat brown face, too dark to be any real good. Thick hands. You can be that way if you're a man, but a girl has to be light and thin and small all over. But me, I show myself too much. My thoughts flare out of my eyes, there's a hard smile on my mouth. And my body moves so hard and clunky, bobbing from side to side. (Murray 1997, 55)

A simple, seemingly unremarkable passage, Cecilia, one of two protagonists in Xyta Maya Murray's novel *Locas,* illustrates how shame infiltrates our countenance. Some critics opine there are social benefits to moral shaming (Deonna, Rodogno, and Teroni 2012; Probyn 2005), but hegemonic culture wraps morality and shame with phenotype. These harms are *visible* in the way Cecilia holds her muscles, her posture, her face, in the way she walks, stands, and sits.

This twenty-something Chicana of East Los Angeles, California, clearly manifests the harm of a priori scenes of intersectional *intraracialization—*racialization committed by in-group members. In this passage, Cecilia plays the limited omniscient tagalong in a critique of in-group gender relations of the Chicano gang led by her brother, Manny. The passage describes her external visual objectification, imbricated by her somewhat bolstered social position as Manny's sister, which stands in tension with her somatic response of mitigated dissent. In our lived experience we may have little awareness of our resting somatic expression or that our resting expression says so much about our life's struggles. Like Murray's Cecilia, literary renderings in scenes of racialization Latin@/xs describe a character's somatic manifestation of racial shaming, which, through repetition over time, becomes habituated in one's resting somatic expression.

You may wonder why I chose this character and this passage for our consideration of the somatic knowledge we gather from vision. Certainly, there are sexier or racier characters to examine. Gilles Deleuze's somatic read of Lawrence of Arabia's report comes to mind, where Lawrence remarks his surprising erection during a gang rape (1997, 123). Deleuze chose this report to make his argument for the autonomy of the (my word) soma, and although convincing, for many, it is also titillating. I concur and admire Deleuze's argument of flowing affective intensity that moves before, beyond, and with the mind for the Deleuzian body. The virtual field of sense perception lying outside of the mind can be a source of subversion, but I challenge my reader to consider the politics of literary titillation that sideline, if not suppress, prejudices and other naturalized attitudes that form habituated cognitive scripts conditioning our perception. Depending on our awareness, we may find we concur with Cecilia's opinion of herself.

When we somatically simulate her description, we may arrive at a very ho-hum idea of Cecilia and women like her. Her quotidian conflict obfuscating between different somatic registers makes she and others see herself as a weak "sheep" (in the novel's parlance) in Murray's adept somatic depiction of the blandness of an intersectionally racialized Brown woman. We are not equally free to express how we feel, as argued earlier, and Murray visibly renders the kind of social invisibility to Brown women: the housecleaner, the nanny, the janitorial crew, and the mother in the park with her Brown baby. On many occasions, we marginalize people like Cecilia, and when those women are also us, we can marginalize ourselves, as does Cecilia, using our sensing organism to distance ourselves from others but also from ourselves. The social eye incorporates and shames us as a form of "domination that separates us from our bodies" as bell hooks states (Lion's Roar, 2014) where we experience ourselves at the periphery of our own perception. And we may lead us to think less of *Locas* as a result.

If we found ourselves initially dismissing this passage as unexceptional and perhaps unworthy, we might ask ourselves how our literary judgements occlude the voice of those who do not necessarily feel the need to capitulate to a U.S. obsessive appreciation for quirky individuality or advertised uniqueness, those who may either believe themselves to be enough as they are, or those who are not interested in fabricating an egoic sense of specialness that could draw them more socially visible. In other literatures, disadvantaged White characters may also be written as socially unseen or underappreciated, but they are usually still rendered in hidden worlds of exceptionalism (e.g., several of the works by Dickens, Steinbeck, Fante, and Melville's *Bartleby, the Scrivener: A Story of Wall Street*).

I would argue exceptionalism is not a common artistic recourse in many instances of Latin@/x literature, making it, in my estimation, one of its greatest contributions. Murray, like other Latin@/x writers, presents us with the challenge to face our reluctance to read of a less-than-titillating rendering of an intersectionally racialized other. We point to his or her unremarkability, and thus hide the degree to which we are wed to esteeming the so-called interesting ones. Our scripted intersectionally racializing filters of perception expose our literary judgement as superficial, culturally narrow, and our criteria of assessment for what makes a character sympathetic, unconvincing, or a literary style appreciable. If we are willing to take a hard look at ourselves, we may find *our judgement* boring rather than the character or the writing.

This passage on Cecilia is particularly of interest to me because we can readily discern the *steps of intraracialization* that Cecilia, in turn, enacts against herself. The passage leads through the visual when she concedes she is Indian-looking, an unattractive racialization of Brown operating in Mexican and Chican@/x cultures, which ironizes the cutesy flattery of her pet name "muñeca" in somatic dissonance of *step one*. The men who generally ignore her, except when to ingratiate themselves with her gang-boss brother, use "muñeca" to actually mark their lack of regard for her; their feigned desire or affection for her are provisional and tactical vis-à-vis their subordination to Manny. Cecilia articulates her internalization of their deanimation in *step two* by describing her estimation of her face as flat and brown, and her body, square and boxy with man-like hands. Intersectional shaming, like other forms of shame, disjoints her sense of self conveyed in rigidity she equates with a Mesoamerican artifact, or conversely, a box—an industrial-like body. In both cases, these descriptions register a "failure to live up to this ideal self—experienced as a sense of inferiority, defeat, flaw, or weakness—that results in the feeling of shame" (Morrison 1989, 36). To self-describe as *muñeca*, Cecilia registers contempt of being rendered a feigned play-object, not a person, but stiff—a use-vessel—a gendered and raced entity of diminished social reception in completion of *step two*'s deanimation.

Cecilia internalizes racial suspicion in a negative, blurred connection to the Aztecs of Mexico in *step three*. From this affective distance with herself, she intimates self-disgust wondering where her darkness comes from, living with this social fact of Brown in Mexico and in the United States, where her skin is "too dark to be any real good" (55). This skepticism lingers as an affective frame where the events that follow confirm her separation from self, a shamed self that Cecilia can approach but not accept. A habituated state, Cecilia's resting soma registers this sense of disgust and mistrust of self.[17] Still, Cecilia falls into deeper levels of loss of self. We might think Cecilia's residing somatic expression would be an uninhibited register of her "lived body" (Merleau-Ponty, [1945] 2014), compromised as it is by the intersectional intraracialization she lives. How she is perceived on a daily basis inhabits the musculature in her body and parts of her facial expression, testifying in turn to how she effectively sees herself from the periphery of other's sense perception of her. But she lives in tension with the tension of her habituated soma.

Adding to the pejoratives of being "no beauty" and "no good," she adds, "I show myself too much." Although her facial expression should subordinate and somatically verify her acknowledgment of her unworthiness toward social disclosure in *step four,* the hot expressiveness of her eyes, the derision visible across her mouth, as well as her gait, bares her body's acknowledgment of and resistance to her diminishment in the eyes of others. Transcending her gendered intraracialized inscription is not up for discussion in the novel, but her somatic expression displays a subtle but resistant stance. Because vision works simultaneously with other sense perceptions, the steps inferred in the way Cecilia describes how she sees herself also register in the somatic description of Cecilia's heavy gait.

Whether attributable to weight or to repressed anger thrust down in the clunk-clunk of her walking feet, the visual description of her gait and the sound of her step reveals Cecilia's response to her intersectional intraracialization that she is otherwise unsafe to publicly express. The auditory cue deepens the sense of her personhood more adroitly in this somatic analysis—it elicits a presence fortifying the psychological remove due to shame and challenges in a more immediate and interesting way than just vision or other narrative strategies such as inner thought or assessments made by other characters.

Diminished or not, she sounds her steps, challenging traumatic shame that otherwise "destroys trust and disorganizes us into a state of arrest" (Conger 2001, 4). She audibly forges on, marking her presence amid her inner contempt and disgust. For Cecilia, gendered racial shaming impedes her ability to feel integrated, apparent in her self-description but also elsewhere in the novel, where Cecilia occupies tertiary interlocutions, where she reacts more often than responds. Even with the flicker of dissent in her eyes, it can be argued she seldom fashions her life according to her wants and needs of her plaintive somatic acceptance.

Western cultures are organized by vision, such that we believe we objectively see, but we do not often consider the social crafting of what we see and the value we assign to that seen. As readers, we enhance the impact of what we know of Cecilia's subjugation by interpreting what she is seeing through the lens of intersectional racializing that we, like she, have been trained to use. It is likely unsurprising that vision is the sense perception most often called upon in literature, but to the question of intersectional racialization, how we interpret smell can be equally damning and shameful, a somatic register to which I now turn.

OLFACTION

On the word *stink,* William Ian Miller argues, "No word dedicated to the disgustful sensations of the other senses has this power" (1997, 78). Textual analysis of scenes of racialization confirms that smell powerfully arbitrates both the threat to and the promise of pleasure. A sense perception that enters us whether we want it to or not, the power of smell has something to do with the smeller's relative inability to ward off or control the smell. Except by distancing oneself from its source or creating a barrier to its spread, the permeation of our environment by odors invokes the ambiguity of stink until or unless we identify the source, and even then, the source is often diaphanous, and difficult to identify. Likewise, one does not know how much of a noxious substance has been ingested with the smell nor how much of a particular smell indicates a physical threat.

Nelly Rosario's *Song of Water Saints* (2002) paints a scene of racialization structured by the somatics of smell. A climatic scene in the novel, the scene takes place during the 1916–24 United States' occupation of the Dominican Republic. In portraying this vicious U.S. neocolonial operation, repeated in different ways across the Caribbean and Central America over the last centuries, the novel highlights the military tactic of interpersonal violence, in the forms of beatings, rape, pillage, and murder to subdue Dominicans.

Graciela, a young single mother living in a shanty on the outskirts of town, escapes the tedium and gendered oppressive role she is expected to carry out as homemaker, lover, and mother on a train headed for nowhere in particular. She encounters Eli Cavalier, a German-French traveler, who proposes himself a nutritionist and a race scientist. He conducts research by bedding "negresses" in different ways to alter their smell with herbs, which he argues makes sex with Black women particular. Graciela, desperate for sustenance and for gendered liberation, and despite the repulsion she feels for him, will eventually accept his offers of food and drink in concession for sex.

From a sociological perspective, as early as Hippocratic medicine, odor was considered a contaminant that could permeate the skin, a pathogen in need of control. The physical reaction to noxious scent became an affective platform for social rejection. Racial shaming uses the somatics of dissmell to program scent as a material marker of race. To this point, anthropologist Martin F Manalansan IV states: "olfaction is a political and cultural process that should be seen in terms of the visceral or the emotional which includes shame, fear, disgust and shock" (2006, 50). During the era of eugenics, natural body odors were signified a lack of personal hygiene and a sign of moral laxity, a physiological quality in the guise of social threat. The intensity of the social interpretation of smell perhaps explains the observation by William Ian Miller, professor of law and honorary professor of history, of the dearth of smell synonyms in the English language. Miller notes that we tend to employ the noun itself, which could refer in reality to a pleasant scent but that we use to specify a bad odor (i.e., "It smells!"; 1997, 68). Tomkins's affect of dissmell complements Miller's findings where bad odors evoke considerable anxiety when compared to other sense data, thus serving a biological necessity to filter out rotten food or the effect of noxious fumes:

> A highly localized receptor, the nose, but often emanates from unlocalizable and diffuse sources. Smells are pervasive and invisible, and capable of threatening like poison; smells are the very vehicles of contagion. Odors are thus especially contaminating and much more dangerous than localized substances one may or may not put in the mouth. (Miller 2005, 342)

This sensorial platform for characterological assessment in turn substantiates the social undesirability of immigrants, affirming Manalansan's argument that immigrants are "culturally constructed to be the natural carrier and source of undesirable sensory experiences and is popularly perceived to be the site of polluting and negative olfactory signs" (2006, 41). The connection Manalansan makes between smell and social standing would easily extend to the situation of Latin@/xs, who are perennial immigrants despite legal standing or even centuries of residence. John Dollard, an early twentieth-century theorist who studied the social inscription of smell, averred that perceiving the racialized as odiferous has been "an extremely serviceable way of fixing . . . an undesirable lower-caste mark and by inference justifying superiority behavior" ([1937] 1998, 380). The focus on the smell of the ethnic and/or racialized other indicates we script smell for sociopolitical goals and their underlying racist ideologies.

The sociology of smell tenses into politics, directing the scene where Graciela encounters Eli. Eli sees the lone, young, Black woman in a train cabin and immediately presumes Graciela heterosexual and sexually available. For Eli, scent confirms her gender, race, and class (*step three*) as denotations of his visual racialization of Graciela into negress, unbound. The simultaneity of multiple sense perception teases out smell to add to what he sees to guide how he imagines her undressed. Eli visually assesses Graciela's skin color and predicts "purplish nipples" that he imagines meet "gray creases where ass meets thighs" (67). As "a concentration of living essence, and a volatile flight from shape" (Connor 2004, 216), Eli predicts her smell will be unpleasant, attributing smell with a social sort of proprioception, that when unpleasant, exaggerates the sense of physical proximity and, therefore, threat. Thus, smell is a key sense leading to the attenuation of *step four*, somatic expression of social foreclosure where Graciela now infected with syphilis, ends her days alone and half-crazed.

Eli focuses on categorizing Graciela's generic gendered Blackness, her smell catalyzing her inscription as a negress. As with all the women he has studied, Eli uses olfaction as "the means to corporealize dislike and a prominent excuse for expressions of racism, sexism, classism and xenophobia" (Drobnick 2006, 14). Eli intersectionally racializes Graciela's scent and establishes the olfactory sense as "the boundary between self and other" (Drobnick 2006, 14), a mental filter to unify his sexual desire and his racialized disgust for her (*step three*), and she becomes a deanimated scientific object/subject (*step two*). So unconcerned is he with the specificity of her ethnic background and other factors that, in *step three*, he sets the stage to seduce her to engage in sex with him in confirmation of his racial suspicions of her global Blackness. Third-person omniscient narration marks the change from sociopathic seducer to sadistic dominator, generating the narrative distance necessary to appreciate this change in demeanor.

Eli feigns sophisticate, enticing her with the promise of the conviviality of food in order to ply her for sex. His presentation tritely pretends his serious regard for her, but his initial gendered, racialized stare and the narrator's omniscience indicate peer mutuality foreclosed from the start. But Rosario writes the scene reflecting the need and/or compulsion to act/reenact the steps of racialization in an indulgent practice of power. The greater part of their interaction exposes both the contemptuous deanimation of *step two* and social marginalization of *step four*. Disinclined to openly assault her, perhaps because he pretends himself a "gentleman," or perhaps because Graciela exudes enough psychological and physical strength to combat such advances, Eli manipulates her consent for sex in a cross-purposed seduction. He appeals to her thirst for experience with his gross worldliness. Coupled with the promise of food and drink in exchange for sex, he cajoles her acquiescence, somatically described. Her tacit agreement finds her in a salt bath at a brothel, her demeanor, a somatic revealing of *step four*, accepting herself a gendered, racialized test object and, therefore, socially foreclosed upon. Rather than casual sex partner, let alone romantic interest or friend, Eli treats her to his racializing project and requires she bathe before joining her in the brothel room:

—You look like the cat that ate the rat, he said.

He was out of his jacket and wore only pants. A new authority rang in his voice, as if he were lounging in his own home.

—Sit up, he said.

From a small pouch he produced some leaves. He opened Graciela's legs and rubbed the dried leaves into her pubic hair.

—Lift your arms.

He did the same to her armpits.

—¿What is it for? Graciela asked. She was disappointed at the brisk indifference toward her nudity.

—Seasoning for my meal, Eli said.

. . .

—Some things are made by nature for pure enjoyment. . . . Stand up. Let me see you.

He made Graciela walk around the tub of dirty water. Had her bend over from behind. Had her raise her arms. Had her untie all her hair.

. . .

—Stop now, he said. (78–79)

Scientists argue the olfactory sense is the most proficient nonverbal communicator. Current neurobiological studies report humans can identify millions of smells, making the number of studies of perception of scent curiously limited. Some studies show humans have a highly developed apocrine system, which along with sebaceous glands, emit body scent through the skin (Stoddart 1990, 50). The apocrine system may be the oldest nonverbal channel in animals where aroma cues transmit data even in single-celled creatures; it is so evolutionarily old, even single-cell organisms possess the sense.[18]

Smell predates visual acuity in the once-upon-an-evolutionary time when our ancestors walked on all fours. According to Freud, smell at an earlier time in human history regulated the timing of sexual activity. When humans began to walk upright, they became physically removed from offensive bodily smell (specifically excrement and menses). Because of the distance from the nose to the genitals, sexual excitement became a function of sight more than of smell. Smell acquired a more punitive function, diminishing sexual desire when foul (i.e., the smell of feces and menses according to Freud [(1905) 2000], who later claimed that female genitalia is potentially odiferous and sexually off-putting; Miller 1997, 70–77). Not surprisingly, humans can scent-identify their blood kin, delineating in-group and out-group members. Additionally, smell signals sexual arousal but also fear as in the adage "I smell danger." These capacities complicate smell into "a code for class, racial and ethnic differences and antagonisms" (Manalansan IV 2006, 44). Western culture's relative obsession with female smell could yield a woman a certain measure of social capital, but unbeknownst to Graciela, Eli's racialized and classed sexual interest in Graciela has removed any temporal or situational agency she may have thought she would have.[19]

Perhaps grateful for the attention or the chance of luxuriating in a bath, Graciela's classed, raced, and sexed body initially acquiesces to the temporary masking of her own smell by the bath and herbs while this perfuming makes her aware that Eli and perhaps other White men find her natural scent unsavory. She becomes aware of her smell, a condition of self experienced freely and perhaps enjoyed before meeting Eli. In this narrative, smell is the sense data that most conclusively marks a time before her internalization of intersectional racialization and a time after. Graciela comes to understand she must see herself as one who, for White men, smells.

The bath alters and adds to her scent, but it also gives Graciela the complicated opportunity to assert her agency. She has a new perverse notion of how she is sexy *and* repulsive to White men, and finds herself curious if not somewhat desirous of what she should expect in the sexual act. Graciela's somatic gesture of outstretched arms as Eli approaches her express an invitation for sex but also for tenderness he contests with his racializing soma that pressures her into subordination. Her yawn that follows suggests critical ennui with the role she is to pretend to embody during sex and postsocial foreclosure (*step four*). But this exchange with Eli demonstrates her power to somatically adjudicate repulsion and disgust as well.

As he lays atop of her during intercourse, Graciela attempts to ward off vaginal pain and to find sexual pleasure, while she contends with Eli's overriding stink. Carrying the moral impropriety Eli displayed upon first meeting (where he fondled himself in front of Graciela), Rosario's description of Eli's repugnant scent of spoiled milk somatically connects his sexual comportment to his antisocial character afforded by his relative social standing. In their initial encounter on the train, Graciela refuses to ascribe social or personal superiority to the (relatively) moneyed White European, repelled as she is by his conduct, his frivolous self-presentation, and his stink. She holds a handkerchief to her nose in disgust, a gesture of repulsion she confirms in words: he must be very sick (69). His smell tells her Eli is rotten, old, and perverse, and her sense of smell becomes a source of rebuff with which she removes her sense of self from what is occurring in an effort to gain from the oppressive experience while minimizing her psychological subjection to harm. Regardless of social asymmetries, the power of olfaction to shame works both ways.

Her voiced rebuke of this first lewd act accompanies her perception of his sickly smell during intercourse. As the sex scene advances, Eli's own foul odor elaborates on his moral decrepitude, in contrast to Graciela's weakening interpersonal power:

> In bed, Eli sniffed her. A beast on the hunt. As she lay on her stomach, Eli's sour-milk smell stung Graciela's nostrils when he pushed himself inside of her. (79)

Ironically, Eli's stink seems to embolden his somatic gesture of control over her in "the heel of his hand" which "pressed the small of her back until Graciela felt a place deep inside her yield and she could not move" (79). It would seem plausible that Eli's apparent disinterest in her as a particular person or special sex partner weakens the sense of sexual authority she enjoys in sexual relations with others as she acquiesces to his subjugating commands, psychologically making way for her submission to the ensuing painful, nonmutually satisfying intercourse.

The next day, Graciela escapes from the brothel, but upon Graciela's return to her village and family life, the narrative forgoes what could have led to her sexually blossoming. Instead, the narrative grows silent, offering nothing more than an eclipsed mention that since her return, syphilis has spread throughout the village. Furthermore, the narrative marks Eli's stink with disease where smell is the narrative's sensorial conduit that permanently marks Graciela's selfhood into intimately colonized Other, who later loses her mind and her life. The narrative rejoins the social inscription of body smell where the soma materializes the putrid physical nature and psychology of Eli, who, representative of historical European and American colonizers, physically and psychologically infects Dominicans as colonized Others.

Rosario aestheticizes the power and politics of smell by turning the tables on who stinks. And though Graciela executes her power to smell and thus judge Eli, this sensual authority does not change the deep asymmetry in the inscription of respective subject positions. Nonetheless, Graciela utilizes smell as a somatic vehicle to register her presence, assert her subjectivity, and perhaps, to establish a basis for negotiating more goods (e.g., food, conversation, lodging, sex) than she might have otherwise. Spoken or left unsaid, somatic perception of smell is a human capacity as well as a social power, insidiously effective in service to subjugating agendas.

With exceptions such as Oscar "Zeta" Acosta's *The Autobiography of a Brown Buffalo* discussed in the next chapter, Latin@/x narrative incursions into the olfactory realm tend to present smells in a positive light: the good smells of amá's sofrito or the glorious smell of ripe mangos, invoking a feeling of home for diasporic communities. Perhaps because of the potency of the association between bad smell and intersectional racialization, these texts more often engage the soma of smell as nostalgic rather than presenting the racializer's inscription of the smells against the Latin@/x community, and thus sidestepping the painful use of smell and subjugation.[20] Smell is uniquely powerful in racializing, but in the following section, Angelo Parra's *Song of the Coquí* will reveal the surprising power of racialized sound.

THE AUDITORY MODALITY

"Why do certain accents . . . inspire such visceral emotional reactions?" asks Joshua L. Miller in *Accented America: The Cultural Politics of Multilingual Modernism* (2011, 8). In the case of Moctezuma in *No saco nada de la escuela*, we not only see, we also *hear* a body's Brownness in an accent. We perceive accent as "a marker of minority language usage" that "labels the minority as an 'other'" (Del Valle 2003, 144). A Spanish accent functions as a sense impression scripted in many sectors of the U.S. population to elicit somatic disgust and contempt as affective measures that nationalize how we hear. Miller argues that "the logic and appeal of English-only Americanism" is "based in a historically specific ideological conflation of nation, race, class, and gender in reconstructing language forms" (2011, 16), which thrust and parry for social control over inflected speech, dialects, and certain varieties of nonstandard accent in English. Because "the salience of accent . . . controls the flow of interaction and signals our communicative intentions," a sensory driver signaling somatic withdrawal (*step one*) and instigating contemptuous deanimation and disgusted confirmation (*steps two* and *three*), an accent "situates the speaker in terms of group belonging and affirms personal identity and stance in an immediate way" (Moyer 2013, 11), an efficacious output in executing social marginalization per *step four*.

Research indicates an early capacity to discern accent where "children as young as five-months old, who have virtually no verbal competence, can discriminate between two languages or dialects, provided that one of the languages/dialects is their own" (Neuliep 2014, 300). In fact, according to some scientists, our aural perceptions guide us to engage with those who *sound* like us (Kinzler cited in Neuliep 2014, 300).[21] Common in *step three*, scenes of racialization illustrate the perfunctory, habituated nature of this kind of assessment: upon distinguishing a nonstandard accent, a racializer moves to confirm racial suspicions and asks, sometimes with contrived sensitivity or curiosity, "Where are you from?" (I challenge the reader who argues the possibility of simple earnest curiosity with this question: Is curiosity over accent ever about seeing the other as an in-group member?)

At other times, inquiry over accent is delivered with polite hostility (a typical affect regardless of political stance) and a somatic expression of dissonance overlays a managed body image of conviviality, in contrast to "What are you?"—the more overt racializer's query of nationality, ethnicity, or so-called race where somatic expression more fully registers contempt and disgust. These questions want to confirm out-group status of their interlocutor rather than seek clarification of possible in-group status. Latin@/x literary accounts that illustrate these questions dissuade mutual rapport to legitimate withdrawal of somatic resonance.[22]

Communication research argues that the general impetus for social intercourse is to positively connect with another. As speakers, we seek data from our interlocutor that confirms we belong and are socially accepted by our interlocutor, such that our bodies draw near or at least, our somas draw toward the other out of a desire to be heard and understood. Within the heterogeneous speech of the Latin@/x community, we add the desire that our linguistic specificity be accepted with neutrality. Latin@/xs with accents in English nevertheless are more vulnerable to racialization and rejection than Latin@/x native speakers of English. In contrast, Spanish monolingual Latin@/xs seeking to be understood in Spanish by nonspeaking U.S. residents likely exclude themselves from certain engagements in hegemonic society at the same time their language decision defends against the possibility of social diminishment when speaking accented English. Accented English, sometimes more than Spanish monolingualism, heightens social vulnerability as it puts the speaker in a public position of lack or limited mastery over grammar, highlights the speaker's level of hegemonic cultural acumen (i.e., limited access to English idiomatic expressions), and even with such capital, accent makes one susceptible to diminished social power.

The politics of speaking Spanish are clear in the summary of Supreme Court Justice John Paul Stevens's dissent in 1991 *Hernandez vs. New York*, about which attorney and legal scholar Carlos R. Soltero concludes: "Spanish-language ability can be a proxy for a discriminatory practice" (2006, 168). The case was brought forth when an attorney prosecuting a Latino accused of murder asked two Spanish-English bilingual jury members to be removed because the attorney believed they could not be trusted to limit their interpretation of the accused's statement to its English translation. Like the U.S. "English-only" movement, *Hernandez vs. New York* extends racist discernment based on visual discrimination to acoustic prejudice. In fact, prosecutors, judges, and Supreme Court justices effectively ruled *against* equal assessment of Spanish-English bilinguals in cases of translated testimony. While seemingly delimited to the specificity of this issue, we cannot pretend high court rulings are somehow outside the prejudicial scripts that organize American life.

I imagine factors other than language dexterity were at play at each level of decision making in this instance. Did the potential jurors speak grammatically correct English? Did they have a Spanish accent in English? Beyond language, were the jurors in question impoverished-looking? Did these men appear to uphold the "American way of life" or did they seem (a somatic determination) more aligned with another social view? The Supreme Court ruling pretends to base their decision as reasonable, obfuscating other racializing markers that work in concert with the overall project and practice of racialization.

Worse yet, their decision adds bilingualism in Spanish as another denotative category to legally racialize the acoustic amid a constellation of somatic output, such that when bilingual jurors are suddenly delimited to their bilingualism and judged as unworthy, per *step two*, the decision forfeits their wisdom, experience, and civic contribution as their speech becomes the sensorial conduit to deanimation and suspicion. Bilingual jurors were and cannot be trusted to consider evidence in the way of their English-monolingual counterparts, an instantiation of *step three* that justified the removal of these Latin@/x jurors per *step four* in their social foreclosure as jurors in the courtroom. The Supreme Court ruling in *Hernandez vs. New York* instantiates a scene of racialization in our communal lived experience that fortifies and legitimates ideologically scripted sense perception nationally, such that, if not for literary scenes of racialization and somatic analysis as in the theatrical analysis to follow, we might not be able to discern the politics of language and accent in the same way.

While we are born into a particular language with an accompanying accent, and whether we embrace it or we strive to lessen it, how others relate to our accent embeds negative affects in the soma. In Angelo Parra's play *Song of the Coquí* (hereafter, *Coquí*), 1994 winner of the University of California, Irvine Chicano/Latino Literary Contest, the acoustics of accent key the *four steps* in the following scene of intraracialization. The plot can be summarized as a bid for romance where upper-middle-class Ray awaits his Puerto Rican parents' return to their New York city apartment when working-class Teresa, their neighbor, who has recently moved to the city from Puerto Rico, drops by Edna and Ramón's apartment to find Ray alone and ostensibly, single. Forty-something Raymundo, has fashioned himself into "Ray," an Anglicizing gesture, indicating his assimilation. We later learn of his difficulty in speaking Spanish, and, perhaps, suggesting his internalization of racial shaming, but calling himself "Ray" helps make Raymundo more socially pliable in his work as lawyer and artist. Here, accent creates the play's dramatic tension in an everyday interaction between Ray and Teresa during a simple, unexpected moment of contact. Knowing beforehand Ray has recently divorced his Anglo-Euro-American wife, Teresa approaches Ray and strikes up a conversation:

> TERESA: Your mom says you're this big shot lawyer.
> RAY: No, not really.
> TERESA: You do divorce law 'n shit?
> RAY: Corporate law actually . . .
> TERESA: (*Cutting in.*) Maybe you could help me out with my ex. Pendejo, coño. I gotta keep on his ass for my alimony, you know? Maybe you could fix him good, you know, like for friendship, 'cause I got no money for lawyers. (278)

The words in a script are obviously critical to meaning, but plays require we read in a more embodied way as we imagine bodies of actors on stage (Blair 2008, 106–7). Due to their relative narrative sparsity, dramatic scripts demand readers fill in somatic gaps for intelligibility (Wolpert, Doya, and Kawato 2003,

596) such that the script adds to the meaning of the words with codifying textures of sound in word selection and stage directions that in turn help us imagine the somatic presentation of the actors. This heightened, embodied imagining allows us as readers to pay close attention to somatic cues and registers in discerning the intraracializing project of this scene.

The auditory depiction of the two characters sets up the scene of a thwarted bid for romantic engagement, teasing out U.S. practices of racialization and racism informing intraethnic/racial practices of racialization and racism. While we are not given precise tonal cues with which to imagine the sound of Teresa's speech in the script, the immediacy of the expletive "Pendejo coño" makes Spanish likely her first language, to which we should imagine the expression accompanied by culturally cued somatic anger. Likewise, Teresa explains exchanging sex for Ray's legal services. Her words, "'cause I got no money for lawyers," implies an accent and a level of informal study of English that quickly affixes a working-class status in an intersectional racialized frame—both expressions working the aural in combination with the phenotype of the actor playing Teresa but also indicating how the actor manages her body image to embody how Teresa should appear within an intersectional racialized scheme. Similarly, we read Ray's words and quickly surmise Parra's intended audience reception to suggest, in my mind as reader, Ray's standard English grammar and standard U.S. accent, a somatic sign that could contrast with the actor's phenotype. Again, his habituated somatic expression and bodily image will indicate how he has crafted self into a desired cultural appropriateness, linguistically dotted with occasional (comparatively) sophisticated words as part of his managed body image.

Later, we will learn both characters suffer from racialized shame, but in this interaction, the play draws attention to the aural as measure of unconformity, as well as the way Latin@/xs, like their hegemonic counterparts, intersectionally intraracialize one another based on sociolinguistic measures or one's style of speech. *Coquí* shows how linguistic decisions parlay social gain. Whether Ray's decision or a decision made by his parents, Ray's monolingual English leaves him feeling less than a full member of the Latin@/x community. Likewise, the constraints for immigrants to choose if and how they acclimate to U.S. mainstream hegemonic culture includes modifying the sensory output such as speech. Our sensory output plays a role in our sense of self. By the same token, we place a value on the sensory output of Latin@/xs unlike themselves.

The aural elements produce dramatic tension, disrupting the presumed cultural affinity between Teresa and Ray in somatic dissonance of *step one*. Ray's limited competence in Spanish may be a source of situational shame, but mutual understanding is not at issue. Rather, the plot positions Ray's romantic rejection of Teresa as his form of social foreclosure in completion of *step four*.

I imagine the somatic posture accompanying dialogic exchanges between Ray and Teresa per Parra's stage directions: Teresa's somatic expression intensifies as she physically approaches Ray, as she pressures answers to her questions and rapport for her attempts at conversation by drawing near Ray. Clearly perceiving her advances, Ray socially retracts in nonanswers while he physically distances himself from her. Gender predicates both characters' responses. Increased focus on accent is the dramatic method that delineates Ray's self-perception as wholly different from Teresa:

> RAY: (*Awkward pause.*) You know, it doesn't look like my mother's going to be home anytime soon. Why don't you come back . . .
> TERESA: Did I say something wrong?
> RAY: No, it's just . . .
> TERESA: You don't like . . . my company?
> RAY: . . . I don't even know your name. (*Teresa extends her right hand and they shake hands.*) . . .
> TERESA: (*Interrupting, heavily rolling her R.*) Terrrrrrrrrresa. . . . Terrrrrrrrrresa. Don't be shy with me. Terrrrrrrrrresa. (*Ray awkwardly frees his hand.*)
> RAY: Sorry, I can't do that. I can't roll my Rs, if you must know. My tongue is too fat or something. I can't even pronounce my own name right. (*Hard Rs, no roll.*) Guerrero. (279)

Teresa may or may not have said anything wrong, but the play suggests to Ray, she *sounded* wrong. As noted earlier, the power of accent begins with an early awareness of ethnicized sound as a key sign of group (dis)affiliation. Cultural psychology researchers Agata Gluszek and John Dovidio's extensive social psychology review of speakers' attitudes toward accented speech found that "accent, like physical appearance, often evokes an immediate reaction, some aspects of which may be subconscious," concluding that because of "negative attitudes towards accented speech," accented speakers were "judged less intelligent, less competent, and less proficient" (in Derwing and Munro 2015, 135). Gluszek and Dovidio assert that "a nonnative accent is one of the most salient characteristics of a person that identifies him or her as an out-group member and that a nonnative accent almost always stigmatizes that person" (in Neuliep [1999] 2014, 300). But the research does not address the complexity of denying familial accent in adopting hegemonic speech.

By indicating his disinterest in learning how to roll his Rs, Ray rejects Teresa's situational linguistic authority, effectively removing the possibility for equalizing social terrain. Sociolinguist Rosina Lippi-Green states when a listener rejects [a] message in this way, "he or she is refusing to accept responsibility in the communicative act, and the full burden is put directly on the other" (2012, 69). In refusing Teresa as teacher, friend, or potential mate, Ray becomes a hegemonic interlocutor (in contrast to other social situations where he assumes the role as an honorary White), and Teresa's repeated rolled Rs stand out as an example of sonic matter out of place, stigmatized with acoustic dirtiness to extend anthropologist Mary Douglas's phrase. Conversely, suggesting that severing one's cultural ties, whether intentionally or by happenstance, deprives one of some important human quality. The play presents Ray's inability to roll his Rs as a sign of his limited ability in Spanish as audience identification should shift from Ray to Teresa, who is clearly being mistreated but, interestingly, constitutes one of the few moments he appears as a sympathetic character. Soon after, we read and somatically program Ray's building contempt for what he, as situational hegemonic, perceives as her Latina inferiority, a cultural prohibition that has "fattened his tongue" out of a Spanish accent and into outing his shame for what he has given up.

True of most plays, playwrights write with the intention of drawing stronger identification with a particular character (McConachie 2008, 22–63), such that in choosing speech style and accent as the sensory medium through which to draw the play's dramatic tension, *Coquí* could lead many audiences to feel more comfortable with Ray because, through his aural soma, Ray represents an honorary majority culture member often esteemed by hegemonic and nonmajority audience members alike. Teresa's word choice, impetuously divulging her personal crises to Ray (to his mind, he feels himself a stranger to her), and her immediate employ of profanity sets against Ray's class standing evident in his measured English but also in his calm leisure where stage directions describe Ray watching television before she enters the apartment. In contrast, my imagining of Teresa's somatic expression as agitated, unnerved, and a little desperate, combines with her seductive body image that together, intends to convey her working-class standing.

Their somas dramatically rendered show the difference between their respective lives in a play of intense intersectional contrasts that underscore Ray's social privilege, which he extends with his leisurely disposition in his parents' home and his social remove from Teresa. In contrast, Teresa is physically positioned as interloper, hence, she remains afoot as he relaxes on the couch. Their respective somatic expressions reflect social hierarchies between characters readily understood by readers and audiences, and rendered in sensory combinations of accent, wealth, and composure, that are then confirmed with words. Lippi-Green notes the intricacy of interpersonal assessments:

Each time you begin an exchange, a complex series of calculations begins: Do I need to be formal with this person? Do I owe her respect? Does she owe me deference? Will she take me seriously, or reject me out of hand? . . . For those you interact with every day, the calculations are fast and sure and well below the level of consciousness. ([1997] 2012, 69–70)

This initial encounter efficaciously inscribes who is vulnerable and on what grounds. In challenge to the social power of assimilation, Teresa will attempt and fail to override Ray's social snobbery with her feminine wiles and appeal to her personal needs. The implication of class deincentivizes romance with Teresa for Ray, confirming research that tests racialized linguistic prejudice with the perception of negative work attributes.

Economic disparities complement racist perception. An early psychological study conducted by Rudolf Kalin and Donald S. Rayko (1978) found accented speakers were perceived to be "better suited to low status jobs than high status positions," supporting findings on underemployment and housing discrimination (in Derwing and Munro 2015, 135). Alberto E. Dávila, Alok K. Bohara, and Rogelio Saenz's study furthers these findings, arguing perceptual negative scripting of Mexican Americans' accents materially correlates with lower incomes, and concludes Spanish accents often lead to lower wages (1993). *Coquí* presents the effects of these important racializing auditory scripts to interpersonal relationships and, specifically, to in-group relations as the scene between Ray and Teresa unfolds.

Coquí problematizes intragroup contempt, Ray, a reluctant Latino, has perhaps worked to rid himself from producing nonstandard U.S. sense data in an effort toward hegemonic inclusion and away from social stigma. As a result, Ray's linguistic register, name, and negative or dismissive perception of Teresa evidences he has forfeited his in-group status and habituated to somatically express his White-ish, upper-middle-class life in standard American English sounds. It seems Ray has not been able to ward off the harms of such forfeit, as evidenced in his diminished personal life and in the sadness and perhaps shame he expresses when stumbling to pronounce his own surname . . . and the coquí will never sing again.

In the script, the somatic content of Ray's language and accompanying stage directions evince a sensorial impression of how Ray sounds, how he manages his body, and that which somatically escapes his control. Though Ray can and does understand what Teresa says, her accent is a complex sign conveying subtexts and somatic tonalities Ray reads as her neediness, that from his superior and assimilated social position, he does not care to entertain.

There is no difficulty in understanding one another, yet his somatic expression (instigated in my mind by the script, but that I fill in with my mimetic neural resonance of actors on a stage) decries her *social* untranslatability for him. He shares the sociologist's quip: "'I can't understand you' may mean, in reality, *'I dare you to make me understand you'*" (Lippi-Green 2012, 69, emphasis in original), indicating *steps three* and *four,* faits accomplis.

Teresa's accent must be understood in its complexity, including code-switching, borrowed words, tone, pitch, cadence, but also accent as provided in some of the phonemic words in the script. Combined with her stage directions that direct some instances of her body language, the reader has a sundry set of data with which to surmise her immediate and largely unmediated somatic portrayal. Parra, to this end, took pains to direct the actor to present Teresa's Spanish-inflected and accented English speech style to clearly delimit her marginalized intersectional social standing.

The racialized, classed, and sexualized tension culminates when Teresa accuses Ray a sellout, a "coconut"—Brown (Latino) on the outside, and White (Anglo-Euro) on the inside (281), which in effect, draws out his social foreclosure of her with her own foreclosure of Ray:

> TERESA: Fucking prejudiced against your own people.
> (*As he speaks,* RAY *starts moving in menacingly, backing* TERESA *up until she falls back onto the sofa.*)
> RAY: (*With contained fury.*) That's bullshit. It's just that I find Hispanic women brazen, coarse, vulgar, intemperate, uneducated, unrestrained, amoral, and generally uninteresting. You dress vulgar, and act it! (281–82)
> TERESA: All of us?
> RAY: Yes!
> TERESA: Including your mama? (*A long angry silence.*)
> RAY: (*Through his teeth.*) Please leave.

This climactic exchange shows both parties angry and rejected: Teresa incensed by his gendered and intraracialized rejection of her while Ray's ire demonstrates his contempt for her that thinly veils his self-contempt. In effect, Ray subjects Teresa to linguistic profiling that scholar Jean-Jacques Weber describes as "the linguistic equivalent of racial profiling and occurs whenever marginalized members are discriminated against on the basis of the linguistic variety that they speak" (2015, 47). The somatic expressions of contempt directed to be spoken "in contained fury" per *step two* expose his internalized racial shame that pressures him to foreclose on himself as well as

Teresa as Latin@ in *step four*. The aspersions she casts on Ray for his cultural assimilation and upper-middle-class membership defend her against feeling the shame of rejection, but, ultimately, Teresa will see Ray as less of a man than his less-assimilated Latino counterparts, judging him unworthy of her time and attention. In her *step four*, Teresa forecloses on Ray as a potential romantic partner and friend.

•

Ideology has co-opted our senses. In variably ordered *steps*, scenes of racialization and those of intraracialization depend on the sociality of the sense-producing soma. Scenes of racialization in literature distill the function of sense data in depictions where the everyday social practice of racializing occurs in what we habitually chose to see, how we codify what we smell, and the judgements we make about what we hear. The scenes of racialization studied in this chapter utilize sense perceptions, turning the social harm of racializing and racism into a base for a social practice that Latin@/x writers employ in developing their particular literary aesthetics they build from the very intimacies of somatic exchanges.

Sight, smell, and hearing, the three salient senses found in scenes of racialization, induce a heightened immediacy and an efficacy to approach these social issues of the harm habituated in scripted sense perception. Such scenes seldom specify how culture crafts the selectivity of the perceiving organs themselves or the way the data received feeds into ideological schemes. And although many disciplines center on the information available from the soma, few scientific or literary studies work from the premise of the indivisibility and simultaneity of the senses informing the soma. In this sense, Latin@/x literature is exceptional. The following chapters in *Shaming into Brown* build on the theory argued in chapters 1 and 2 to address specific texts and their individual contributions to understanding the social relevance of the soma and deepening the potential for somatic analysis. In chapter 3, we move from chapter 2's external senses to look at internal experience to examine how the gut becomes a somatic subjectivity in Oscar "Zeta" Acosta's *The Autobiography of a Brown Buffalo*.

CHAPTER 3

Soma and Viscera in Oscar "Zeta" Acosta's *The Autobiography of a Brown Buffalo*

> Constipation? How in the fuck can I be
> constipated when I have so much to offer?
> —Oscar "Zeta" Acosta

MILITANT, OVERWEIGHT, LOQUACIOUS, and ailing attorney in *The Autobiography of a Brown Buffalo* ([1972] 1989), Oscar "Zeta" Acosta contends with his cerebral sense of self and his defiant viscera expressed in ulcers, flatulence, vomit, and yes, constipation. You see, Oscar is sick. In his autobiography (hereafter *Brown Buffalo*), he is frustrated in his attempts to know, control, and integrate his inner feelings with the person he presents himself to be. In a covert aesthetic, Acosta positions Oscar's stomach as a central somatic source of autobiographical expression in tension with Oscar's experience of self.[1] I remind the reader the term *soma* from the Greek usage signifies the intelligent, communicative body thought in different traditions to contain or manifest one's spirit, a presence usually separated from intellectual activity, but often associated with one's emotional life. I employ *soma* following this etymological lineage because the term *soma* gives me a way to access the body as a perceiving but also responsive entity that grounds one's experience of the world. In *Brown Buffalo,* Acosta purposes Oscar outwardly, reacting to his subjection in an infelicitously managed persona, while his innards somatically and irrepressibly narrate social situations he cannot will, effort, or cajole himself out from under.

Oscar is an accomplished and eloquent man, and yet, his life is impaired by his damaged digestive system, but is it a simple matter of organic disease or an expression of the composite effect of his social milieu? In his autobiography, Oscar tells of health care practitioners who suppose jurisdiction over his state of being and compartmentalize his innards as diseased while obfuscating his poor self-image in medical pathologies. Medical doctors claiming to see *into* his body assign him diagnoses, attributing his suffering to the problem of Oscar's individual body, which, early on, Oscar suspects has to do with factors other than physical origins: "Who can say for sure what causes ulcers? At the age of twenty-one, six (6) doctors showed me pictures of what they claimed were holes in my stomach. Perhaps it really is a physical thing . . ." (2). In contrast, Dr. Serbin, Oscar's psychiatrist who appears as an internalized voice heard inside Oscar's head, derides Oscar's denial of sex and race (19–25) at issue in Oscar's mental and physical condition. These core issues affecting his core could be described as a berserk narrative style; however, I argue the style authentically portrays the disintegrating effect of life under intersectional racialization in what should be reread as a subaltern realist style. In the end, Oscar comes to a clear awareness of his subjection, and in claiming himself a Chicano Brown Buffalo, he dedicates his life to political activism, a story he tells the following year in a more conventional aesthetic in *The Revolt of the Cockroach* (1973). In chapter 2 of *Shaming into Brown*, I argued the external soma, in pressing for or against social inclusion, highlights the social value of the senses in racializing the other. Here, the external continues to do its work while the internal soma is the sentient expresser that pressures Oscar to come to terms with his life under gendered racialization, *Brown Buffalo's* central conflict.

Oscar's external body is presented in its somatic form through the senses of vision and smell to express his social marginalization. Oscar is a Texan racialized a *Mexican*, circa 1930s–60s; the narrative implicates White racializers who deem Oscar "smelly," while his sometimes friend Hunter S. Thompson eulogized him as a "rotten, fat spic" (Acosta [1972] 1989, 5–7).[2] On multiple occasions, Whites call Oscar a "nigger" (32, 78, 86, 88, 93, 187), while California Chicanos racialize him *Mexican* for his regional differences (78). Oscar's autobiography narrates several scenes of racialization where forms of the racializing questions "What are you?" and "Where are you from?" discussed in chapter 2 continue to extricate Oscar from the national whole, demonstrating the habituated practice of American interlocutors to usurp social power in intersectional racializing terms. While dialogue and self-reflection indicate some aspects of social marginalization, Oscar's bad stomach most clearly conveys the destructive impact of his intersectional social inscription.

Despite Oscar's successes in school, the Armed Forces, and civil service, Oscar feels himself a failure. Failure, as presented in social science research, is a mental health symptom in disorders such as depression, low self-esteem, and anger issues, and is a common result for people assigned color (Sanchez-Hucles and Dryden 2012; Utsey, Giesbrecht, Hook, and Stanard 2008). The following excerpt from psychologist Robert T. Carter's research indicates the common misdiagnosis of the source of individual mental and physical health issues, which Latin@/x literature presents as the systemic psychopathology of U.S. intersectional racism:[3]

> Racial stratification and systemic racism have been and continue to be endemic and ingrained in all aspects of American life: in customs, laws, and traditions.... Perhaps a major contributing factor to the problem of racism and its impact on the mental health of its targets is a failure to clearly understand the emotional, psychological, and, to some extent, physical effects of racism on its targets. (2007, 13–14)

When we, like Oscar, do not look at the systemic nature and effect of oppressive social forces, the cultural discourses of rugged individualism, nationalism, and meritocracy lead us to personalize harms we are suffering. U.S. culture offers assimilation and other forms of conformity as routes toward ridding ourselves from such subjection at the same time U.S. cultural investments in intersectional racialization present a barrier to social equity. Scholars are just now attending to this particular conundrum in new ways, as argued in "Mad Futures: Affect/Theory/Violence" (Aho, Ben-Moshe, and Hilton 2017): "The nascent field of mad studies draws on decades of scholarship and activism examining how psychiatric disabilities or differences must be understood not only as medical conditions but also as historical formations that have justified all manner of ill-treatment and disenfranchisement—even as they have also formed the basis for political identities, social movements, and cultural practices of resistance" (293). A move away from the mind/body split, I join new lines of critical inquiry in articulating the specious divide between biology, mental health, social ills, and people's lived experience.

His autobiography narrates a four-day, cross-country misadventure where Oscar abandons his job as attorney at a San Francisco legal aid office to take to the road. In a frenzied account of random actions, drug-induced mental states, and flippant social interactions, most of *Brown Buffalo* logs Oscar's self-abuse, reckless actions, and chance social encounters. Though some readers and scholars may be intrigued or dissuaded by the style, the embodied aesthetic innovatively registers racial trauma. Whether incident-based or a pervasive, low-intensity, social psychological affective landscape, and usually in combination, recent studies show racialization and racism generate degrees of trauma on a scale of domestic abuse and rape victims (Bryant-Davis and Ocampo 2005; Brown and Christmas 2014). Oscar's stomach steadily chronicles the harm of injustice, a register of dissent against the promises of meritocracy and social mobility, while the narrative style untethers Oscar from autobiography's demand for narrative coherence and instead portrays the profound psycho-physiological effects of racializing phenotype in U.S. society.[4] In this chapter, I continue exploring the function and content of the soma and its role in racialization that I have begun in earlier chapters by focusing on the stomach as the primary somatic ground for other levels of Oscar's subjectivity. Oscar's viscera urgently inform Oscar (as well as the reader) how he experiences trauma outside of his mental machinations, disaffected in dialogic exchanges and interior thought. His unusual somatic aesthetic of his innards recuperates a degree of sovereignty over his frustrated attempts at belonging, a critical stratagem of the somatic innards that broadens aesthetic realism to present life under intersectional racialization, the theoretical contribution of this chapter.

The autobiography likewise structures the simple plot on the road where, instead of a grand quest, Oscar meanders aimlessly, physically imbibing, regurgitating, and expelling the trauma he lives. His only requirement: no map.[5] He intersperses these actions with somatic reaction where his body—principally his stomach—marks his physiological health as a response to what Oscar socially experiences. By drawing the expressive value of Oscar as somatic organism, Acosta subverts the convention of the coherent autobiographical talking head for a racially traumatized "I" bounded in emotional distress and a gaseous stomach. Oscar's stomach affectively centers his despair, but rather than the psychological reflection expected in autobiography (Smith and Watson [2001] 2010), I begin by arguing digestive sentience somatically expresses Oscar's interior subjectivity. This connection to his body as a register of his interiority parodies the coordinates that, according to Continental thought, evidence Oscar's intellectual refinement. First, I will outline the intellectual history of the stomach and then address the way his stomach tells of Oscar's intersectionally shamed personhood.

SCENE OF RACIALIZATION: IN THE BATHROOM WITH DR. SERBIN

The confluence of subjective voices registers Oscar's body, his social location, and his mental activity in a form of realism that is confusing to follow. This brand of realism sets this aesthetic as the tone signifying self-doubt, reprisal, and shame found in many passages in the text, yet none more so than in another bathroom visit where Oscar grapples for the first time with what his psychiatrist will later deem Oscar's core issues of race and sex. Before confronting a waiting room full of public defense clients, Oscar escapes to the bathroom:

> No, not today. I just can't face those five fat TRO's under these conditions. Pauline will just have to deal with them, I whisper to myself as I duck into toilet. If they even see me, their expectations will increase. Things are bad enough for suckers without having to cry over me.
>
> Dr. Serbin squeezes into the green-walled toilet with me. "Oh, of course, you can't give them any false hope. After all, you're just a little brown Mexican boy." (24–25)

In near theatrical style, the unsuspecting reader could suppose Dr. Serbin squeezes into the bathroom stall with Oscar where they have a dialogue, but it is more likely that Oscar mentally conjures Serbin's clinical invasion, the result of the impact Serbin has had on Oscar's sense of self during psychotherapy treatment. Dr. Serbin reduces the complexity of Oscar's angst—physical and psychological—to what Serbin perceives as Oscar's self-pitying racialized emasculation.

Dr. Serbin breaks rapport with his client by barging into the toilet (*step one*) only to then withdraw understanding and compassion for Oscar as his client, disregarding Oscar's feelings of fear and insecurity over his limitations in fulfilling the needs and demands of his clients. "You're just a little brown Mexican boy"—Serbin's incredulous, imagined, utterance racially shames Oscar in quick accomplishment of *steps two* through *four*. This arrest of interpersonal mutual regard threatens their therapeutic alliance with an incongruent but sadly common demand for instantiating social asymmetry, overshadowing social etiquette. His psychiatrist's degrading sarcasm and intrusion shames Oscar into accepting himself as socially incompetent and forever infantile, intersectionally diminishes and deanimates Oscar into a racialized category (*step two*), and socially forcloses on Oscar as an ineffectual child (*step four*). The voices of Serbin, medical doctors, and later, teachers, lovers, and his parents have reached the inner recesses of Oscar's psyche and organism. They have little to do with the specific characteristics of Oscar, but point to the habituated, widespread, pernicious practice of intersectional racialization and their effects. A central mode of social interaction argued in chapters 1 and 2, racializing functions like a U.S. social pathology, as I argue in chapter 5, but here, as we see with Oscar, it deeply affects one's mental and physical health. The effects of this passage through rough racial shaming take on somatic proportions. Still involved in imagined conversation with Dr.

Serbin's internalized racialized and shaming voice, and still in the bathroom, Oscar lowers his head:

> For the third time this morning . . . I struggle, I push with my diaphragm at the refuse in my gut. But only rancid, hot air blows . . . the dry heaves! My stomach burns with acid, hot sauce, sawdust hamburgers, Chinese curry, wars and rumors of war. I double my fist and strike my belly . . . and this time it comes . . . a work of genius. *I ponder the fluid patterns of my rejections and consider the potential for art.* (24, emphasis added)

His body responds to what Oscar ingests as his soma simultaneously manifests the psychosocial conditions in bleeding ulcers, nausea, cramps, vomiting, and constipation. His body does not necessarily parse out his fear of war from his food digestion. The sociality of his gut responds to all stimuli. A Chicano male, socially condemned to embodiment and the threat of social disconnection, somatically presents how Oscar integrates his body's reaction as the site of the internal processing of psychosocial pain. He feels, hears, smells, and sees the pain of his internalized and materialized disorder, seeking in vomit to expel social subjection in redress of this pain. Perhaps an attempt at humor (with the "potential for art"), this somatic description integrates the discharge of racial shaming with the desire to see something beautiful emerge from his pain sought in the detritus of his innards rather than the ugliness of social marginalization, forming the experiential nexus grounding Acosta's subaltern realist approach. Without more context, Serbin's incursion may seem either awkwardly contrived or surrealist in nature; however, when we look at it through a realist frame, Oscar's mental tribulations narratively intertwine with his bodily experience, which together, present his selfhood. Acosta narrates the activity and intrusion of the interior soma, raising the specter of what physicality can convey in comparison to verbal elaborations alone.

Oscar internalizes the racializing protocol, moving from scene to scene of self-destructive behaviors where he internalizes the objectification of his appearance but where the role of his innards embodies his mind such that both his exterior physical self and his mind wrangle with his innards, delimiting him to a body to be used and abused by others but also at his own hand. At the same time, the body also reanimates its agency through inner somatic expression, drawing Oscar's attention to the extent of his suffering. He internalizes society's deanimation of him by removing himself from deep emotional connection with others and treating himself as a contemptuous entity for deprecation.

SITUATING THE SOMATIC GUT AND ERUDITION

In the West, from the premodern period until the twentieth century, the stomach has been argued in relation to the mind. From humoralism to modern medical nomenclature, the stomach has been the center of notions of health in the West. Greek physician Galen of Pergamum (CE 129–216) argued digestion was an "integral aspect to the maintenance of humoral balance" (Miller [2011] 2016, 7), a position that influenced medical theory from the Middle Ages until the seventeenth century (Nutton [2004] 2013). Later, in the medieval period, the stomach diminished in cultural esteem and became the site of appetites that conflicted with spiritual goodness (Miller [2011] 2016, 7). Seventeenth-century physician, physiologist, and chemist Jan Baptist Van Helmont went so far as to argue the stomach as the site of the soul, thus motivating his study of digestion and bodily disorders (Miller [2011] 2016, 7). An organ that both emits and receives, the gut makes us uniquely aware of what it wants, needs, and feels, a position found in recent scientific studies asserting the stomach's responsiveness to the quality of our physical lives but also of our psychosocial experiences (Johns Hopkins Medicine n.d.). This overview points to the long-standing scientific and popular fascination and almost preoccupation with digestion, and where, as producer of key excretions, the stomach not only influences one's health but also one's character.

We may be unaccustomed to the term *soma,* but we are familiar with popular ways we refer to the stomach as a source of inner knowing. A second brain of sorts found in idiomatic expressions like "I had a gut feeling" signal the stomach is a physical location of intuition. Most recently, Western studies confirm the intelligence of the stomach as scientific fact. An organ with the number of brain cells equivalent in number to a cat's brain, our "little brain," a nonscientific term referring to the enteric nervous system (ENS) is "not so little. The ENS is two thin layers of more than 100 million nerve cells lining your gastrointestinal tract from esophagus to rectum" (Johns Hopkins Medicine n.d.). These nerve cells allow the digestive system to function as a center of intelligence, receiving and sending messages that relay information about internal and external stimuli to our brains and back to our gut.

A primary expresser of feelings, a hub essential for life energy, and an intuitive force present beyond the (disembodied) intellect, this visceral knower appears to be more than a myth or an obscure belief. The gut is "just as large and chemically complex as the gray matter in our heads" (Enders 2015, 125). In fact, the brain and the gut are together the engines of our human intelligence: "Scientists have found evidence of what many of us already suspected: our brains and our guts 'talk' to each other. In fact, they are so intimately connected that some believe the gut and the brain should be viewed as part of one system" (Paddock 2009).[6]

Before such scientific reports, the intelligent stomach may have seemed almost romantic to a twenty-first-century reader, but European intellectual history shows creativity and intellectualism have been argued in relation to the stomach for centuries. Particularly poignant is the eighteenth-century idea of the stomach as site of a kind of subjectivity. At that time, the stomach was thought to react to and work with the mind. In fact, the stomach was said to affect one's lifestyle, ethics, morality, and intellectual ability. Different from other organs, the stomach specifies preferences and aversions for various foods and responds to physical activity, as well as to sexual and intellectual activities. Théophile de Bordeu, the renowned vitalist physician of the mid-eighteenth century regarded the stomach "not just as part of 'the triumvirate of life,' but also as a dynamic organ that possessed animal intuition, its own distinct tastes and distastes, and the capacity to play a significant role in most illnesses" (Vila 2005, 95).

During that time, it was thought that when one carried out one's life well, one's satisfaction evidenced in "good bowels" or a "good stomach." As Ian Miller notes in *A Modern History of the Stomach*, the stomach "appeared . . . to occupy a central and persistent position in the development of key fields of medicine including physical anatomy, physiology, surgery and psychosomatic medicine" such that "even at the peak of reductionist medicine at the start of the twentieth century, it proved hard to convince both the public and medical professionals that approaches to the [stomach] which neglected the complex interaction of body and mind were entirely accurate" ([2011] 2016, 2).[7]

In addition to knowledge and self-fashioning, recent research shows the stomach plays a role in the production and communication of feelings: "All those neurons lining our digestive system allow it to keep in close contact with the brain in your skull, via the vagus nerves, which often influence our emotional state" (Mosley 2012). In fact, research attests feelings and the stomach work both ways: what we eat may influence our feelings and what we feel emotionally affects our digestion (Johns Hopkins Medicine n.d.). From the beginning of *Brown Buffalo*, Oscar correlates what he ingests with who he is and how he is—spicy, overbearing, and domineering:

> I analyze my medical condition. It's true I refused the advice of all six doctors. For Christ's sake, I was only twenty-one. What value is a life without booze and Mexican food? Can you just imagine me drinking two quarts of milk every day for the rest of my life? They said, "nothing hot or cold, noth-

ing spicy and absolutely nothing alcoholic." Shit, I couldn't be bland if my life depended on it. (12)

As Christopher E. Forth and Ana Carden-Coyne explain, for hundreds of years "the digestive and appetitive dimensions of the abdomen have been inextricable from our concepts of the embodied self" (2005, 7), which, in purview of *Brown Buffalo,* holds cadence as a system of self, made up of the material, social, and psychological ingestion, digestion, and expulsion. Current research reports the stomach maintains the integrity of dual properties: food and the psychological/mental are forces interacting on and through us, a somatic specificity of the digestive system. From mouth to rectum, the system's many parts respond to what is ingested, react to digestion, and can wreak havoc in protest during excretion.[8]

What ails Oscar in *Brown Buffalo* medieval doctors would have called a person's individual humoral constitution, but recent research attributes many chronic digestive problems to the psychological impact of social stress on individuals and on the gut in particular. Historically, it was believed that a person physically taxed the organism by excessive intellectual activity, emotionality, physical inactivity, and/or poor food, straining the stomach in the form of constipation, a nervous stomach, and other digestive troubles. Cultural historians Forth and Carden-Coyne argue this supposition continues in an inverse mode where people discipline their bodies in order to alleviate or ameliorate their mental sense of self: "Techniques of the self, then, have clearly persisted in our modern ways of approaching our food, our appetites, and our bodies. The steps we take to feed, manage and sculpt our bellies have been intimately connected with who we are and what we wish to be" (7).

Additionally, the sociocultural inscription of the digestive system adds coordinates to racializing schemes as we see in recent critiques of ethnicizing diseases such as obesity and diabetes as prevalent among the Latin@/x population (Lopez 2014). Such diseases revitalize the imagistic connection between the stomach and marginalized subject position where historically, "the stomach's primary importance stems from the fact that it played a central role in mapping and maintaining the gendered, class-based, and ethnic social hierarchies of early modern culture" (Purnis 2010, 801), and in which *Brown Buffalo* inscribes Oscar's bad stomach. This review of the cultural history of the stomach in the West contextualizes today's scientific findings, presenting the stomach as a vital constituent of human experience that in *Brown Buffalo* Acosta allows to influence Oscar's subjectivity.

OSCAR'S GUT AND INTERNALIZED INTERSECTIONAL RACIALIZATION

His gut punctuates the mock in the autobiographical heroic from the start: "I sit on the bowl and face myself in the mirror above the sink. An outrageously angry face stares me down and I laugh at the sight of a Brown Buffalo sitting on his throne" (12). Hence, beginning on the second page, Oscar tries to physically expel feelings he identifies as nausea for the emotional shame of inadequacy based on his gendered and racialized physical unattractiveness: "I strain to vomit, pushing upward with my diaphragm, with as total control of the belly as any good clarinet player could have . . . but nothing comes except gurgling convulsions from down under" (12).

On a physical level, in the opening chapters Oscar grows sick from the upset caused by denigrating opposing counsel and judges, who disparage his performance as public defender in San Francisco. Collegial rejection and the job's hollow promise of helping his underemployed, largely female clientele motivates Oscar to throw his law certificate in the trash and take to the road:

> Right about now my stomach reminds me of my clients sitting in the dingy waiting room of the Legal Aid Society at Fourteenth and Fruitvale in the slums of East Oakland. It's already fifteen to nine. Already they're waiting to devour me as they have each day for the past twelve months. (18)

Thus, in the first dozen pages, Oscar stakes out social scripts that define how life in the United States of America has blocked his efforts for acclaim, his contributions to society, and his longing for social acceptance. His soma perceives and responds to society's schema to fail him across these three endeavors. In stark contrast to the cocky, irreverent persona he publicly dons, his digestion reveals how he truly manages his work and civic lives, his romantic affairs and his friendships. Back on the toilet:

> I hold my breath too long. . . . Grumbling and convulsions in the empty pit . . . I stare into the repository of all that is unacceptable and wait for the green bile, my sunbaked face where my big, brown ass will soon sit. "Puke, you sonofabitch!" I command. "Aren't you the world champion pukerupper?" Jesus Christ, not even my body obeys me anymore! (11–12)

Oscar's body imposes itself effectively against Oscar's wishes. Acosta inducts the reader into Oscar's internalized self-view from the perspective of his racially coded physical disarray that Oscar believes he should be able to control. Literary scholar Genaro Padilla refers to Oscar's malaise of the culturally adrift where "only by denying and rejecting some elemental part of the self can the Chicano's relationship with America prove to be propitious, and, even then, propitious only in the eyes of the self-deluding protagonists" (1984, 249). Oscar's bad stomach presents a sufferance willful Oscar tries to manage, an internal discord paralleling Oscar's inability to socially inhabit the powerful man he believes himself to be, and by many measures, effectively is.

But who is Oscar talking to in the above passage? Oscar's exchange with his body renders his stomach as plausible interlocutor, characterized by its obstinacy. Given autobiography is a literary tradition which presumes a rational writing subject, Acosta uniquely treats his body as a subjective entity with whom Oscar must contend, a Cartesian disembodied "I," disinterested in the life of the body that is typical in conventional U.S. autobiography. Acosta writes unapologetically of the physical ramifications of intersectional racialized self-loathing and so mocks the unicity of the disembodied mental or intellectual "I" as the hero of his own story. These veiled critiques of *Brown Buffalo* cohere in recognizing Acosta's intentional destabilization of the transparent, factual, autobiographical voice for the litmus of his ailing stomach, a somatic demonstration of his personal truth to which most readers are unaccustomed. Where autobiographical subjects are depicted as minds with dominion over their bodies, the internal origin of Oscar's somatic expression aesthetically expresses the effect of the hyperbolic emphasis on phenotype per racialization and serves as a counterpoint to realism of the disembodied "I" in autobiographical norms. The political efficacy of somatic expression of the innards clarifies and grounds obscure dialogue, random social interactions and, at times, drug-induced interior thoughts which, at times, make the text difficult to follow.

Written on the heels of the Chicano Movement recently brought asunder by the Federal Bureau of Investigation, police violence, the murder of Rubén Salazar and three others during the August 29, 1970, Chicano Moratorium, and the incarceration of Chican@/x activists, Acosta's texts reflect upon the upheaval of this historical moment. In *Brown Buffalo*, save for several critical flashbacks to early childhood in 1930s backwater Texas, the bulk of his youth and early adult events occur during the 1940s and '50s, a time of high tension for Chicanos returning from World War II and the Korean War, finding themselves still treated as second-class citizens. In the 1960s, the autobiography's present, the historical activist lawyer Acosta was integrally involved in the Chicano Movement, imputing the California Grand Jury with racism, and running for sheriff of Los Angeles County (Stavans [1995] 2003). While

Brown Buffalo speaks to the time before Oscar's politicization, *The Revolt of the Cockroach People,* a memoir, describes Oscar's life during his political activities. Shortly after publication of both books, Acosta traveled to Mexico, disappeared, and has since been presumed dead.

On the literary front, Acosta's instrumental founding of the Gonzo journalistic style seeded his formidable presence in certain sectors of the national imaginary (e.g., *Brown Buffalo* is often required reading in Chicano@/x literature courses, as are films like *Fear and Loathing in Las Vegas* featuring Acosta as Thompson's companion). The amount of scholarship on *Brown Buffalo*, as opposed to the stylistically more conventional *Revolt*, evidences the pull of Acosta's contribution to the Gonzo style, which is most often attributed to Acosta's associate, famed counterculture journalist Hunter S. Thompson. Journalism scholar Tony Harcup partly explains Acosta's stylistic choice: It "involves a mixture of personal observation, verbatim transcripts of conversations, overheard dialogue, and extracts from documents or original notes, mostly delivered at great length and frequently focusing as much on the quest for information as on the information itself" (2014, 116).[9] However, Gonzo journalism does not fully capture the deeper level of political and philosophical critique in *Brown Buffalo* and thus, to my mind, is ultimately only a partial marker of Acosta's contributions.[10]

In *Brown Buffalo*'s present, Oscar denies participating in what often was considered a social phenomenon of contemporary, Anglo, White-collar dropouts (e.g., Ken Kesey or Timothy Leary), who opted to live on a drug and alcohol binge in search of "the truth" in lieu of the hypocrisies of a sober life and in abeyance to the status quo. Literary scholar Marci L. Carrasquillo (2010) argues Acosta was inspired by the Beat Generation, where the similar objective of finding self outside of mainstream society in the work of Thompson, Kerouac, Ginsberg, and Leary mourns the lost American promise of superiority for the male hegemonic subject in texts such as *Fear and Loathing in Las Vegas: A Savage Journey to the Heart of the American Dream* (1971) and Jack Kerouac's *On the Road* (1957). For my study, Oscar's innards are more persuasively a subjective register of lived experience than a scatological expression that upsets and amuses readers (Aldama, 2003; Calderón 2004).[11] The multiple sources of information from the body combined with altered mental states, such as writing while under the influence, infers an affinity with the Gonzo style, perhaps most strikingly so in his commitment to "personal observation," summarized by Hames-García as Acosta-Oscar's position as "artist-participant-protagonist" (2000, 467) and to which I would add "-soma." The soma allows for the appreciation of Oscar's affective self in a register of his physical body, a field of subjectivity with which Acosta disavows a Cartesian mind-driven agency still at the core of the Beats and those their work inspired.[12]

Therein the reader's challenge follows what often seems to be a nonsensical narrative style that literary scholar Hames-García codifies as grotesque satire where "the personality of the Gonzo protagonist is exaggerated to such a degree that its subjectivity is defined through its physical and psychological excesses" (2000, 467). To that point, facts reported in *Brown Buffalo* are not always accurate. Within the text, Oscar reports his stomach problems begin with his breakup with Alice, his high school sweetheart, but then reports an even earlier stomach upset due to his primary school crush on June Addison. Literary studies scholar Frederick L. Aldama notes further evidence of creative license noting Acosta was thirty-six years old at the time of writing *Brown Buffalo*, but deliberately chose to represent himself at the age of thirty-three to more closely connect Oscar's likeness to Jesus Christ (2003, 65). Such discrepancies engage in a "self-reflective technique to call attention to the artifice of the narrative as an invented story and to hold up a fun-house mirror to society" (54).

Given discrepancies in the material facts and the autobiography, critics argue for an altered sense of truthfulness in his text, fostering Dieter Heims's critique of Acosta's autobiography as better thought of as an autobiographical novel, one Ramón Saldívar classifies as a semi-autobiographical work (Saldívar 1990, 155). Aldama contends *Brown Buffalo* is more interested in breaking down autobiographical conventions than presenting the most empirically factual account of his life (2003, 29)—perhaps part of his subaltern realism questioning a hegemonic standard that removes the relevance of trauma that is better rendered by doctoring the facts. To this point, literary scholar Héctor Calderón deems the split function of autobiographical narrator and character to be more of a Gonzo-style "self-portrait" than a conventional autobiography (2004, 98–99).[13]

The figure of the addicted "I" is not new to autobiography or to other genres, but in these cases, clear-headed reflection situates time-while-inebriated in accessible terms (e.g., *Junkie* (1953), *Go Ask Alice* (1971). In *Brown Buffalo*, the dominance of imbibed narrations and somatic expression intentionally frustrate easy comprehension, a distancing mode that sociologist Matti Hyvärinen argues allows deviation from generic expectations (2010, 9) and exposes the aesthetic challenges to accurately portray a life of gendered racialization. Engaging in erratic, oftentimes almost nonsensical verbal expressions, Oscar speaks to others and to himself with judgmental perceptions of manhood, heteronormativity, middle-class membership, and racial schemes, all of which he himself feels he fails and, importantly, have failed him. Despite his success playing out paradigmatic roles of respectable American manhood, Oscar either continues to experience social marginalization or does not find the social legitimacy they afford fulfilling.

These promised and then unfulfilled methods of social agency coalesce in anecdotes of Oscar as a sexual partner. Oscar, who reports regularly suffering impotence or otherwise unsatisfying sexual encounters, offers an encounter midway through his narrative to attest to his limitations. His fantastic, inebriated mental distortions stylistically decontextualize normative speech and paralinguistic communications during the tryst to focus instead on the experience of body parts, where psychological Oscar appears as the dimmed, drugged observer/participant of his own activity. The following passage appears fanciful but, within the context of somatic racial shaming, the experience of his body described in this dispirited mental elaboration illustrates the present-tense disintegrative harm of intersectional racialization where Oscar, instead of desired, feels himself used and confused:

> Maryjane reaches over and begins to stuff raspberry sherbet into the yellow lard under my belly button. . . . She takes my huge brown head ready for mounting and holds it in her arms like the Madonna. She puts her mouth full of emerald lips over my nose. She sucks on it to save my life. My green snot puffs her face and fills it up like a carnival balloon. With her eyes against mine, she sucks and sucks until finally my head collapses like a rubber ball stuck with a dart. My shriveled face is thrown among the stale stogies on the floor. Black boots kick at me and the blood pours red carpets. (63–64)

This scene portrays Oscar and his friends under the influence of narcotics to be sure, but his altered state still includes his self-view—a mounted brown head like a buffalo—positioning his bodily fluids as mediums of sociality. The solicitation of green snot is a euphemism for psychosocial infection whittled into his ailing body, as are the release of seminal fluids from fellatio performed on him. The scene ends in a joyless ejaculation where his pleasure is eclipsed by his deflated head-cum-penis, converted suddenly into debris on par with the used-up cigars strewn on the floor. The last sentence of the passage concludes the sexual scene's inscription in racialized interactions where black boots suggest State combat gear physically assault Oscar, leaving him bleeding and humiliated.

This self-presentation breaks down the view of Oscar as engaged sex partner or simply hedonist to reveal him as a bizarre object to be used and discarded, underscoring the way the body as interlocutor centralizes much of the text. Further, the expressive soma challenges the assumption of consensual sex and while still physically stimulating, the soma's reaction remarks racialized affront and degradation. His skull and the factions of the mind become the head of his penis creating a disturbing scene where the choice of narrative style evinces this experience as sadomasochistic or perhaps abusive. Faith lost in cultural myths of egalitarism, his composite head collapses in gendered racialization, and with it, his desired social position as subject. The decision to represent Oscar's internalization of how society views him through fellatio performed on what he claims to be his unusually small, brown genitalia[14] is an aesthetic decision where "bodies at the margins of national norms seem to provide a conduit to the material real, and, in this proximity to reality, access to exceptional insights" (Russell 2011, 59):

> This quality of seeming both more real and more otherworldly than the quotidian social world suggests just one of the complexities of representing physical difference and its figural burden . . . [to] become legible in the national imaginaration." (59–60)

The deliberate focus on the body may seem curious if not bizarre, but when understood as an ethical representation of society's exaggerated imbrication of Oscar as brown body, the strangeness of the aesthetic reveals ingenuity of approach.

Oscar's material body socially circulates while his innards emote, relaying a level of subjectivity registered in the response of his body as soma. Thus, Oscar's contentious experience of, and relationship to his body relays as much a personal situation as a socially induced struggle. Oscar's race, gender, sexual orientation, and ethnic assignments categorize him in variations of *steps one, two,* and *three,* where, from a somatic angle, we can discern socially scripted cognitive paths where, despite mastery of social scripts, he understands himself bad-because-intersectionally-Brown, an a priori social foreclosure completing *step four* in scenes of racialization (theorized in chapters 1 and 2). As such, in critique of U.S. racism, Oscar's individual accomplishments end in social failures, leading Oscar to self-abuse and, ultimately, a bad stomach.

Intermittently throughout the narrative, Oscar recalls several early events that he recounts to explain his adult despair. Oscar has suffered interpersonal social marginalization from childhood, several instances of which he details to describe the cognitive rapidity of his somatic innards responding in different scales of traumatic events, the shame of which tends to result in self-alienation. As a schoolboy, school authorities use the fact that they speak Spanish to deny Oscar and his Chicano friends recognition for their athletic talents. When Oscar and his Chicano classmates win a game of football against a group of Anglo-Euro boys on the playground, the Anglo-Euro boys call foul play. Their reason: Oscar and his team directed their strategy in Spanish. The grammar school principal weighs in and warns Oscar he will be punished if he continues to speak Spanish during class or on the playground (186). Oscar recounts this experience of racialization to explain why he stopped speaking Spanish or listening to Mexican music, but the scene also depicts typical forms of responses to racial shaming. Internalizing the feigned startle of the White boys and the school principal who decide to play the race card, Oscar suddenly recognizes his public display of intersectional difference stymies his budding sense of heteronormative manhood but also threats to expel him from school, institutionalized social foreclosure of *step four*. The schoolyard anecdote explains how Oscar purposefully ends two forms of somatic mimicry that alienate him from his community and from himself.

As with Piri in *Down These Mean Streets* (Thomas [1967] 1997), hegemonic racialization engenders intraracialization, and Oscar's Mexican family affords him little succor, withholding from Oscar a deep sense of acceptance, and emotional and physical safety. Oscar recounts scenes of abuse and diminishment with his parents where Oscar must prove himself "man enough" to his Yaqui-Mexican father and where his dark, overweight body disgusts his mother: "My mother had me convinced I was obese, ugly as a pig and without any redeeming qualities whatsoever " (82). Dr. Serbin's early observation of Oscar's central issues of gender and race lays blame on how Oscar handles such issues, typifying the onus on the individual to prevail over strident social practices, sidestepping the critical societal change to dismantle and decognitivize oppressive ideologies. Oscar's early stories and crazed present-tense narration of his adult life tell of life from this tenuous psychosocial place before his politicization, where his stomach portrays the effect of concentric realms of intersectional racialization for which, as a socially systemic problem, there is little individual remedy. Over the course of the text, Oscar structurally intimates the similarity of power relations involved in this incident to many other events during of his life. In the text's numerous scenes of racialization, individual achievement garners social diminishment, then expressed in his escalating digestive illness and his increasing cynicism.

As Acosta biographer Ilan Stavans argues, racial exclusion was Acosta's intellectual and political raison d'être ([1995] 2003, 54) and a primary cause for multiple nervous breakdowns (23, 34, 44). In fact, Calderón identifies the beginning of Oscar's stomach problems the night he was forced, because of his Brownness, to separate from his high school sweetheart, Alice Brown (101). By command of Alice's racist parents and supported by racist local police, Oscar is told he cannot be seen alone with Alice or he will face some level of police intervention: "The convulsions down under began that night. The wretched vomit, the gas laden belly formed within my pit when the chief of police asked me if I understood. Savvy?" (119–20).

Ethnic minorities experiencing racism must cope with the psychological sequelae stemming from the destruction of basic beliefs in safety, meaning, and personhood. This oftentimes perpetrator-less crime is precisely color-blind racism, sociologist Eduardo Bonilla-Silva argues. Bonilla-Silva's influential text ([2006] 2013) outlines a contemporary map of the entrenched nature of racism where individual racists or isolated racist acts are no longer necessary to carry out racism. Social institutions and practices of all kinds are increasingly cloaked in verbiage misdirecting racism into isolated penurious acts, the foibles befallen on an unlucky individual, and/or the consequences of colorless poverty and drug-addiction, limited intelligence, or wanting work ethic. In addition to psychologically damaging childhood events where Oscar reveals racist verbal and physical attacks, his descriptions of his present troubles are dotted with overtones demonstrative of intersectional racism, racialization, and their impact.

SCENE OF RACIALIZATION: RACE AND UNREQUITED CHILDHOOD LOVE

Parting from his current drugged mental state and neurotic activity at this moment in the narrative, Oscar turns toward a more conventional realist mode with an omniscience born of a mediated past to relate an important romantic encounter in grade school:

> I had been mad for Jane Addison ever since the day her father checked her into my fourth grade class at the very moment I was gazing up Miss Rollins' skirt. She was blonde, shy and red acne all over her beautiful face. She was the smartest girl in the class and lived no more than seven blocks from me in the American sector. . . . She just ignored my obvious suffering. The pain in my gut, the secret gnawing at my belly didn't concern her one damn bit. (88–91)

Although in this recounting from grade school Oscar in the narrative present contradicts the beginning of his stomach problems with the forced breakup with Alice, Oscar remarks Jane's indifference by physical suffering. His gut centers the sense of frustrated longing in a somewhat atypical collapse between the distress of his innards as material evidence of his affections that, somehow, she should know of and respond to. In a poignant passage about the same affair, Oscar etches her bloody, scabby initials on his arm. Instead of engendering affection, Jane reacts with disgust when he shares his self-mutilation.

Given his accounts of racialized school dynamics in Texas circa late 1930s, Oscar conveys his racialization as impetus for Jane's rejection. Her words assess Oscar's physical unacceptability that Acosta ties to several other childhood scenes of racialization as he comes to understand his social diminishment as a racialized person somatically: "My ears pound red. I am done for. My heart sags from the overpowering weight of the fatness of my belly" (94). In the last instance, Oscar will fight a White boy who calls him "a fucking black nigger" (93). After this row (which Oscar believes will prove his a-racial masculine prowess and thus, romantic desirability), he enters the classroom, sweaty and flushed with adrenaline and bravado. Jane Addison asks their teacher: "Will you please ask Oscar to put on his shirt? . . . He stinks" (94). Young Oscar reacts in shame at her rebuff over his body smell, an impactful racializing sensorial datum, as argued in chapter 2.[15] This scene of early, repudiated affection decodes a primary scene of racialization. His overweight, brown, sweaty body repulses Jane, and in hearing the request to the teacher, and therefore the class, Oscar, like Moctezuma in Valdez's *No saco nada de la escuela* also discussed in chapter 2, has been socially foreclosed upon by in- and out-group members. Jane asks one question that, as readers, we imagine fleshed out with affects of contempt and disgust. Somatically, Jane's question becomes a statement, a social indictment, instantiating Oscar's social marginalization and intersectional shame. Through the affective racializing soma, Jane provides a somatic cognitive pattern to collectively loath. The vexed intersection of racial shaming and diminished masculinity act as a foundation for Oscar's sense of self and is further characterized by his inner sensory perception of a bad stomach. Oscar receives physical pain in the forms of the fight and the scarification, but he also receives clear messages about himself via the reception of others' sense perceptions; the White boy sees Oscar as a "fucking black nigger" (93), Jane is repulsed both by Oscar's willingness to hurt himself and by his dissmell, his racialized, noxious scent. The text demonstrates the efficacy and sociality of this entrained cognition accomplished in the jeer of the class. In this instance, like chapter 2's discussion of Graciela in *Song of the Water Saints*, dissmell instigates the racial hate that journalist, author, and cultural critic Ta-Nehisi Coates argues "gives [hegemonic] identity" to Jane and her classmates as White and superior, while Oscar's expression parallels Coates: "I am black. I have been plundered and have lost my body" (2015, 60). In these early scenes of racialization where Oscar loses himself, racial shaming separates the self from the body and from the presented public self. The safety of somatic expression becomes threatened, so Oscar, like many of us, focus on the power we can amass in managing our body image.

This narration involves various levels of utilizing his body to convey more convincingly than words his desires and his racialized rejection. Oscar is willing to involve—and to some degree cannot avoid involving—his body in his somatic expression, taking his body image as a tough guy, a proud Chicano boy of the fight, his body as material site of inscription, while his innards manifest his love torment and his social rejection in this particular rendering of *step four*.

This passage switches from the stylization of the present perfect to the present, heightening the enduring effect of these early hurts, and extenuating the effect of these early betrayals from the concentric realms of family, classmates, of the community, and the State. The soma facilitates these engagements of realism. With Acosta's more confluent tone of realism under a drugged state on the lam, the childhood scenes of racialization are told in a more conventional realist narrative tone. This conventional tone striates the somatic discussion, stylistically easing the reader into the role of the soma in the passage and giving context for his frenzied description on the road.

In like manner, literary scenes of racialization are deftly presented along with racially motivated interpersonal rejections and professional prejudice. The moment-by-moment style shows the random volley of a personhood denied basic human regard. Quotidian scenes of racialization appear alongside these earlier traumatizing moments that, over the course of the text, intercalate with the interminable narrative present offered by his stomach.

Toward the end of the text, Oscar holds the fantastic belief that Mexican women would cure his ulcers and his heart. After visiting El Paso, Texas, his home town, Oscar decides to cross the border to Juárez when he is suddenly overcome with desire for the Mexican women he sees: "My heart ached to speak with any of these women. I knew they had the answer to my pain. If only I could speak whatever language I could muster, I was certain they'd give me the cure for my ailing stomach, my ulcers and the blood in the toilet" (189). Oscar fantasizes bodily rehabilitation through the emotional and sexual experience of romantic love.

After an extended tryst with two Mexican sex workers, Oscar feels himself "a serious Mexican for the first time" in his life (190), a measure of sexual success he equates with social acceptance and physical healing. But alas, he is ultimately rejected by Mexicans, frustrating his self-reconciliation as an American or a Mexican. Landing in a Mexican jail, he stands in front of a judge who admonishes: "Why don't you go home and learn to speak your father's tongue?" (194). Repeated in a Mexican context, Oscar understands his social incongruity on both sides of the border. The Juárez adventure debunks the fantasy of belonging to either U.S. or Mexican cultures; there is no home necessarily for Chican@/x. This knowledge is key to pushing through an assimilationist front where there is only the narrow possibility of satisfying social scripts in exchange for social acceptance for those racialized Chican@/x. Thus, in both the U.S. and Mexican contexts, *Brown Buffalo* asks the reader to first understand society's role of incorporating or, conversely, rejecting us that often affects our respective illness or wellness; second, to broaden our notion of the body as site of health or harm in service to the mind and the body; and third, to appreciate the soma as an earnest communicator in expressing self and interpreting others, as a biological entity refracting social conditions that greatly inform who we experience ourselves to be.

A growing body of medical researchers happen to confirm theories argued by Sara Ahmed (2004), José Esteban Muñoz (2006, 2007), and others that sustained states of emotional discomfort accrue over time, creating a cumulative harm on the body and on the mind.[16] From a literary standpoint, this social practice and predicament of racial trauma situates the stomach's condition in expressing the mostly "long ago-ness" typical of the past-tense genre of autobiography and into an aesthetic of moment-by-moment presence in *Brown Buffalo,* effectively delineating an urgent sense in the chronological present: "The possibility of a memory of trauma, of an unbroken account of its history, disappears in the hypnotic-suggestive knots that tie trauma to an interminable, repetitious present tense" (Orr 2006, 21–22). Oscar's stomach becomes particularly prescient as a form of subjectivity that speaks each moment to the effects of his early childhood intersectional racist traumas. Whereas present microaggressions can be easily misread as something other than the intricate tapestry of social practices imbuing another with racialization, their cumulative, deeply felt effects recover in Oscar's expressive stomach.[17]

Studies show racist encounters engender feelings of disrespect, anger, insult, disappointment, frustration, outrage, hurt, and shock, and contribute to long-term emotional distress (Landrine, Klonoff, Carter, and Forsyth 2012, 512) that becomes physical:

> The severity or chronicity of the stressor and the ensuing physiological response systems can cause damage, exacerbate existing disease processes, or predispose the individual to . . . become maladaptive . . . particularly true in situations [where] . . . the ability to adapt has already been altered due to genetic or early life events, thereby biasing an individual's susceptibility to the negative effects of stress throughout life. (Mayer 2000, 861)[18]

In *Brown Buffalo,* ulcers, flatulence, and vomiting removes socially scripted divisions between inner states and outside behavior as a somatic aesthetic where Oscar feels and expresses the effects of his unequal American life. Unstymied by the reproach of the autobiographical "I," Oscar's body could be mistaken as his alter ego in its rebuke of Oscar's decisions, both emotional and physical.[19] While a productive argument, to delimit Oscar's presentation of his body to the role of his alter ego minimizes the political efficacy of Acosta's artistic use of the soma. From a narrative perspective, "traumatic 'experience' breaks into and breaks open the bounded subject or 'self'" (Orr 2006, 21), such that fronting his stomach as somatic interlocutor effectively allows feeling to inform and transmit his racialized trauma to the reader.

Oscar's later recount of childhood scenes of racialization gives a narratological basis regarding the power wielded by systemic racism on self-esteem and personal conduct. The probability that Oscar suffers from race-based traumatic stress is "a potential predictor of emotional abusiveness and trauma . . . levied by those in society with more power against those with less power" (Sanchez-Hucles and Dryden 2012, 511). The soma, registering physical ill health coextensive with the intense emotional discomfort of his socially inscribed delimited subjectivity, is not unique to Oscar. Psychological studies indicate racism-induced trauma is widespread, confirmed by 89% to 91% of racialized minorities surveyed: "Racism is linked to . . . societal trauma, intergenerational trauma, racist incident-based trauma, insidious trauma, psychological trauma, and emotional abusiveness" (511), such that in 2007, Carter forcefully argued: "A key notion associated with . . . definitions of racism is the emphasis on personal character rather than on systemic processes" (20). Somatized ideologies hide their dehumanizing social logic in chastising people like Oscar for their discomfort with his difference, for finding fault in his sameness, and for daring to respond in angry belligerence—a sociological bait and switch that fools itself out of ever needing to consider its motivation or process.

THE INTELLECTUAL STOMACHACHE AND BEAUTIFUL VOMIT

Acosta's inner physical turmoil is never only about physical malaise. And, a bad stomach and a bad attitude write Oscar out of the Cartesian split and into an aesthetic that corporealizes the devastating effects racialization and racism mete out to Latin@/xs. Curiously, such a connection also authenticates Oscar's intellectual prowess. The long European trajectory of intellectual thought positions the sensitive stomach as a sign of refinement. While the effects of social stress are well documented, the stomach is hardly an arbitrary marker but an organ long understood in the West on par and in relation to the mind: "The human stomach is an organ endowed by nature . . . forming a centre of sympathy between our corporeal and mental parts, of more exquisite qualifications than even the brain itself" states Scottish physician Thomas Trotter in his 1808 study *A View of the Nervous Temperament* (203).[20]

And much earlier, in the fourth century CE, treatises on physiognomy based on Polemon's notions found in the Book of Physiognomy proposed the size and shape of the belly as indicative of one's moral character, where the bodily protrusion itself made certain moral aptitudes more or less probable (Hill 2011, 79). And much later, the organismic concept of the stomach replaced the physical dimensions of bellies as thinkers, and even contemporary artists articulate connections between stomach, feelings, and mind: "Pure intellect without feelings is impotent and even potentially dangerous" while "expressionsism ([identified with the] stomach) without intellect is pointless and usually boring" (Haring 2010, 114). Thus, the connection between feelings, the stomach, and creativity extends to established cultural traditions of intellectualism and the stomach as site of feeling. More recently, Bryan Waterman reasons in *Republic of Intellect: The Friendly Club of New York City and the Making of American Literature,* "The stomach is the organ of the greatest sympathy with the brain as is observed in the sudden loss of appetite . . . by the arrival of joyful or afflicting intelligence" (2007, 213), such that, from a U.S. perspective as well, the condition of intellect, gender, and social class reflect in the state of the stomach, a bemusing relation for Oscar when seen as parody. However, Oscar's poor digestion reflects his social travails in reports of alcohol and drug use, his psychological state, and the state of his innards. Contrary to his stomach as a sign to himself of his refinement, Oscar's stomach registers social pressure that may have motivated his initial disbelief in his ability to write the next great American novel (100).

What he ingests and his mental state, however, situates Oscar in a genealogy of writers, an *homme de lettres,* who, like his literary predecessors, is overtly challenged by his stomach. Indeed, the bad stomach abides as a kind of physical hallmark of the true intellectual. Writers such as Coleridge, Voltaire, and Rousseau among others regularly lamented of their battles to stay healthy by attempting to regulate the working of their stomachs. Oscar, in simpatico, barbs the trope of the delicate stomach of the exquisite mind: "I speak as a historian, a recorder of events with a sour stomach. I have no love for memories of the past. Ginsberg and those coffee houses with hungry-looking guitar players never did mean shit to me. They never took their drinking seriously"

(18). If the stomach integrates Oscar into the sensibilities of the great writer, then it also mocks this possibility in light of the racialization he suffers. Oscar, the international traveler who holds multiple university degrees, and who has studied with prominent writers, demonstrates his considerable cultural acumen in the way he writes. References to contemporaries exhibit knowledge of the Beats and twentieth-century Spanish poet Federico García Lorca, but *Brown Buffalo* also evinces the project of self-fashioning that perhaps builds on similar projects in the work of Walt Whitman, Ralph Waldo Emerson, and Henry David Thoreau, and the grit of urban strife for people of color in autobiographies by Piri Thomas (1967), Dick Gregory (1964), Richard Wright (1945), and Claude Brown (1965).

Near the end of the work, Oscar capriciously and jocularly proclaims he is the man of his generation who, like Gandhi and Jesus, is destined to deliver "the message": "Once in every century there comes a man who is chosen to speak for his people" (198). Structurally, Oscar waits until page one hundred to reveal his literary goals, which he tucks into anecdotes of having rubbed elbows with the day's literary luminaries. Chance meetings introduce Oscar to Richard Dettering, (the coeditor with S. I. Hayakawa of the magazine *ETC.*), who in turn presents Oscar to acclaimed writers like Van Tilburg Clark, Mark Harris, and Herb Gold, congregated in San Francisco at that time. It was Dettering who convinced Oscar to write: "Little did he know I was scared shitless of all those guys with tweed coats and fancy pipes" who he now belittles in hindsight: "These guys weren't the world famous fags they are today" (100). After becoming a mentee of this group, Harris asks Oscar to read his latest novel *Wake Up, Stupid!* where upon reading the first paragraph, Oscar proclaims, "I was no longer afraid of the intellectuals. I knew I could tell a better story" (100), supporting Paul Guajardo's point: Acosta sees himself first and foremost as a writer (2002, 56–57). And besides, as Stavans argues, "[Acosta] enjoyed being repulsive. . . . Who else but him [would] champion a vision of victory through repulsion?" ([1995] 2003, 13). From his insides out, Oscar's stomach makes him at once refined enough to write the next great American novel while simultaneously presenting Oscar as pitiable, a mock hero, in inimical response to the unequal social standing for those racialized Brown.[21]

•

This perhaps surprising focus on Oscar's somatic stomach binds Acosta's text to the predicament of living a life conditioned by his Brown male body. An indifferent reader, apathetic toward or simply unschooled in issues of racialization, conditioned to value sentimentality, or inured to rhetoric of transcendence would not expect to read of the inner disagreeable workings of the autobiographical "I"'s somatic body or body-based self-loathing. Yet, the soma enters as interlocutor in Oscar's self-presentation, asserting the adverse psychosocial and physical effects of patriarchy, racism, and class prejudice. The aches, groans, and eliminations prompted by his guts not only respond to oppressive social practices, they protest Oscar's internalization of them; they register his elemental dissent, and they prompt him (if not impel him) to find a source of nurturance and self-acceptance.[22]

Oscar presents himself as a failed assimilationist, where despite fulfilling cultural mandates for acceptability in the forms of Christian religiosity, hard work, education, sport, writing, civic commitment, and heteronormativity, Oscar is never fully socially received within or outside his marginal standing as an American or a Mexican. Instead of directly critiquing cultural hegemony and its cultural scripts that barter social approval, Oscar intercalates a drug-induced narrative style with a somatic aesthetic, physically and subjectively responding to society's deep commitment to racialized schemes so harmful, they become sources of ongoing and lifelong trauma, and they make Oscar sick.[23] Oscar brokers self-acceptance by recognizing the physical impact of racialization in the accounts his stomach tells, alerting the reader to the intersectional effects of socially manufactured trauma. At the same time, Acosta writes Oscar and his core grappling of "race and sex" in *The Autobiography of a Brown Buffalo* as the stuff of great American writing.

CHAPTER 4

The Ugly Soma Speaks Out in Octavio Solís's *Lydia*

> A Body that could never rest, Since this ill Spirit it possest.
> —FRANCIS QUARLES

THE *UGLY SOMA* identifies the power gained by coercing another to psychologically displace the body from the self, obfuscate it, and/or disavow its integrity. It is a tool of hegemonic oppression that disturbs the spirit and keeps the body in a state of unease. Octavio Solís's 2008 play, *Lydia*, uses its own ugly phrasing to elaborate the contours of this tool that holds back the bodies and spirits of the Flores family living in El Paso, Texas, circa 1970. Nominated for a Pulitzer Prize, *Lydia* studies the politically complex situation of Latin@/xs, eloquently tying disability to undocumented Mexican labor, gender, in-group racializing I call intraracialization (as argued in chapter 2), homophobia, and poverty. In the *four steps* of scenes of intersectional racialization argued thus far, the racialized are pressured to accept reinscription of themselves as contemptible bodies, the cognitive perception of another arousing affect that creates the social fact of intersectional color and, thus, relegation to inferior social status. Using the threat of harm and sometimes even of death, the intraracializer seeks to foreclose on the intraracialized oppositional somatic expressions and, instead, delimit the responses of the intraracialized to concessions of shame, the *fourth step* with which I foreground my analysis here. This apparently odd juxtaposition between disability and domestic work reveals how intersectional intraracialization and racism press for distance between the self and the body in an exacting and insidious form of oppression, dimming the biosocial reality of interrelation between people and undermining the political power that can flow from notions of our mutual intelligibility and socially confluent subjectivity.

Cognitive theater scholars place the body at the dramatic center, the site where movement itself sets off feelings, insights, and natural responses to the character's situation: "In performance, the body is smart, intelligence puts on flesh—and we are smartest when we stop thinking" (Huston 1992, 6). Given that theater is one of the few U.S. cultural paradigms directly concerned with the soma's efficacy in presenting the portrayal of authentic feelings, Huston's remark gestures toward the spontaneity and near irrepressibility that define somatic expression as an involuntary medium of communication revealing how we (and others) genuinely feel. So critical a source of our daily perceptions, actors seek to replicate lived somatic expression, analyzing how the soma behaves in their preparation. On stage, this potent complexity appears in the form of disabled Ceci and Lydia, her caregiver—doppelganger protagonists whose intersectional struggles are emblematic of the unspoken shame and subjugation of the Flores family. Where in chapter 2 I analyzed the four steps of *scenes of racialization* through the senses, and in chapter 3 I focused on the internal somatic expression in Acosta's autobiography, in this chapter, I turn my focus to the *fourth step* in *scenes of racialization* to explore the somatic idiom employed in *Lydia* that dramatizes social foreclosure, the premise underlying the lives of the coprotagonists.

Lydia clearly belongs to the well-developed U.S. theater tradition of familial reckoning.[1] However, instead of the White, mostly middle-class families found in the plays of Arthur Miller, Tennessee Williams, Sam Shepard, and Eugene O'Neill, the Floreses are Mexican and Chicano, a Mechicano, or 1.5-generation family composed of immigrant parents from Mexico and their U.S.-born children. Solís's *Lydia* joins in the Latin@/x dramaturgy of mother-daughter relationships, afflicted women, and family dysfunction, building on the work of Latin@/x playwrights José Rivera, Cherríe Moraga, and Migdalia Cruz, among others. Solís's intense psychological study of this family unpacks the cultural forces of class, gender, sexual preference, labor, intersectional racialization, legal standing, generational issues, migration, assimilation, and acculturation as they impact Latin@/xs and infiltrate familial relations. Bit by bit, during the second half of the play, Ceci reveals that two years prior, she found Cousin Alvaro, her love interest, in a romantic tryst with her brother, René. She expressed her distress at this deception in homophobic accusations against René, the culpable party behind the wheel in the car accident that has left Ceci in a persistent vegetative state (PVS). In the wake of the accident,

Ceci lives out Quarles's admonition of the epigraph as she writhes on the stage for nearly two hours in arrhythmic spasm—a result of her neurological condition, and perhaps, her body's expression of her pained spirit.

Solís structures Ceci as a character seemingly lacking personhood: a body whose spastic gesticulation seeks to clearly denote her inability to communicate and her assumed mental death. Ceci's condition refers to the Western practice of making the disabled both non-normative bodies and disordered minds, the latter of which has been interpreted as evidence of poor character, if not demonic possession for centuries. Harking back to formative early Christian cognitive scripts that construed such bodily behavior as evidence of damnation, Ceci's family believes her life experience of another realm. Locked in neurological torment, incapable of self-expression and without needs beyond the physical, Ceci's agitated body performs an anguished shadow existence of the person they once knew. The play employs the popular suppositions reflected in Quarles's words, dramatizing in extremis a relationship between the body and the spirit. In addition to intervening in disability prejudice, I argue, the play deploys Ceci's physical condition as the dramatic point of departure for sharing her worries, resentments, and joys. We thus return to the question of the spirit in Quarles's quandary for the purpose of challenging social scripts that diminish the disabled as they do the racialized. Ceci's body, which I shall refer to as Ceci-the-body, asks audiences to reinterpret her bodily behavior as also a personal expression of her dismay.

Ceci-the-body, we come to learn, is an emotionally distraught character who voices the household's collective distress as well as her own woes. Her physical agitation gives raw performative expression to the shame and anger of intersectional oppressions stifled in misdirected speech and actions by each member of the Flores family, including the family's new caregiver, Lydia, who is the play's second protagonist. Developing a protagonist who is nonverbal, such as a PVS sufferer, is unusual in contemporary U.S. theater, but adeptly generates the tension necessary to illuminate the role of the somatic body in the intersectional racializing under which the Flores suffer. I base my remarks on the script (Solís 2010) and on the May 9, 2009, performance I attended at the Mark Taper Forum to argue that disability, like undocumented domestic work, prompts specific acting styles to effectively draw out the household's beleaguered state of intraracial shame.

Beyond dramatic novelty, I argue, the protagonists' respective acting styles provide an alternate cognitive script that helps us apprehend how we somatically express and manage intersectional racialization. Ceci and Lydia alternately employ and disengage the soma, and, in so doing, present the soma as the primary communicative site for assessing authentic and inauthentic feelings. Conversely, the soma is also the conduit through which the two women develop deep interpersonal intimacy, a relational paradigm through which to consider our felt sense of connectedness and its political potential. I argue these points by analyzing the Solís family drama through the two protagonists who play three roles: Ceci-the-body, speaking Ceci, and Lydia. In my analysis of these characters, I continue elaborating my central argument of the soma where, in the theatrical discourse of *Lydia*, the actors' intentional engagement of the soma reveals sublimated practices of intersectional intraracialization and racism. In the next section, I present the landscape of U.S. actor training that puts the unnamed soma at the center of these important cultural practices. As Sarah E. McCarroll argues, "We watch these onstage bodies, read them and are impacted by them without our conscious notice" (2016, 158).

Contemporary training techniques draw out tensions between the realism of somatic portrayal and the artifice of theater that characterize a significant portion of dramatic performance. These tensions shed light on the way we somatize our response to our respective social station in U.S. culture.

THE POLITICS OF ACTING STYLE

Thematizing the family's efforts to manage Ceci-the-body may seem a predictable choice, given the limitations of care a nuclear family can provide. Indeed, two years after the accident, the family has devolved into a state of spiritual and emotional bankruptcy, in contrast to Ceci, who remains very much physiologically alive. In fact, she passes most of the two-hour performance convulsing unremittingly. With snarls and groans, punctuated with involuntary bodily functions, throughout the play, Ceci appears up close, spot lit, stage right. The able-bodied actor's performance pulsates like a heartbeat, presenting Ceci's body as a constant presence foregrounding the family's constant state of emotional upheaval. For the audience, she is bothersome, pathetic, and irrefutably magnetic. Solís describes Ceci's condition in the following stage directions:

> For most of the play, Ceci lies on her mattress locked in her body in a semi-vegetative state. Her body's muscles rigid, her hands curled and fingers knuckled, she undergoes degrees of spasticity that come and go in ways that score the play. Her voice is fallen back into her throat and her eyes unfocused; her powers of expression are utterly buried in a neurological prison. (4)[2]

In this demanding role, Ceci's epileptic-like gesticulations highlight an Othered body situated front and center, then juxtaposed with the same actor intermittently rising to become Ceci, the able-bodied soliloquist. In the performance I attended, the first scene interwove two apparently contradictory somatic depictions of Ceci who, first lying there in spasm, turned suddenly, her expression focused, her body normatively controlled.[3] Stage directions do not mention the latter posture; the actor simply stands to give her soliloquies as a normative person. Her first soliloquy, a theatrical preface, contextualizes the events that follow. Ceci begins with the meaning and power of her unspecified relationship with a woman, Lydia, her caregiver, who the Flores family hire as their maid. The physical connection and somatic expression of touch and the profound connection it can engender guides how Ceci relates to Lydia:

> CECI: She touched me and I flew. Touched my fault-line. And I flew. With her hand, laid holy water on my scar. And I flew on wings of glass. My body *como una* bird racing with the moon on a breath of air. (5)

There is an intimation here that Lydia's touch recognizes Ceci's personhood, the physical acknowledgement that reignites Ceci's return to self. Ceci then gives her central dramatic dilemma: how to reconcile herself to her life in the current state of her body, socially dashed on the cusp of womanhood:

> *(She looks down at her arms and legs curling under her as a light falls on her mattress.)*
> A card with me printed, *La Vida Cecilia,* rag doll thumbing the stitching in her head, forming the words in her vegetable tongue, what happened to me, *porque no puedo* remember, I must remember. (5)

In subsequent soliloquies and asides, speaking Ceci provides the audience with an account of the struggles, questions, passions, and encumbrances to maturity faced by the seventeen-year-old thought to be trapped in her nonverbal and otherwise incommunicative body. Yet, as these first lines demonstrate, Ceci's words focus on the life state of Ceci-the-body, and while Ceci-the-body remains the subject of interest, the two radically different sets of capabilities of Ceci create an experiential breach between her two forms. I will later address Ceci-the-soliloquist, but here I argue that Ceci-the-body tests the bounds of the soma in an acting medium by posing the question of whether and how to read the soma of a person with non-normative body functions. Further, I argue the tension generated between a convincing somatic portrayal and a perceptibly managed body image clearly demonstrates the manipulation of acting style as a dramatic means of social critique.[4] I discern Method acting, arguably the most popular theater actor training in the United States, as the political idiom the play uses in navigating Ceci's two vastly different performances, and, as I will later argue, predetermines Lydia's acting style.

A dominant approach iterated in different ways by many directors of U.S. theater since the 1930s, Konstantin Stanislavski's "Method" teaches actors to *inhabit* a character rather than *represent* a character.[5] This approach intends to bring a level of authenticity to a given role, thus making dramas more realistic, and, in current neuroscientific terms, more empathically compelling to audiences. Stanislavski did not espouse developing characters so much as situations, instructing actors to cull from their life experience and to relive personal feelings in order to approach the emotional state of the character in situ such that "the actor gradually obtains the mastery over the inner incentives of the actions of the character he is representing, evoking in himself the emotions and thoughts which resulted in those actions" (Stanislavski quoted by Magarshack [1950] 2010, 375). Without identifying it as such, successful Method acting largely depends on an intense engagement with the soma.

The soma, a spontaneous and largely uncontrollable force of body subjectivity in life, physically materializes the actor's personal feelings rendered in dramatic simulacrum. Theater scholar Elizabeth Carlin-Metz argues that actors specifically use what neuroscientist Antonio Damasio refers to as somatic markers, physiological evidence that points one to one's feelings to "gain information and knowledge about habitual self-use through awareness of physical processes of which most people rarely are conscious" (Carlin-Metz 2013, 39). Given this description, acting cannot be considered a fully spontaneous expression of lived experience but rather the employ of the studied soma of the character. Thus, Method acting premised on bodily communication does not engage the actor's soma (which would evidence how the actor really feels as a *person* who is acting on stage) but trains actors in somatic portrayal, a rendering of already-felt feelings employed by the actor to deliver a more authentic, truer to life performance.

I complicate the performance goal of Method acting's seemingly real somatic portrayal because, in my experience, I notice that often, such portrayals rub up against another style of acting I refer to as *body image management*. In nearly all plays I have seen, there are moments of Method-style somatic portrayal, but there are as many moments where the actor invokes pitch, gestures, scripted movement in space, timing, facial expressions, and other modalities that deliberately lack the naturalness of lived somatic expression, and strike me as devoid of the intention to somatically become, so to speak, a character. While signs of inauthenticity would seem generally undesirable in theater, I use actor and theorist Bella Merlin's analytic to describe the interplay between somatic portrayal and dramatic artifice in most acting performances I have seen, including in the performance of *Lydia* I attended. Actors tend to hover between somatic portrayal, where the actor (and consequently the audience) feels and identifies with the character, and managing her body image (Merlin 2013, 67), where the audience (and perhaps also the actor) feels the actor's presence as the character's absence.

Even for those who adopt Stanislavski's Method (and variations of it) as creed, somatic portrayal still alternates with managed body image. This dual artifice may be neurologically driven: behavioral neuropsychologist D. W. Zaidel states the frontal lobes are the part of the brain that clearly tells us when we are playing a role and when we are witnessing events rather than experiencing them directly (2013, 18). Thinking through dramatic concepts as old as catharsis in these terms, we can appreciate that our identification with the character alternating with our emotional remove could be neurologically necessary for emotional identification to occur. From Aristotle to contemporary theorists, too deep a level of identification with a character or dramatic situation can detract from the refracted real-life problem at the play's core. It was this well-known concern that motivated theorist and playwright Bertolt Brecht to argue for *Verfremdungseffekt* to deliberately disrupt audience identification. Contemporary theater scholars make similar arguments regarding the necessary audience experience of theatrical fabrication, put adeptly by theater scholar David V. Mason:

> The deep experience of theatrical art that strikes us with the force of reality arises, always, from our consciousness of the fabrication of the entire enterprise, and strikes us so firmly with its unreal reality that theater inevitably calls us to doubt it all—stage, house and life, altogether. (2013, 210)

In contrast to other performance genres,[6] theater cognitively cues meaningful make-believe through the palpable artifice of material theatric conditions and affected behavior. As theater scholar Douglas Robinson argues, a good performance engages the audience to feel itself a party to the dramatic action at the same time as its varied levels of palpable artifice cue the audience to distinguish it from their lived experiences of actual exchanges and actions (2008).[7]

Theater scholars Rhonda Blair and Amy Cook tease out the tension between the notion of suspended disbelief necessary to experience a play and the concurrent practices assuring we are aware of that suspension:[8]

> Of course, contemporary theater does many things to create an impression that there is in fact no boundary between the world of the viewers and the

world of the stage, but it is only successful to a degree—the boundary may be a see-through one, and, so to speak, hear-through or even touch-through one, but it does not go away, and the sense of conceptual independence of the real world and the storyworld remains valid. (2016, 23)

Typically, the actor's voice is characterized by a less-than-everydayness of pitch, cadence, volume, and articulation, that, at a minimum, are led by the pragmatics of conveying audible words to the back of the theater. Similarly, larger-than-life gestures make actions somatically legible. As a means of projection, a verbal and somatic tone of declarative intent inadvertently secures the cognitive distinction between witnessing an actual conversation or action and the awareness that we are watching a dramatic performance.[9]

At the level of bodily conduct, actors communicate the character's psychological state in the most elemental way by employing the modalities of the soma. Stage positioning of actors makes use of the audience's reception of spaces on stage to deliberately cultivate or diminish audience identification (Barton and Sellers-Young 2017, 131–34). Similarly, actors often mark their path with unusually heavy footsteps that, like the hollow sound of a set door, strike the ear as unnatural, making plain the crafted nature of the performance. Stage illumination can also enhance somatic portrayal, using spotlights, for example, to intensify our attention and ostensibly our connection to a character. By the same token, when lighting drops the rest of the cast into penumbra, the audience may connect more deeply to the illuminated character, while the visual dimming of the rest of the set simultaneously brings out the fictional quality of what they are experiencing.

The stage also depends on somatic portrayal in conveying the sense perceptions of smell and taste. The somatic portrayal of tasting while ingesting air rather than the purported wine or steak, or of smelling while sniffing a paper flower, creates a cache of normal, everyday life, sensorial somatic output that enriches the believability of the dramatic whole. On the other hand, the overt gesticulation typical of managing body image technically helps define and broadcast the thoughts and feelings of characters across the theater space, but because it generally carries more intensity than lived experience, such gesticulation equally signals the fictiveness of the performance.[10] Congruent somatic *portrayal* connects the audience to the play, while the palpable deliberateness of somatic *display* per bodily image management creates the requisite psychological distance to inscribe an interaction as staged—interpersonally staged as purposefully less than authentic, as well as staged in theatrical props.[11]

In sum, body image management tells us what is going on (a reminder we are watching a play that is not part of normal life; Mason 2013, 210), while somatic portrayal drives why we care. Whereas most actors blend these two styles of acting to convey characters, speaking Ceci, Ceci-the-body, and Lydia each engage somatic portrayal and body image management in unusual ways. Ceci twists and struggles, and because this kind of bodily expression is not often seen in public and is personally experienced by few, Ceci-the-body's performance likely exceeds the audience's implicit expectations for combined somatic portrayal and body image management. Lydia's much more familiar countenance of false cheer disproportionately employs body image management to the near exclusion of somatic portrayal, as we shall see. Because body image management seeks to naturalize a social mask, it gives a mere *impression* of authentic countenance rather than presenting the *authentic* countenance of the soma.

The common volley between somatic portrayal and body image management in contemporary U.S. theater is notably absent in these two characters. In its place, we see extremes: speaking Ceci and Lydia almost exclusively manage the image of their bodies, while the actor delivers Ceci-the-body almost entirely through somatic portrayal. While these extremes may reflect preference or skill, I argue these respective imbalances serve to dramatize the pressures in asserting the self suffered by the intersectionally disabled and the intraracialized. As argued throughout *Shaming into Brown,* in scenes of racialization, the aggressive, contemptuous soma of the racializer affectively supplants the racialized person's somatically expressed humanity, treating the racialized as an intersectionally marginalized body first, and sometimes, instead of full consideration of another as a human being. For present purposes, these actors dramatically mimic response styles of the marginalized to expose social practices of intersectional intraracialization, racism, and ableism.

The play succeeds in making unexpected connections between racialized gender, unregulated labor, and disability, making a still more unusual connection between the play's protagonist, the disabled Ceci, and the plight of a *doméstica,* a single, undocumented, female Mexican domestic worker. Yet, a dramatic engagement of the factors of racialization, gender assignment, and disability should not surprise us: race and gender have long been categories of non-normativity in the United States, and have been presented both historically and culturally under the umbrella of disability (Thomson [1997] 2017). From the Hottentot Venus of the nineteenth century, through the parading of Native Americans during the seventeenth to twentieth centuries, to contemporary engagements such as Guillermo Gómez-Peña and Coco Fusco's performance piece commonly known as *The Couple in the Cage* (1992),[12] the racialized and gendered have shared venues with the disabled. Sometimes the circus freak, racialized people, like differently capacitated people, showcased physicality as material to assess social unacceptability, later criminalized when, for a time, ugly was declared illegal. Contrary to the social foreclosure this stigma intends, Ceci's physical state emotionally expresses the physical, intellectual, social, and spiritual productivity of intersectionally disabled and/or ill bodies argued in Latin@/x critical and literary theories.

Latin@/x literature scholars Suzanne Bost, Laura Halperin, Julie Avril Minich, and José Esteban Muñoz directly address social assignments of gender, ethnicity, and disability as a productive confluence for theory and art. While Bost and Minich caution against overstating parallels between latinidad and disability, Bost states, "[Both] Latino/a studies and disability studies . . . draw attention to previously overlooked corporeal experiences as well as the role of cultures and environments in shaping identity" (2013, 89).[13] In fact, Minich, in her study of disabled figures in Chican@/x literature, dissuades essentialist readings, arguing that Chican@/x cultural texts "invite dialogue between Chicana/o studies and disability studies and demonstrate how the theories developed in each field might help the other to contest more effectively the 'rise to power' of unjust social systems" (2013, 23). Racialization, gender, and disability are clearly dissimilar as felt experiences, but as respective states of embodiment, each incurs social rejection and shame in theater's perennial project of "negotiat[ing] around what the body *is* and *means*" (Shepherd 2006, 1, emphasis added). These three categories of social ugliness found in the cultural and legal phenomena of the body are discussed in the next section, but here I remark on the way the ugly soma in *Lydia* takes on this charge, interrogating what the intersectional body means when dramatized disabled in Ceci's case, and when intraracialized, in Lydia's.

CECI-THE-BODY

The role of Ceci-the-body demands the actor engage the soma and body image in unusual ways. First, the actor must incorporate the stigma of disability into her somatic portrayal, where her physical expression becomes the dominant and instantaneous message indicating she is to be read as a bodily presence that, by convention, indicates her social absence. After Ceci gives a soliloquy expounding on familial misery, the power of paralinguistic sound returns speaking Ceci to Ceci-the-body who gurgles "ssccrrmmgfmhm" (7), a somatic expression of her worry and sadness that younger brother Misha and Rosa read as a signal of physical distress:

MISHA. Mom, what's wrong with Ceci?
ROSA. *Alomejor* [sic] she went poo-poo.
MISHA. She doesn't smell like it.
ROSA. Maybe she wants her therapy. . . . (7)

The able-bodied but socially marginalized members of the Flores family project unease with Ceci's difference by shaming Ceci or feeling ashamed of her (37). As we know, difference in physical ability itself does not signify disability. Rather, the term *disability* designates the way society structures life such that those who cannot adapt to its structure are identified as disabled (Sullivan 2001, 23). Based on the perception of the social incommensurability of her body, Ceci-the-body, who is obnoxiously present and yet beyond her family's comprehension, solicits their embarrassment at her lack of personhood.

Ceci's character, a young woman gripped in a perpetual state of seizure, is a material presence—a body—creating the visual affective frame of the play. As a split character, speaking Ceci relies on the actor's body management in contrast to Ceci-the-body's somatic portrayal. The difference of style between the two Cecis startles. Far from a surfeit problem of her physical state or a titillating opportunity for dramatic gymnastics, while Ceci-the-body convulses, groans and growls, drools, defecates, and later experiences orgasm, speaking Ceci delivers a smart, sassy, self-possessed personality of a normatively bodied teenager. The soma enacts the theatrical idiom through which the actor melds these two disparate performances into a unified character. From the opening scene, the audience first sees Ceci-the-body convulsing on the ground, only to suddenly assume the soma of an able-bodied person who directs her words to the audience.

The actor portrays Ceci-the-body's disability in a realistic mode, but one that is not necessarily reflective of the actual experience of PVS sufferers,[14] to offer a contrast to the affected acting style in the role of speaking Ceci, and so, deliberately draws attention to the importance of her wounded agitation in fleshy script. She touches her physical scar like a palimpsest that can unlock the secret of how she came to live as Ceci-the-body amid her family's dour unease:

I gotta read my scar for the story, it's in there, I know it! ¡*Aguas!* I see her. The girl that touched me . . . her face in a mirror looking back . . . showing me her own sccc—ggghn mmm her- own- ssccrrmmgfmhm . . . (7)

The belief within the medical establishment is that those with PVS do not enjoy a satisfactory quality of life, and exist only as living bodies, a state of being we refuse to consider legibly subjective.[15]

Absent verbal confirmation or elaboration of how or why Ceci-the-body feels so, her uncontrolled physical gesticulation stands alone, decontextualized, univocal, and minimized to neurological mayhem. But in these lines, Ceci recasts her physical state of agitation as a constant somatic message connecting her story to her family's lives and to Lydia, the "girl that touched me," "showing me her own scc-ggghn [scar]." To this end, Ceci-the-body creates an agonistic tone in an affective frame, transliterating the family's unacknowledged despair and anger of marginalization in her somatic body movements, as if she is in a permanent somatic state of anger and grief. The accident serves as the dramatic offstage catalyst overlaying her and her family's grappling with intersectional racialization, expressed in the sound "ssccrrmmgfmhm" that speaking Ceci ties to the emotional predicament of the Flores family: "Mi familia. All sad and wounded cause of somethin.' Somethin' that broke" (7).[16] This "somethin" Claudio later attributes to the soul-robbing life that Mechicanos lead in *los Estados Unidos* (45).[17] Ceci's reference to Lydia's scar intimates a previous change to Lydia's life circumstances, but what we witness is the direct degradation she suffers in the Flores home.

Ceci's prefatory remarks set up the play's hermeneutics. We will learn in intervals the why and how of Ceci's PVS and of Ceci-the-body's relationship to speaking Ceci, to the family's circumstances, and to Lydia. In contrast, the portrayal of Ceci-the-body as a character depends on the uncoordinated, uncontrollable body in a dramatic approximation of free somatic expression, the latter characterized and authenticated by spontaneity and irrepressibility. The respective modes of acting layer different registers of embodiment at the same time as they also express multiple subjectivities. The two Cecis interpolate physical normativity in "flourishing transactions between organic bodies and world," where disability provides the dramatic hermeneutics in giving an intersectional "account of truth" of both performances of her character (Sullivan 2001, 10).

In a typical depiction of Ceci-the-body, speech follows a phonetic transcription of an imagined groan: "CECI. 'Gh. Ghgngn'" (58). Typifying her dialogue as body throughout, the script gives Ceci-the-body sounds rather than lines. But what does "Gh. Ghgngn" mean? Are they meaningful utterances or the physical sounds of a young woman who is mentally dead? Social psychology researcher Wendy Berry Mendes (2016), like feminist philosopher of cognitive science Shannon Sullivan (2015), avers that the body's affect is largely outside one's control; however, it is far from random or limited to the inner autonomic workings of the body. Our nervous system can override our brain's mental deliberations of what is best for us. Our nervous system works in concert with our sensorium and mind to assess for threat, so that when these systems deem necessary, we faint, tremble, vomit, suddenly urinate or defecate, hyperventilate, go into shock, twitch, growl, or scream (Ganzel, Rarick, and Morris 2016).

The soma informed by these bodily intelligences constantly and instantaneously considers external and internal data, responding at the level of organs and systems we may or may not be aware of internally but that produce a legible external register we notice in the form of posture, countenance, and mien. Whether squirming on the floor or simply in an overly rigid torso and neck, these somatic expressions seek to respectively soothe and protect the organism while they convey to the outside world our ongoing deep internal response to our experience of the environment.[18] Mendes's research supports my argument that Ceci-the-body intentionally and legibly expresses herself and her milieu through affect, which Sullivan contends, is always already socially responsive, and therefore meaning-rich, a whole body experience toward externalizing stressors and self-calm (Sullivan 2001).[19] In the adeptly calibrated performance I saw, I understood Ceci-the-body's sudden "grrhhh" and similar sounds accompanied by sudden contortions as a meaningful whole-body, multisensory somatic reflection of the circumstances in the Flores home.

On par with the intensity of her convulsions, English professor Steven Connor's work on sound would propose the vocalization "Gh. Ghgngn" (58) draws from the hollow of the throat, the place where phlegm, mouth structure, and aspiration come together to convey our most elementary human expressions. Connor avers that the sounds *gh* and *gr* connote death but also "1) unpleasantness (*grim, grisly, gritty* . . .) 2) complaint (*grumble, groan, grieve, gripe* . . .) and 3) relating to undesirable friction or rubbing (*grind, groove, grate, groit, grub* . . .)" (2014, 111), on the one hand, but on the other hand, suggest "the raw, pure audible-sensible of the breathing body" (110) of the divine. Meaning-rich sonorous emanations, *gh* and *gr* mark both the emergence of life and the imminent death. Both in English and German, philosopher Michael Serres traces a genealogy of gutturals beginning in the second verse of the book of Genesis where *gh* of *ruagh* (divine breath) indicates:

> . . . at the back of the throat, before language, in front of the root of the tongue, where the gasping intake of breath acknowledges the divine; *ruagh*, breath, breathing, wind, breeze of the spirit. ([1985] 2016, 316)

In both fields of sonorous connotation, the sounds *gh* and *gr* signal the presence of life, whether dawning or fleeting. *Gh* of "Gh. Ghgngn" are sounds "speaking from the belly" (Connor 2014, 115), presenting the unwelcome, ugly utterance of vital disquiet, if not anger and aggression, but also of hunger, elimination urges, erotic desire, pain (115–27), and to my mind, the dawning consciousness of shame. Ceci's *gh* is part of an alternative discourse wherein the soma powerfully modifies body posture, movement, and verbal sounds in ways that square with the nature of shame, an unresolved affective intermediary between the desire for acceptance and its denial.[20]

An unseemly sound, in my analysis of *Lydia*, "Gh. Ghgngn" draws out the somatic aural of shame in "a somatic temporality, where the potential of again being interested [in relationship] is felt in the present pain of rejection" (Probyn 2005, 63). "Gh. Ghgngn" accompanied by physical convulsions distends time and dispels hegemonic discourse in a mode of expressing anguish for denied social connection. The fact that "Gh. Ghgngn" is heard many times throughout the play indicates intended affective speech—Ceci-the-body's unadulterated nonsemantic utterances expose (perhaps more than express) the household's intersectional pain of shame. Her "Gh. Ghgngn" voices the predicament of accepting her social death or moving with the thriving physical state of her organism in a metaphoric parallel to the difficulty of submitting to the hostile indifference of the household, versus accepting the promise of renewal with Lydia's help. "Gh" and "gr," I argue, generate the semantic frame of Ceci-the-body's somatic expression from which we can contextualize other sounds as content-rich somatic data.

This frame appreciably enriches Ceci-the-body's performance. The way she expresses her shame, desire, and anger, unexpressed feelings shared by her father Claudio and her caretaker Lydia toward the end of Act One, is a salient example. The scene begins with Ceci-the-body supine on the floor, gently convulsing, as Lydia and Claudio begin a sexual encounter. Ceci-the-body's writhing and audible expressions gain intensity, perhaps expressing her and their sexual arousal, physically contextualizing speaking Ceci's sudden rise to speak. She discusses the ghost-like nature of the pair, Lydia and her father both intersectionally shamed and more dead than alive. Speaking Ceci forebodes "La Muerte! La Muerrr . . ." ("death! dea. . . .") (47), the word trailing into powerful somatic spasms of anger, fear, and shame, she ends in the guttural gurgle "Grnnnnn." The ugly soma speaks out in Ceci's *grh*, convulsing across her two dramatic stylizations, and conveys as much of her thriving vitality as it does the ebbing of their quality of life.

THE LEGACY OF THE UGLY LAWS

From the Floreses' point of view, Ceci lives the innocent but shame-filled life of a body out of control. Rosa summarizes her estimation of Ceci toward the end of the play: ROSA. ". . . [to CECI] You were going to be my partner, but look at you," to which Ceci responds, "Gnnghg" (78). Rosa's "but look at you" shames Ceci into a mindless dysfunctional body, a sensorially offensive and socially useless once-upon-a-time daughter, and where despite Ceci-the-body's good looks, Rosa treats Ceci as if contemptuously ugly. A brief history of the politics and deliberations regarding the nature of the body and social acceptability contextualize the contested social acceptance of Ceci, Lydia, and the Floreses. I present a limited genealogy of the set of legal edicts commonly referred to as the Ugly Laws to argue that Ceci's physical disability, like Lydia's intersectional legal standing and the Floreses' social marginalization, builds on a Western legacy that defines *ugliness* as a shameful physical expression that reflects moral decrepitude. Established nearly a century ago, the Ugly Laws codified the common rationale that *ugliness* was grounds for social exclusion in the United States. As Susan M. Schweik argues in *The Ugly Laws: Disability in Public* (2009):

> Gender, race, sexuality, religion, and national identity are inexorably intertwined with disability and class in the culture(s) of ugly law, producing a variety of ugly identities . . . (141)

Deeming certain body types and personal comportment offensive and therefore shameful, the Ugly Laws negotiated body type and affect to signify moral offense in fabricating the notion of social ugly.

Quarles's words in this chapter's epigraph evidence a Western philosophical rationale, prominent from medieval times to the Enlightenment, that attributed physical and/or mental difference to a faulty Christian spirit. Differences observed in so-called madmen and the mentally non-normative were thought to reflect demonic possession and/or forms of perversion. Enlightenment philosophy displaced the devil with the mechanization of the body where the body was seen as a tool of the mind or spirit, a concept still in operation centuries later. As the late historian Roy Porter argued in *The Flesh in the Age of Reason* (2004), insanity and other varied mental capacities challenged the belief in rational man, implicitly denying the autonomy of the body as solely a physical organism (a concept premising current medical thought) and the expression of the body as a constituent of one's personhood.

Enlightenment theories diagnosed uncustomary behaviors as the malfunctioning of the body, the result of physical illness, rather than of a diseased mind, but did not exonerate disease from the charge of reflecting the poor condition of spirit.[21] Both ontologies evidence the West's intense social discomfort with non-normative bodies. This discomfort motivated scripting illness and non-normative bodies and behaviors with embarrassment, if not shame, in need of discipline, arriving at the establishment of the asylum and sanitarium (Foucault [1964] 1988)—architectural and organizational solutions allowing the removal of the non-normative from the public eye. Porter, building on Foucault, notes the tendency to treat madness with social discipline as in the case of the famous asylum, the York Retreat in England, established by Quaker William Tuke in 1796. York Retreat changed the medical paradigm from treating the mentally ill as if they were subhuman, and thereby subjecting them to hunger, neglect, and abuse, to advocating treatment of the mentally ill as children for whom caretaking staff should parent. The staff modeled what they believed to be healthy adult comportment in the hopes of teaching the mentally ill normative adult behavior (Porter 2003, 318). This approach to socializing the disabled became the model for caring for the mentally ill. It is still remarked in psychiatry books today and continues to fashion the treatment of the mentally ill in today's U.S. mental institutions and therapeutic approaches, as it appears in the Floreses' treatment of Ceci.

Until the late twentieth century, physical and mental differences were considered sufficiently discomfiting to U.S. society that removal of people with disabilities off the streets and out of social view was authorized by the Ugly Laws. These municipal ordinances generally defined "ugly" to include specific notions reflected in the Chicago edict below:

> Any person who is diseased, maimed, mutilated, or in any way deformed, so as to be an unsightly or disgusting object, or an improper person to be allowed in or on the streets, highways, thoroughfares, or public places in this city, shall not therein or thereon expose himself of public view, under the openly of a fine of $1 [about $20 today] for each offense. (Schweik 2009, 2)

English professor Rosemarie Garland Thomson's disability study describes the powerful cultural milieu in which ethnicity and non-Whiteness could incur the generalizable epithet "freak," indicating a semiotic chain from non-normativity to racism to ugly, later formalized into law ([1997] 2017).

Distaste for disability resulted in legal codification of aesthetics, and thus played a role in making beauty and gender performance socially critical. The tramp scare of 1880s-90s was a formative moment in this cognitive history, joining gender to physical appearance in stipulating social ugliness. As Schweik explains under the auspices of female gender, women under the "tramp scare" were "ugly" not only by deformity, but also by their "consciousness of lack of attraction and beauty," "extremes of leanness and stoutness, shortness and tallness, "extreme awkwardness," "cross-eyes and eye-lesions," "excessive" or "slight growth of hair," "tiny and massive breasts," appearing "unkempt, tough and unpleasant" (2009, 145).

Schweik argues the tramp scare was trumped up to generate a cultural cognition under which physical difference denoted poverty, illicit begging, and, later, immorality and criminality, giving birth to the alms house and, later, the poor house as penitentiary (35). Ugly bodies were simultaneously imagined to equate to an empty bank account, and thus to portend economic blight as well. With the physical condition of difference connotatively intensified, lawmakers and the public believed those deemed ugly in need of removal, and they were summarily disappeared from the streets. Politicians legislated disgust to justify shaming non-normatives, a practice that continues today in the enforcement of formal and informal standards of aesthetic acceptability.

By the twenty-first century, ugly was no longer used as a legal category; however, I wonder if its cultural logic has not been influential in creating laws against vagrancy, sleeping in public, and begging, as well as imposing limits on other forms of public appearance of color and poverty (like current California laws outlawing informal street vending [Kang, 2011a and 2011b], removal of bus stops used primarily by Latin@/x workers in elite neighborhoods, and the elimination of day-labor rendezvous points). Today, de facto cognitive scripts train us to judge unsanctioned racialized laborers unsightly; unsightliness is intentionally conflated with illegal status and poverty, used in rationales for laws to corral and/or expel Brown people in a social logic complementary to that of the Ugly Laws.[22] What is certain is that across time, the charge of ugliness[23] associated with disability has also been attributed on the basis of race and gender in a similar social logic affixing social stigma (Thomson [1997] 2017). Ultimately, the practice of social ugly continues shaming particular bodies off the street and out of sight.[24]

Incredibly, the Ugly Laws enacted between the early nineteenth to mid-twentieth centuries were invoked (albeit unsuccessfully) as recently as 1974. Corrective reintegration of the so-called ugly back into society led to the passage of the Americans with Disabilities Act of 1990, challenging society to allow the disabled into public view to work and more. Today, activists continue to work against the lingering stigma of social ugly, pressuring the revaluation of differently capacitated individuals first, as social contributors rather than economic liabilities, and second (hopefully), as not ugly.[25] Yet, we can feel the potent legacy of the Ugly Laws in the ways their historical enactment has left a cultural mindset linking disability and unattractiveness to race, ethnicity, gender, sexuality, and informal labor, where socially formed cognitive scripts select intersectional racialization to connote social illegitimacy and encumbering economic dependency.[26]

With these cultural practices in mind, Ceci-the-body presents a perceptual disturbance violating entrained standards of visual decency regardless of (or perhaps heightened by) the actor's physical attractiveness in the performance I attended. From the frame of social ugly, the dramatic suturing of the two Cecis asks the audience to accommodate Ceci's beauty and increasingly legible personhood against discomfort with Ceci-the-body's unsightly and figuratively smelly non-normativity. Next, I will address how Ceci's soliloquies only partially restore Ceci-the-body's socially ugly presentation.

SPEAKING CECI, CECI-THE-SOLILOQUIST

Throughout the play, while the characters wonder at times how and whether Ceci thinks and feels, Ceci intermittently rises and becomes a speaking, mentally coherent, normative-bodied character, exceeding the human abilities of a person in her condition. She speaks of her life as a "vegetable" and describes her hopes and aspirations before the accident.[27] These moments are delivered in soliloquies in which Ceci serves as an intermittent omniscient narrator. Formal features of the set guide the audience to interpret speaking Ceci within the confines of Ceci-the-body's disability. Lighting spotlights speaking Ceci's position downstage right, sensorially and spatially drawing the audience's attention to her social remove from able-bodied characters stilled in action.

Her more lengthy soliloquies where she describes her life as a child cast her as a reasonably mature seventeen-year-old. In the performance on which I base my analysis, the actor delivered highly enunciated lines in a tone significantly younger than her years. These soliloquies provided the backstory of the Flores family before the secrets, the accident, and the maturation of the Flores children. Yet the content contrasts with the quality of her voice. Ceci's impish tone reaffirms the diminished sense of self she somatically portrays when presenting her flailing body. As discussed earlier, infantilization of Ceci-the-body informs the shamed tone of a naive child who struggles to understand why she and loved ones are needlessly burdened. Speaking Ceci's deliberate childlike demeanor explains why she cannot identify systemic intersectional racism as the cause.

The manufactured quality of tone creates an aural subtext, the sound meanings subtly invoking the political stakes of negotiating gender, ethnicity, ablebodiedness, sexual orientation, class, legal status, and social status. An adept dramatic strategy, this tone leads the audience to decipher the disingenuous calibration of her voice and what it implies. A confected tone efficiently communicates intentionality to the hue of the actor's portrayal, facilitating the shift to mature speaking Ceci, a sudden change in character from the young woman who a moment before thrusted and thrashed on the floor. Speaking Ceci modulates through the childlike delivery of her teenage quandaries, the value and meaning conveyed in the somatic portrayal of the continuously distressed Ceci-the-body. Her tone provides effective sensory data under conditions of intersectional racial shaming that undercut her age-appropriate opinion, judgment, or assertion, demanding instead the charming but effectually bland stances of a child.

Sexual desire is one way speaking Ceci intimates a more adolescent-cum-adult persona claiming, "I'm horny! I'm just horny! I want to be wanted. I want to be touched. . . . I want to be fucked" (24). Ceci's socially ugly body seems to respond to her sexual desires with unease and judgement, and without remedy. When Ceci is uncomfortably libidinous, the actor delivers her speaking lines in the tone of a frustrated innocent, which, given her physical condition, we cannot expect her to fulfill her own desires. Solís gives voice to the taboo subject of sexuality and the disabled, an empowering discourse, influential in power relations, as healthcare researcher Sarah Earle argues: "The denial of sexual identity is a significant feature of power relations," noting that "disabled people are generally infantilized by society and perceived as asexual" (2001, 433). Because Ceci (as Ceci-the-body) lacks physical control or clear communication, her orgasm and suicide at the end of the play seem somewhat implausible, given the flailing state of Ceci-the-body and her childlike tone when speaking. Yet the two sides of her character have by this juncture in the play contested such an assumption. Ceci's orgasm and suicide engage the soma in confirmation of her subjective personhood. Conversely, the sound of Ceci's childlike voice speaks of feigned immaturity whereas her words say otherwise. The combination of registers—spoken, tonal, and physical—bridge the two performances of Ceci into a more unified character whose PVS body becomes legible as also an expression of her personhood that simultaneously exposes our complicit prejudice in diminishing the full humanity of disabled people.

We come to learn her dramatically argued subjectivity is not limited to an inaccessible mind state, but is coterminous with the capabilities of her body. As the two Cecis become one, Ceci-the-body exhibits more clearly her daily gendered and racialized diminishment in parallel to the unspoken burden of the magico nanny that Lydia bears.

MAGICO NANNY: LYDIA AS RACIALIZED DOMESTIC WORKER ARCHETYPE

> We smile, but oh great Christ, our cries
> To thee from tortured souls arise.
> . . .
> We wear the mask!
> —Paul Laurence Dunbar (1896)

This discussion thus far may make one wonder why the play is titled *Lydia* when Ceci is so compelling. As Ceci-the-body's somatic portrayal expresses Ceci's feelings regarding herself and her family, over the course of the play, we come to understand Ceci-the-body also expresses Lydia's anger and hostility, as well as her objection to the socially imposed vulnerability of an undocumented mexicana domestic worker. Because U.S. culture delimits people like Lydia to low social status despite their important contributions, Ceci-the-body and, eventually, speaking Ceci express the stifled fury that brings Lydia's subdual into relief. Limited in dialogue, Lydia occupies a tertiary role in the Floreses' home. Overshadowed by the intense stage presence of Ceci-the-body, Lydia becomes a screen onto which each family member projects his or her crisis or fantasy. From this remove, the archetype of the racialized domestic worker emerges, revealing Lydia as a magico caretaker, and intersectional intraracialization, the principal subject of the play.

Unlike the Flores family, Lydia finds Ceci's bodily actions legible and on point in her subjective engagement with her state of health and her familial environment. Disrupting the notion that PVS divorces intention from bodily behavior, Lydia knows Ceci as a communicative, attractive, and desiring person who is quite attentive to her milieu. Lydia's special understanding of Ceci despite the PVS she suffers is clearly seen when Lydia presents Ceci dressed in her forlorn quinceañera gown for Cousin Alvaro's visit to the Flores home. Cousin Alvaro is struck by Ceci's confounding attractiveness despite her physical condition, but as he holds Ceci against him in a quasi-dance, Ceci suddenly urinates and soils Alvaro's shoes in somatic debacle. Ceci responds to mutual somatic sexual recognition by peeing on Alvaro. Whether as payback for betraying her or as symbolic of other releases, the soma drives the scene. René shoves Ceci away from Alvaro, somatically expressing René's disgust with Ceci, the upset resulting from his unrequited love for Alvaro, and his contempt for Lydia, who assumes social power in claiming to know Ceci's heart. Angered, René confronts "the maid" who has authored this social mayhem:

MISHA. Still, you didn't have to push her away like that, fuckhead! What's your problem!
RENE. My problem is this maid doesn't realize what that fucking dress means in this house!
LYDIA. But [Ceci] does.
RENE. Who asked you to talk?
LYDIA. She knows everyone's pain. All the time. Even yours.
RENE. Did she really ask you to put her in this dress?
LYDIA. How else would I know where to look?
ROSA. She told you?
. . .
LYDIA. Not everything she says comes out of her mouth. (38)

Though the Floreses hardly appreciate Lydia's relationship with Ceci, her special ability to somatically communicate with Ceci is one often inscribed in U.S. culture as a magical attribute of domestic workers, becoming a defining quality of racialized domestic workers that fuels the archetype of the magico nanny.

Typifying the complexity for immigrants of managing their reception by the dominant culture, McNulty states: "Lydia needs a place to live and in exchange will anticipate the household needs and desires with an intuition that recalls all those old tales of magical nannies" (2009). McNulty's assessment of nannies and magical realism places *Lydia* squarely in the trajectory of American literature's fancy with houseboys and other domestic workers usually (but not exclusively) of color, intertextually drawing the character Lydia in the archetype of the gendered and racialized domestic worker of U.S. letters.[28] We recall scenes from these varied genres demanding, sometimes under threat of death, that a person of color feign happy subservience, merrily conceding to racialized shamefulness and inferiority. Joel Chandler Harris's *Uncle Remus, His Song and Sayings: The Folklore of the Old Plantation* [1881] (2002) and its many subsequent iterations in the magical Negro through the twentieth century aptly demonstrates this archetype presented through the soma.

Despite suffering from racialization and racism, Uncle Remus portrays a jolly African American man with soft, kind eyes, and an easy laugh, holding an affable, welcoming body posture that becomes popular and imitable as a managed body image found acceptable to racializing forces.[29] Such characters seek to make palpable uncontested social subjugation by using infantilized tones and grandiose addresses to social superiors (e.g., "Yes, Sir!") and adopting a sturdy posture, ready to serve but careful to avoid somatic suggestions of possible aggression. I contend the archetype delimits natural somatic response, replacing it with managed body image, the latter, a physical discipline of presenting docile, happy, attentive yet dutiful social surrender. An archetype advanced in varied cultural venues throughout the last one hundred years, the magical domestic worker was an acceptable and even desirable persona for former slaves and others of color. Despite the differences in iterations, characters like Uncle Tom of *Uncle Tom's Cabin,* Mammy of *Gone with the Wind,* and Uncle Remus, among others, embody the racialized domestic worker archetype in controlled bodily expression, where physical and psychological distance from hegemonic characters in postures confecting somatic-like acceptance of social inferiority allow hegemonic subjects to control physical and emotional intimacy. The racialized domestic worker archetype uses her/his somatic portrayal in endless selfless acts of service, if not martyrdom, possessing especially deep spiritual or otherworldly insight, with a gift for tender, loving rapport at all times and with everyone: the archetype bridges racial shaming through the perennially subservient magical caregiver.[30]

Lydia presents the archetype with the particularities of her intersectional circumstances and her treatment at the hands of a Mechicano family, who are situationally hegemonic figures at the helm of the Flores home. Lydia's delimited role, carried out by managing her body rather than through somatic portrayal of her character, extends Frederick L. Aldama's critique of magical realism for U.S. Latin@/xs, identifying the pervasive colonizing cognitive filter where any variety of things Latin American and, by extension Latin@/x, are seen as otherworldly, magical, if not quaintly bizarre. Casting Latin American and Latin@/x cultural production in exotic terms minimizes its serious concerns, while promoting its commodification for economic and political gain. Latin American and Latin@/x texts are then marketed as Other-worldly, their content, fetishized:

> Theorists can identify [magical realism] as an exotic packaged Otherness that covers over real political and social processes that exploit, oppress, and suppress Third world ethnic and/or minority Others. (Aldama 2003, 27)

Aldama proposes the term *magicorealism* to signal Latin@/x writers' understanding of their co-optation. While writers sometimes employ tropes and/or plots engendering such codification, Aldama argues they often build in strategies to arrest this effect:

> [Writers] use magicorealism to speak to their character's estranged sense of self as they inhabit newly bordered geopolitical landscapes . . . offer[ing] a complex mapping of subaltern-identified story and discourse. (39)

With Aldama's frame in mind, I assert Lydia, a magico nanny, is an intraracialized domestic worker who plays to her archetype, but does so in an acting style that somatically withholds authenticity. In the gap between her affected countenance and the hostile somatic portrayal that occasionally spills out, her countenance instructs the audience to reconsider the power asymmetries underlining her archetypal performance of the depoliticized magical nanny. The actor embodies and then effectively distances herself from her role as magico nanny in social critique.

Thus, as is common for characters of color, Lydia negotiates racial shaming when answering peaceably or with enthusiasm in reflection of a mainstay of accepted responses to U.S. racializing practices for intersectionally racialized labor markets. In line with actual social practices, the actor quietly and unobtrusively obeys orders as well as those the Floreses *somatically* request. Lydia busies herself through the house, bright, amiable, and available, attending to chores without being asked. As the excerpted dialogue noted earlier makes clear, Lydia's response must conform to a somatic affect of subservience if she is to keep her job. In the May 9, 2009, production, the actor who played Lydia quickly moved from this somatic portrayal of shame described above to an upright posture, head and neck expressing the dignity of self-assurance and stability in the face of the actual precarity of her social position. The confection of bright eagerness and her subtly forced smile suggest the management of shame, an overexertion of happy earnestness toward two goals: the manufactured wide-eyed expression, smile, head and neck thrust forward in attention, deliberately soft but energetic muscle tone in face, arms, and hands somatically acknowledge the intraracializer's power. In this scene and many others, Lydia manages her body to make it seem she is unaffected by the family dysfunction and violence in her quick return to a happy state. As in lived experience, the actor playing Lydia manages her body image by inhibiting as best she can her natural somatic expression of resentment and anger, and in so doing, Lydia reveals the pressures and effects of intraracial shaming that foregrounds and backgrounds the conditions of her daily countenance. Her character exposes the false liberal notion that levels of embodiment (e.g., phenotype, the soma, feelings, health, and physical ability) exist somehow outside of the effects of social relations on those racialized Brown and on other people of color. *Lydia* demonstrates that expressing oneself somatically, untaxed and untethered by social circumstances, is an unspoken yet irrevocable right born of human constitution, and yet, is not equally available to all subjects.[31]

In the performance I attended, Lydia occupied the physical margins of each room, passing through center stage only when en route to the periphery of the room. Indeed, her spatial marginalization paralleled the actor's bodily position on stage. Most often, the actor stood in profile, embodying the family's implicit demand for her discreet presence, a servile position from which she listened for directives and prepared to console the Floreses through their familial tensions. When not in profile, Lydia appeared with her back to the audience dutifully caregiving, cleaning, or conversely, feigning polite ignorance of the tumultuous family troubles at center stage. The play exposes the intraracial particularity of this imposition. Unlike Rosa and Claudio, who are Mexican nationals, the actor playing Lydia is pointedly more ethnically *Mexican* in her performance. She carries out her limited dialogue mostly in English but with a notable accent; her grammatical inconsistencies single Lydia out as decidedly and vulnerably *the* Mexican of the household. In this ethnic calculus, Claudio and Rosa appear comparatively more assimilated to U.S. culture than Lydia, and although unhappy, they are more socially secure. When addressed, Lydia verbally responds yet rarely portrays herself as she likely should feel. Instead, the actor adopts a formulaic bodily attitude of a cheerful, hardworking laborer-ingénue.

In the theatrical performance, Lydia's "nice" demeanor served the purpose of relieving the audience from the Floreses pervasive drudgery and hostile resentment as well as her affective attempt to mitigate the precarity of her employment. Lydia's chirpy demeanor reflects the exigency of managing the shame of intersectional intraracializing; by acting other than she feels due to such pressures, Lydia acknowledges herself as so shamefully dependent on the good graces of her employer that she must somatically abandon her true feelings.

Parallel to Ceci's demanding physical presence yet subjective familial absence, Lydia's work is omnipresent while she, as an individual, exists unknown. Even when assertive, her character remains superficially expressive, eye-catching but short of any emotional and somatic range that would complete her personhood. Lydia has lived for some time in the Flores home, but midway through Act 1, it finally occurs to the youngest brother Misha (and only Misha) that the Flores family has almost no knowledge of Lydia, the person. Misha's youthful crush gives rise to his desire to know her to which she retorts: "You know my name" (23). Lydia meets Misha's romantic attentions with the same good-natured attitude found in her general managed work countenance while guarding who she is outside her work arrangement with the Floreses. Like real-life domestic workers, Lydia must constantly control how she affectively appears or face the consequences of being labeled a difficult worker.[32]

Lydia's managed body image educates the audience on the performative exigency of the Latina archetype of the magic*o* nanny, a dramatized expression built on a cultural dictum to intersectional oppression. Willing the suppression of the soma for the hoped-for safety of body image management is a psychophysical means of meeting the qualitative interpersonal expectations of domestic labor. Lydia's efforts to maintain feigned good humor require an oppressive level of self-vacating in the attempt to minimize the somatic fissures that threaten her well-being at the hands of this Mechicano family.

This dynamic of imposing social superiority through somatic countenance and action is apparent in the interactions previously analyzed, but the politic of implied acting style poignantly appears in this brief, early exchange between Claudio and Lydia:

> LYDIA. . . . you like the coffee or not?
> *(He downs the coffee in one gulp and throws it violently into the kitchen, shattering it.)*
> CLAUDIO. *No. No me gusta.*
> *(He goes back to the bedroom.)*
> LYDIA. *Pues* . . . I'll have to do it better. (26)

In *Lydia*, we learn marginalized groups can also racialize, and that they can do so by the same somatic means as hegemonic groups—exerting somatic power to emotionally and physically overwhelm another to force acceptance of marginalized status. Claudio's words by themselves simply answer Lydia's question, but in his violent shattering of the cup, he uses somatic anger and contempt to assert his dominance over Lydia, her job, and the household. His use of Spanish to her English imparts to Lydia his power over her—power ascribed to his social position as a Mexican man who is thus authorized and in fact, socially pressured, to lord over this young, poor, undocumented Mexican woman. Intraracializing shame, like racializing shame, is an efficacious affective strategy that similarly asserts and maintains power in survey of each party's somatic countenance.

Cultural texts reflect the lived experience of expressing defiance, indifference, or aggression in response to these oppressions, but asserting self as peer often meets with further marginalization, varying in form from verbal reprisal to the extreme of murder.[33] Indeed, it is Lydia's direct questioning of Claudio's palpable and perpetual hostility—an uppity inquiry for a lowly *doméstica*—that motivates his aggression. Accepting her employer's bellicosity intraracially shames Lydia into feigned docility. Lydia's fabricated jollity is only secondarily an attitude of words; she consciously uses her body to effectuate this social negotiation, acknowledging her perceived status as vulnerable inferior while her positive countenance seeks safety from further debasement.

Lydia's words concluding the interaction express her pressured compliance under the countenance of calm acceptance: "LYDIA. *Pues* . . . I'll have to do it better" (26). The posture accompanying her words in the performance I attended conveyed acceptance of the intraracializer's dominance, potentially ingratiating herself with him in the hope of more beneficent consideration.

In the four steps of intersectional racialization argued in the first two chapters of *Shaming into Brown,* the racialized is pressured to accept reinscription of herself as intersectionally colored and so reduced to an inferior, contemptible body. Using the threat of harm and sometimes even of death, the intraracializer seeks to foreclose on the intraracialized's oppositional somatic expressions and, instead, delimit the responses of the racialized to concessions of shame. I observed in the performance that false jollity quickly morphed into the somatic portrayal of averted eyes, blushing, and slouched, a concave expression of the torso typical of feeling shame. These kinds of interactions in *Lydia* problematize the assumed freedom of all parties to respond honestly and authentically to others. However, the soma can never be completely suppressed, and inevitably fissures appear.[34]

On other occasions, Lydia is provocative, showing her will to defy her circumscribed passive servility. Although more emotionally expressive, these lines continue to be tailored to the demands of her job:

> *([LYDIA] raises the volume to full.* CLAUDIO *rips off the headphones, jumps to his feet, his eyes glaring with rage.)*
> CLAUDIO. [sic] HIJO DE LA CHINGADA!
> LYDIA. How come [CECI] like this. [sic]
> CLAUDIO. *Un accidente. Chocó mi Pontiac.*
> LYDIA. How long ago?
> CLAUDIO. *Hace dos años.* (26)

With infrequent, accented speech, guarded and limited personal disclosure, peripheral staging, and deferential body posture as described earlier, the actor playing Lydia almost exclusively manages her body image, the bodily method that hides somatic expression for the sake of securing her job.

In this sense, the actor's portrayal meets a U.S. audience's racialized "horizon of expectations" (Elam [1980] 2002, 85), as her physical stage position, her non-native English, and the socially dictated self-effacement of her character reflect the position and personal presentation demanded of domestic workers. Dramatizations of racialized comportment must consider the audience's lived experience with domestic workers of color in their homes, neighborhoods, and/or in cultural portrayals. In mass culture, maids, like "good" houseboys, conform to demanded servility. Actors playing the racialized archetype embody a deictic thread that enables audiences to follow and accept the dramatic logic of the play as reflective of actual social arrangements (Elam Jr. 2010, 549).

In recent depictions of racialized domestic workers, and more specifically, of magico nannies, cultural productions featuring domestic workers often dare to shed compelled subservience or somatic display for fear of reprisal in favor of advocacy of the workers' individual goals and morals in demands for respect and fairness.[35] In contrast to her usual crafted, guarded disposition, Lydia also offers moments of such assertion. Fissures in body image, though they remain primarily somatic, are concretized in rebellious words. Claudio's use of the power of the soma to intraracialize Lydia is aptly illustrated when they first meet. Lydia's social demeanor in the Flores home is stylistically hers and *appears* authentic, as previously mentioned; yet, her hostile reserve lies just beneath the surface:

> (CLAUDIO *enters, gruff and disoriented after a long daylight sleep. He stands in the middle of the room and stares at* LYDIA, *who stops and stares back.*)
> LYDIA. Lydia. I am your maid. (*No reply.*) ¿Cuántos años tiene su hija?
> CLAUDIO. ¿Hay café?
> LYDIA. In the kitchen. What happened to her? (*No reply.*) It's okay. She'll tell me.
> (*He glares at her and then goes to the kitchen.*) (25)

Before she speaks, Lydia first somatically contests her presumed social inferiority by defiantly staring back at him. In this exchange, Lydia momentarily falls out of serene subservience. She claims her personhood by first stating her proper name, but then mitigates the assertion, as she realizes that she must accept the reduction of her being in the service she is to provide: "I am your maid." Underlining her use value at the expense of her personhood, she quickly relinquishes her defiant stance, complying with his somatic demand by returning to her work duties: "If [the coffee is] too strong, tell me. I like it strong, but for some peoples [*sic*], coffee is not good that way" (25)—words he does not bother to acknowledge. He shames her through violence, somatic contempt, and anger, and by ignoring her; she concedes her reduced status with a spurious peppy response. Thus shamed, Lydia continues her archetypal performance of the undocumented special perceiver, who sublimates her subjection with the indefatigable self-assurance of the magico *doméstica*. This factitious empowerment completes the scene of intraracialization.

Lydia's emotional labor in self-absenting reflects the social demands on vulnerable workers, challenging the audience to consider the multiple jobs women like Lydia are implicitly asked to perform for U.S. families. Sociologist Mary Romero delineates this corrupt cultural script, where labor expectations that fall well outside the job description are often justified under the false promise of emotional care and concern for the domestic worker who, in reality, must function as a highly conditional intimate ([1995] 2016). The emotional manipulation of care guises the threat of deportation behind the demand for unpaid duties. Cajoled, one-sided intimacy, offered to extract extra, unpaid labor, is a potent leverage that gains compliance and loyalty from domestic workers (Hondagneu-Sotelo [2001] 2007) for employers who "threaten to deport undocumented domestics if they refuse to do more work, reject sexual advances, or attempt to return home" (Romero [1995] 2016, 122). Lydia's occasional fall into somatic portrayal does not necessarily make her character's thoughts intelligible; instead, it signals the irrepressibility of the dissenting soma in the face of hegemonic cultural scripts for the *sola*.

Lydia's contentions create the appearance that she is expressing her will. And maybe she is. But she circumscribes those assertions within her role as maid and caretaker: when she displays more authentic feelings of resentment and agency, she does so through somatic portrayal seen only by Ceci. As the play progresses, speaking Ceci clarifies and contextualizes the unspoken resentment of intersectional intraracialization that lies behind Lydia's managed body image, forging a union between the two silenced, socially ugly women.

DOPPELGANGERS AS POLITICAL CRITIQUE

Solís situates Lydia as diagonal protagonist through her caregiving of Ceci-the-body, where Lydia's magic*o* communication with Ceci turns on a paralinguistic intimacy built through her reading of Ceci's somatic expression. In the following scene, Ceci-the-body (who functions as Ceci's public persona) begins to merge with speaking Ceci's private monologues. The play seams together the two expressions of Ceci, giving the increasingly integrated Ceci the ability to interpret Lydia's silent, somatic, decontextualized, resentful somatic expression for the audience. This dramatic structuring challenges our normative assumptions about the separateness undergirding Western notions of individuality where personal perception meets existential self and the other. Here, the protagonist's interpsychic and intersomatic communication establishes very critically needed social acceptance and, though just two, a sense of community.

I return to the sex scene mentioned earlier in the study of Ceci to delineate the play's structural suturing of the two women. The scene begins after Claudio and speaking Ceci finally reveal details of Ceci's accident to Lydia. Lydia, about to leave the room, catches a pleading look in Ceci's eyes, and suddenly agrees to provide emotional and sexual succor to grieving Claudio. Lydia turns to see Claudio in his usual disconnected self-soothing practice of drinking alcohol while listening to music via headphones and watching television. Lydia, seemingly without a priori motivation or invitation, approaches Claudio, silently removes her panties and his headphones, and mounts him. She does so while Ceci-the-body lies on the floor near them. As they have sex, speaking Ceci takes over convulsing Ceci-the-body, and, in a one-sided deictic conversation with Lydia, Ceci speaks of Claudio but, more importantly, reveals Lydia's unspoken thoughts and feelings. The soliloquy presents a deictic "you," broadening the mark of the women's relationship into a dyad. Structurally, the integration between Ceci's body and her speech mirrors a reciprocal telepathic connection between Lydia and Ceci. As their psyches conjoin, so do the experiences of their bodies:

> CECI. I had a dream the night before you came. That you stand at the door and stop breathing. And a part of you falls away . . . (47)

Here, Ceci recalls "you . . . stop breathing" at the Floreses' door in somatic preparation for the requisite disintegration of Lydia's personhood in order to meet the demand that she become a magico nanny: "And a part of you falls away." Ceci relays Lydia's somatic portrayal prior to arriving to the Flores home in a dream state, deepening the importance of their relationship as it enters expanding realms of consciousness in the forms of the subconsciousness, the soma, and the oneiric, palpitating with life while still fluttering toward death:

> That you come like a ghost into our house and stand over my daddy, who's a ghost himself, and you take his crown and hear the voices in his heart crying for love . . .
> *([LYDIA] takes off [CLAUDIO'S] headphones. She places them over her head and listens for a moment.)* (47)

Ceci, downstage center under a spotlight, asserts speaking Ceci's omniscient narration, interfering with the titillation of viewing prohibited sex:

> And then you blind him . . .
> *([LYDIA] turns off the T. V. He remains still with his eyes fixed ahead.)*
> And land on his lap and take his breath away. (47)

As magico nanny, Lydia plays the stereotype in critique. Lydia absents herself to become a warm body for succor while simultaneously sidelining her anger and resentment in somatic expression for only Ceci and the audience to see:

> Each breathless *beso* reaches into his heart and lays grout over the crumbling walls of his pride, you touch him who can't remember touch any more than I can. It was a dream more real than this maid on my father making sex like the last act of God, I see your eyes, Lydia, dreaming the same thing, burning their grief into me, their want, their reckless need for darkness—
> *(She turns and meets LYDIA'S gaze.)* (47)

Playing on her employer's unspoken but somatically visible desire for her emotional labor, Lydia's real feelings are drawn in Ceci's lines to emphasize the de facto work culturally demanded of domestic workers, as well as their silence. This bifurcated scene helps the audience digest the scene's moral complication—Lydia's apparently unsolicited offer of sex is unexpected and solely motivated by the women's exchange of looks, a somatic communication called again in stage directions to indicate the sexual engagement's deadening effect on Lydia's spirit. Ceci responds *for* Lydia, but also *as* Ceci. Ceci becomes upset witnessing Lydia and Claudio's betrayal of Ceci's mother, Rosa, and she returns to physical spasm:

> I see—you! With the inscription, La Muerte, La Muerte, La Muerrr . . .
> *(They continue to make love as CECI goes into convulsions.)*
> gngghgnghg. gfhghngng. (47)

This reciprocity of subjectivity between the two women persuades us to understand Ceci and Lydia as telepathically connected characters. During the emotional and physical service Lydia performs for Claudio, Lydia's sexual contact and the energy surrounding its prohibition meet Ceci's earlier longing and portends Ceci's concluding fulfillment. Most certainly, Lydia's sexual activity in this scene mutualizes with the lust Ceci expresses earlier in the play. In part through physical proximity, the two young women come to identify with one another to such a degree that the socially restrained fury of one is voiced by the other, their bodies sharing desires, pleasures, and eventually deaths (Lydia is removed from the Flores home and deported; Ceci achieves orgasm and then commits suicide, thus concluding the play).

Telepathy—the nonverbal relating of two beings—uniquely structures Ceci and Lydia as doppelgangers.[36] In what may seem simply a dramatic concession, their telepathic relationship is consistent with research showing the deep psychophysical connection that often develops between caregivers and their patients. M. Jean Daubenmire and Sharon Searles found in their study of nurses and patients that they attune to such a degree, they form a "dyadic relationship," an interaction process where "two people get to the same state through communication (talking, dancing, singing, massage, etc.), [that] certain physiological processes become synchronized and the two interactors function, in part, as a single organism" (P. Byers in Davis 1982, 305). The time spent together and the nature of intimate care create a cognitive bridge conveying the patient's needs, wants, and preferences to the caregiver. Assuming this dyadic relationship found between nurses and patients also applies to home caregivers of the infirm, the research findings give gravitas to the intense relation between Lydia and Ceci "in which the nurse [or caregiver] and patient are transformed into a new state . . . [that is] more than the sum of individual behaviors" (305), and where, in 1/48th of a second of speaking, the listener of the dyad synchronizes his or her movements (Condon in Davis 1982, 306).

The likelihood of a psychophysical connection between caregiver Lydia and patient-charge Ceci lends credibility to the staged evolution of the two women as capable of deep mutual understanding beyond what the audience or the Floreses may concede. Of course, the play establishes their dyadic connection *avant la lettre,* but these research findings challenge easy dismissal of Lydia as simply a magico nanny per the racialized domestic worker archetype, instead validating both the depth of connection and humanity possible between these characters and the play's implied critique of individualism as disempowering. The device of telepathy serves as a theatrical means of conjoining the women as doppelgangers, but also powerfully politicizes their joint subjectivity.[37]

During sex, both Lydia and Claudio continue to relate from managed body images, translated by Ceci into an erotic reparative of their mutual spiritual void. Most importantly for my study, this scene interpolates the shame and subsequent disempowerment caused by Lydia's intraracialization. Although both characters maintain their respective social roles, Claudio's forlorn patriarchal mask churns hostility in a fairly typical response to his relative failure to realize his wife's dream of financial security or to maintain a traditional patriarchal familial structure. The racialization the Floreses have been subjected to also manifests in the familial countenance, distressed and weighing heavily throughout. In addition to his statements and actions, Claudio displays the gestural repertoire of an embittered, insecure macho. Interpreted as manifest discourse, Claudio's silence "is really no more than the repressive presence of what it does not say; and this 'not-said' is a hollow that undermines from within all that is said" (Foucault [1972] 2010, 25). His anger at Ceci's womanly (dis)appearance, and again, in his unwavering stare at the television screen as Lydia sexually engages him, speaks to the unmentioned offstage causes and conditions of his stunted prowess, which, as Ceci explains, the act of sex with his intraracialized maid seeks to redress. He will end the sex scene quietly crying while mounted, apparently after the sex act has culminated in (at least) his orgasm (48). His tears are fissures in somatic portrayal parallel to Lydia's deadened, resentful glare—they express the Foucauldian hollow of what is left unsaid, the oppressions he and his family suffer as a racialized Mechicano family in El Paso, Texas.

Conversely, when Lydia offers Claudio sex, she adheres to the unspoken expectation discussed earlier that she, as also an emotional laborer, will feign somatic desire. But she does so for reasons important to understanding the work of her intersectional intraracialization. Lydia stays within the body image management scripted for the *doméstica*, presenting herself as a desirable woman, interrupting intraracial shaming and thus her social diminishment because, as his lover (where quite opposite of Graciela of chapter 2), she gains fuller humanity, as one who can move Claudio from diminishing her to seeing her as capable of fulfilling his desires for sex but also intimacy and emotional succor. Her pursuit of physical intimacy recognizes Claudio as a macho but also a longing man in a different register of his humanity, temporarily upending the one-down position Lydia occupies as domestic worker. Far from transcendent for either party, their sexual engagement, authored and dominated by Lydia, puts Lydia in a position of instigating situational dominance over Claudio, thus occupying a gendered, sexual role not outside of, but momentarily superior to, her inscription in intraracial shame and subservience. Thus, a morally suspect dalliance reveals a complicated palliative for their respective intersectional racial and intraracial shaming. Lydia's deployment of situational power in assertion of her humanity presages the concluding sexual encounter between Misha and Ceci, and Ceci's subsequent suicide. Here, Ceci is at the mercy of Misha's sexual dominion and when the encounter ends in Ceci's audible orgasm, her body publicly acknowledges her personhood and portends her death. Lydia, too, is scuttled out of the Floreses' home and ostensibly out of the country for having appeared a full(er) person. Deportation ends her bid for economic and social independence in the United States.

Acting "grows out of our biological being" where "emotion, reason, and physicality are ultimately inseparable in the brain's structure and function" (Blair 2008, xii), showing the multiple realms of confluence in this form of human subjectivity. In *Lydia*, Ceci presents almost the inverse of this formulation. As a PVS sufferer who portrays her subjectivity through the autonomic physical communication of her feelings, emotions, reason, and her physicality, Ceci also asserts a particular social agency impacting her social milieu. Presenting a character with PVS challenges the audience to consider the role of the body, the soma, and mental subjectivity. Ceci-the-body's somatic portrayal disquiets hegemonic models of dramatic characters and acting styles. At the same time, the performances of Ceci and Lydia disrupt lived U.S. social scripts seeking to silence the emotional fallout of intersectional racial shaming on Latin@/xs.

In this chapter, I have discussed the ugly soma, a theatrical device that deftly presents the social diminishment of PVS-stricken Ceci. In so doing, the play connects the cultural legacy of making socially ugly to the personhood of Lydia, an undocumented Mexican domestic worker. Solís writes their respective social vulnerability and subsequent invisibility in Ceci's somatic groans and Lydia's hollowed body image. Ceci-the-body's stylized confluence in tone with speaking Ceci knits the paralinguistic somatic portrayal of a disabled woman to her managed body image and, thus, exposes the common imposition of childlike physicality and subjectivity on the mentally and physically different. Likewise, Lydia's stunted somatic expression dramatizes observable pressured behavior in the lived experience of racialized domestic workers in the United States. Serving neocolonial and neoliberal agendas, *Lydia* exposes the lives of this labor sector, entrenched as it is in unfair labor arrangements and the diminished archetype of the fake-happy intersectional racialized domestic worker. In somatic critique, Octavio Solís's *Lydia* unpacks the obfuscated resentment behind the mystique of the magic*o* Mexican nanny, exposing intersectionally intraracializing shame at the hands of a Mechicano family who misguidedly place their resentment, the tenuousness of their own security, and their uncertain social belonging on the back of their *doméstica* while they reject their once dear daughter, Ceci.

Two ugly somas speak out: Ceci, sufferer of PVS, and Lydia, a magic*o* nanny, who portrays the experience of living in and under social foreclosure, the *fourth step* in scenes of intersectional intraracialization. I argued the four steps in chapters 1 and 2, but here, I focus on how specific dramaturgical work shows us the world from the vantage point of the *fourth step* by asking, what discursive strategies are available to the socially excluded? How are we to manage self, express our feelings, beliefs, and our organism's reality, while to hegemonic sectors, we are politically and socially irrelevant and, thus, highly vulnerable when not expendable? Building on chapter 2's discussion, I closely read the intimate intricacies of somatic portrayal in the specific venue of an intraracialized quasi-foreigner living and working in a family home, a closed domestic space, a dramatization of the very real ways *domésticas* live and too often suffer in homes across America. Lydia's Mexicanness, like Ceci's disability, sets off a point of comparison that enables the Floreses to assert their resentment as a Mechicano family marginalized in a border city of Mechicanos, Chican@/xs, and Mexicans. The fifth and final chapter on Andrés Montoya's *The Ice Worker Sings and Other Poems* provides another vision of the soma—the soma that transforms pain, suffering, and sin through the sacred figure of Sophia, the Christian feminine Godhead.

CHAPTER 5

The Political Work of Sophia

The Blessed Soma, the Conversion Narrative, and Shame in Andrés Montoya's The Ice Worker Sings and Other Poems

FOR MILLENNIA in Europe and in the Americas, art has been the medium to express theology. Doctrinal arguments have been hashed out, mystic love expressed, and thorny political issues read through Christian poetry, iconography, and art as well as in theological treatises. Surprisingly, outside of expressly religious cultural texts, in the early twenty-first century, we are strangely reticent to engage art as an appropriate discursive medium for theology. However, as religious scholar and poet Michael Martin argues (2015), the recent divorce of contemporary art from the spiritual does not diminish the enduring Puritan influence in today's cultural practices. Indeed, sociologist Max Weber (1864–1920) argued Puritan cultural capital a persisting presence, wedding U.S. capitalism and political governance under its auspices ([1958] 2003). I find Andrés Montoya's *The Ice Worker Sings and Other Poems* ([1999] 2017) to be a religious conversion narrative tying art and theology in somatic practices that evidence racial shaming in a widespread sociological schema, and, specifically, I see the divine Sophia, a radical mitigator of its harm.

Martin notes the tension between art and theology is recent and, given its long, entwined cultural histories, believes it a temporary breach (2016). For many Chican@/xs and Latin@/xs, however, the concept of spirituality, perhaps more than religion, continues to be a critical avenue for affective sustenance, and often, political resistance. In Chican@/x texts written by men (with some exceptions), there is seldom explicit address of the religious or the spiritual, and yet, the late Andrés Montoya (1968–99) is described as a poet in love with justice and art (Chacón 2008, 13), and in his own words, one who wrote "for God" (12).

In his highly acclaimed *The Ice Worker Sings and Other Poems*, Montoya unites political poetry with the spiritual in the unexpected form of a lyric conversion narrative. Historically considered a quintessentially American genre (Caldwell [1983] 1985; Heimart and Belbanco [1985] 2001, xiii), the Puritan conversion narrative has been touted in retrospect as the nation's first literature not only charged with documenting spiritual transcendence but also civic rights. A literature embedded in settler colonialism, the Puritan conversion narrative marked a social practice of racialized spiritual exceptionalism leading to the development of a future racializing United States (Bailey 2011)—not likely the genre one would imagine a Chicano activist poet would choose to do progressive political work. In fact, Montoya's turn to the conversion narrative might seem improbable if we are unaware of the palpable vestiges of Puritan thought and cultural practice permeating contemporary U.S. society, or if we unconsciously racialize him and assume him perhaps a Chicano gangbanger, or simply undereducated and therefore unfamiliar with the American literary canon when, in fact, Montoya held a Master's of Fine Arts and taught creative writing at several colleges and universities. We might also erroneously presume such a poet would not have enjoyed a rich spiritual life either.

While biographical notes suggest a long commitment to Evangelical Christianity, Montoya's writings also show his cultural familiarity with Roman Catholicism. And although an analysis of either faith or their combination would be worthwhile, neither would reveal the importance of Sophia, the feminine Godhead in some Christian faiths and an inspirational figure in numerous theologies and art for centuries,[1] who more recently has become a central figure in nontraditional forms of spirituality. I propose Sophia as a key figure in reading the spiritual quest found in *The Ice Worker Sings and Other Poems* (hereafter *Ice Worker*), but more than a figure, Sophia presents an important and productive theoretical axis for literary analysis writ large, and in this chapter, I argue Sophia to be a personage and vital force axiomatic to Montoya's critique.

Sophia, the second figure of the Holy Trinity, according to some traditions, and the syzygy of Jesus Christ in different parts of the world, remains a lesser known figure and seldom recognized in U.S. Protestant and Catholic faiths, while in the speaker's poetic meditations, Sophia intervenes as a force more than a figure. And although Sophia appears in human form only once in the collection and even then, obliquely, her momentary and single physical appearance is insufficient evidence to conclude the collection as a lyricized conversion narrative in the Puritan tradition. I argue Montoya's single mention establishes her presence as a sign signaling an alternate cognitive filter through which the speaker interprets his life and his community in evidence throughout the collection.[2] Sophia understood as such generates the text's driving aesthetic. We cannot pretend we treat poets outside of their subject position and with racializing practices, we may view marginalized poets narrowly. We may doubt such an intersectionally racialized poet would intend such a sophisticated project.[3] However, if we allow for the full humanity and intellectual and theological refinement of *Ice Worker,* without prejudice, the collection reveals a poetic theology of conversion where, through the spiritual conduits of Sophia, of breath, tears, and blood, he sings his sins in an expression of spiritual redemption.

Well-established theologies elaborate Sophia's material signs as intermediaries between human want and sin as the impetus for salvation. Thomas Merton, an American Catholic writer, mystic, and Trappist monk, speaks to Sophia's ability to join raw human nature to the divine in a teleology less recognized in Roman Catholicism or in many British, European, and U.S. Protestant faiths. However, the Song of Songs, perhaps the best-known text associated with Sophia, is a point of departure to consider the nexus between Sophia, theology, and creative literature.[4] In the Old Testament's Song of Songs, an unnamed female lover often, argued Sophia, *sings* of carnal delights as the experience through which she loves, a figure who presents the possibility of spiritual transcendence by the flesh. To modern sensibilities, spirituality, Christianity, and the flesh seem dichotomous, but she promises this possibility in similar terms in the Tanakh, in Job, Ecclesiastics, and Proverbs, and Deuteronomy of the Torah, the Septuagint, and most prominently, in Gnosticism and Orthodox Christianities. Yet in most theologies and artistic representations, Sophia is referred to by her attribute of Wisdom. Sophia doctrine, or Sophiology, speaks of Wisdom as an elevating force in sensual life, present in joy, love, gratitude, insight, and generosity and in emotional fields and acts fueled by anger, hatred, treachery, and desire. Generally read as moral binaries in contemporary terms, for centuries prior, the range of feelings and actions had been understood as potentially spiritually productive, synergetic energies of Wisdom and catalysts for spiritual immanence.

A driving force in Montoya's oeuvre, divine Sophia is revealed within this varied but well-established theological frame as sensual Wisdom of the Old Testament, as a force working spiritual transcendence through the speaker's material body. She becomes palpable in his angry and tortured face, suffering from social oppression lyricized in his breath gasping in exasperation, despairing through stutters, and expressing gratitude in cries from rotten teeth. In *Ice Worker*, social oppressions and their effects are not transcended or even alleviated but imbued with layers of feeling and meaning, capable of unsettling and potentially unseating their deterministic value over Chican@/x life. I aver *Ice Worker* renews this semi-obscured figure in U.S. literary criticism, offering her carnal divinity, wisdom, presence, and power to a readership hungry for more than lyrical magic. Divine Sophia furthermore provides a cognitive paradigm manifest in the soma.

I first identify the Sophiatic soma, an actor throughout the collection, in the collection's third poem "the ice worker sings." In a simple and mundane activity, the speaker sings as he stacks ice and becomes aware of the sensuality of his singing soma as a semi-connected entity in contrast to his normal experience of self.[5] In this poem, he witnesses his song's frosty breath and sound as he attunes to the somatic materialization of his own vitality and presence. Here, he begins delineating the soma, a coextensive subjectivity with his intellectually, or mind-identified, self. Seemingly akin to Merleau-Ponty's *lived body*, an awareness of the body engaging as primary source of experience of the self and the world, poeticizing the Sophiatic soma exposits the speaker's phenomenological experience of his theology. Thus, in the poetic "I," Sophia generates the palpable presence of his soma where seeing a spiritually imbibed physical sense and expression of joy in his breath fosters intimacy within himself, the same presence intervening in other poems via the spiritual fractures born of rage, despair, and disgust.

In accordance with Sophiology, Sophia appears in her two forms: *sapientia incarnata*, Sophia as force, and *sapientia carnata*, her figural depiction.[6] Sophia appears as sapientia incarnata in the poem "the ice worker sings," where her presence imbues his visible breath and becomes a somatic expression of his joy, while divine Sophia appears in human form, sapientia carnata, during a weekly dalliance with an eponymously named sex worker "sofía" in the poem "the ice worker in love." Sapientia carnata also appears in a less obvious form in poems referencing the ice worker's mother, his grandmother, and in the homeless, female, street-corner evangelizer. These incarnations create figural signposts of her work as force guiding the collection.

His mother, whose prayerful smile interrupts the family's desperation; grandmother, whose hands are joyful agents that invite God's grace; and the homeless woman, who calls out "repent! repent!" through rotten, green teeth ("denial," lines 75, 81) quite similarly to Sophia's rebuke in Proverbs 1:20 (New Living Testament [1996] 2015), who "shouts in the streets. She cries out in the public square." These women tie the impactful presence of Sophia identified in "the ice worker in love" to the fire and brimstone rhetoric from which the conversion project emerges. Sophia in her two forms somatically expresses transcendence, mercy, and glory, whereas in Puritan rhetoric, the soma of the unrepentant registers recrimination, judgment, and damnation until salvation imbues the soma of the saved with joy. Likewise, the speaker's salvation manifests in the somatic joy expressed while despairing, for the limp of his tortured self, and in appreciation of a peach, ants, the clouds, and trees in many poems he titles "songs." But this Sophiatic soma does not discount or eradicate the power and pressure of intersectional racializing shame.

As I have argued throughout *Shaming into Brown,* intersectional racialization and racism morph life conditions and, too often, the self-view of the speaker and his community. In Montoya's collection, we can trace the somatic interplay argued in *scenes of racialization* (argued in chapters 1 and 2) driving poetic tension. The speaker, like those community and family members he describes, responds by fronting somatic postures of hostility or acquiescence in response to State abuse and apathy (chapter 4), subjecting others to intra-group violence, and/or turning against the self in shamed somatic expression. Similarly, the structure of the Puritan conversion moralizes somatic shame as proof of repentance, an affective crucible considered prosocial and requisite for verifying spiritual deliverance. With adequate somatic delivery, the approved conversion afforded the converted tangible material and social benefits in Puritan societies. Both paradigms—racializing shame and Puritan shame—are transacted by somatic expression and are socially necessary in achieving their respective aims.

Puritan origins of coercion by public shaming spreads to a variety of social practices, leading to a U.S. social field of endemic shaming, and critically, racializing shame where, like in the Puritan era, difference connotes a shameless lack of deference used to justify barriers to social inclusion in humiliating social practices. And while the speaker's conversion is more spiritual than religious, this thirty-year old Chicano from Fresno, California, speaks to a nation fixated on racializing subjection, the latter, an obsession in relief of colored apperception that characterizes to a degree the uniqueness of that "shining city on a hill" birthed by Puritanism, currency continued in speeches made by twentieth- and twenty-first-century U.S. presidents, including John F. Kennedy (1961), Ronald Reagan (1980, 1989), George W. Bush (2004), and Barak Obama (2006). These orations on American exceptionalism, like their Puritan predecessors, muddle moral shame with social shaming that, directly addressed or not, coalesce in how America racializes shame.

In contrast to Puritan faith practices, politics, and their legacy, the poetic speaker dispenses with promises of material and social reward to instead mark the intransient condition of racial shaming on the speaker, who even after his spiritual conversion, continues to live a subjugated life. The Sophiatic soma in *Ice Worker* thus posits the nontranscendental nature of material and sociological conditions despite the speaker's spiritual regeneration. As dissimilar as moral shame and racial shaming are, they both arbitrate social acceptance per social shaming. Inadvertently, they create an opportunity for the Sophiatic soma to negotiate moral shame and shaming racializing practices in a meaningful spiritual process without material or even necessarily emotional resolutions. In this chapter, I argue Montoya's collection redoubles the performative tensions of shame and the conversion narrative and their sociological offspring for nascence of his racialized perspective into American letters. I argue Montoya employs the conversion narrative as a rhetorical template to revalorize the struggles of the intersectionally racialized speaker and the Latin@/xs community. Different from other analyses of the soma thus far argued in *Shaming into Brown,* Montoya's presentation of the Sophiatic soma disrupts the affective experience of the Puritan conversion narrative, of moral shame, and of racial shaming, and are habilitated as ports of entry for Sophia in offer of a paradigm for scholarly inquiry, and importantly, for empowerment.

In the midst of the harm of intersectional racialization and racism in a capitalist system, which leaves millions of Latin@/xs undereducated, emotionally harmed, economically impoverished, and outside the imagined community of Americans, the Sophiatic soma expresses the possibility for theological *immanence*—the moment when divine revelation can occur—leading to spiritual renewal or *transcendence.* Under Sophia's influence, the poetic voice presents moments of poignant beauty and grace in the most desperate of circumstances, revealing the sacred possibility of spiritual redress within the politically entrenched.

"THE FINEST BOOK OF POETRY TO COME OUT OF OUR COMMUNITY"—RIGOBERTO GONZÁLEZ

I offer an excerpt from the poem "luciana: this is how i see you":

> how will I remember you, grandma?
>   will it be your name, luciana, that i recall
>   on nights when the forgetful remember
>   everything?
>   luciana: beautiful
>   like the wind winding whispers through the arms of the trees.
>
> . . .
> or perhaps

>   it will be your face, a bruised petal of forgiveness
> ...
> i tell you, grandma, this is how his see you:
>   you are dancing, your straight leg is bending and your hair is waving wild
>   as beautiful laughter like song strums from your mouth into the sky,
>   and your eyes, your eyes are catching the shine of the Son,
>   like two huge apples begging notice on the tree, and you are shouting
>   with your smile, "hallelujah! hallelujah!" and all the angels
>   are dancing and
> laughing with you, and Jesus is saying, "i love you so much, mija."
> and you are saying, "mi amor, mi amor," like a beautiful sigh.
> (lines 1–54)

Written in celebration of the poet's grandmother at her death, this long passage from the poem "luciana: this is how i see you" (hereafter "luciana") imbues the elderly woman's old age, poverty, and intersectional oppression with Sophia's spirit, and thus she becomes agile, melodious, her legs, mouth, and eyes radiating spiritual transcendence. Sophiatic forces weave *abuela* in the arms of the tree, her eyes become apples, her cheek, a worn petal, refashioning her intersectional struggles into a vibrant life force in communion with nature, longingly and joyously entering the kingdom of heaven where the speaker imagines a Mexican or Chicano Christ welcomes *abuela*, equally desirous to reunite with her. Like many poems in the collection, "luciana" corroborates for me Rigoberto González's statement on Montoya's work: "In this generation, *the ice worker sings [and other poems]* should be known as the finest book of poetry to come out of [the Chicano] community" (Chacón 2008, 38).

Clearly influential for a generation of Chican@/x poets, *Ice Worker* won first prize in the University of California at Irvine's Chicano/Latino Literary Prize competition,[7] was posthumously awarded the American Book Award, and has had two university literary awards named after him based solely on *The Ice Worker Sings and Other Poems*.[8] Given Montoya's untimely death before publication, scholarship on his work is understandably scant, yet his poetry has been noted for its quality of spirit and political reformist agenda, features that, for Montoya, were one and the same (Chacón 2008, 11).[9] As Montoya's mentor, renowned poet Garrett Hongo remarked, Montoya "brooked no compromises—in politics or in poetry—and wanted from both that they work for practical change in the lives of the oppressed" (166),[10] however, the collection's underlying conversion story and its somatic presentation have not been critically presented to date.

U.S. SOCIAL LOGIC OF SHAME

Modern America has long celebrated the repentant and rehabilitated with the literary form of the conversion narrative. During the hundred or more years of Puritan influence (roughly 1630–1740), Puritan conversion narratives circulated evidence of conversion as a didactic tool for remedying the wanton ways of the "unregenerate." Once converted, the "postulant" came to be known as a member of the "elect" (also referred to as "generates" or "saints"). Bona fide conversion meant full church membership, which played a key role in establishing colonial governance and a nascent sense of nation (Andrews 2007).

I later argue the conversion's considerable impact on American culture, of which *Ice Worker* partakes, but I point out here, several *stages* of the Puritan conversion process appear in *Ice Worker* that reveal the collection as a conversion narrative. I preface my analysis by noting *Ice Worker* does not adopt a persecuting tone, nor does the speaker explicitly express the desire for conversion customary per these narratives. The critical moments of the ice worker's conversion do not follow a chronology of *stages* but appear in confluence. In fact, we could not read *Ice Worker* as a conversion narrative until the arrival of the sign in the fourth poem, "the ice worker in love." And the sign is Sophia. After her arrival, we can read backward to earlier poems and forward to later poems and note how the collection accomplishes the conversion's requisite trajectory.

Distinct from the more common enterprise of personal insight per spiritual autobiography (Dorsey 1993) and imbricated in long-standing traditions of Sophia poetry and theology, I contend Montoya's collection is a conversion narrative by virtue of its employ of several steps of a conversion process theologically referred to as the *ordo salutis* (Latin for *order of salvation*). Variable in emphasis and particular to a given tradition or minister, Puritan conversion narratives writ large relied on the *ordo salutis* to make the quintessential determination of whether a postulant had been spiritually delivered in a stage referred to as *credulo salutis*, the arrival of the divine sign.[11]

St. Augustine of Hippo, considered the founder of the conversion narrative in Western letters (5 CE) and himself, a devotee of Sophia,[12] devised these stages based on Romans 8:29–30; however, though Puritan traditions varied significantly with little consensus on the number or order of steps, most traditions concurred with those *stages* followed in *Ice Worker*. Montoya (like Americans generally) was likely more familiar with the Puritan sermons of Richard Mather, Increase Mather, John Cotton, and Cotton Mather—as they often appear in high school and college courses on American literature—than with the *ordo salutis*. Whether Montoya specifically knew of the *ordo salutis* or

Puritan doctrine is less important than his clear familiarity with well-known Puritan sermons where recourse to the *stages* of conversion narratives were formulaic and repetitive.

For the purposes of this study, I summarize the following *stages* lyricized in Montoya's conversion: *stage one,* the postulant expresses his sinful nature; *stage two,* he finds himself desperately afflicted and spiritually lost; *stage three,* the speaker rids himself of what we might think of as ego in preparation to receive the divine sign of salvation; *stage four,* the postulant receives the sign, and finally, in *stage five,* the poetic "I" describes his joyful soul, postconversion. Indeed, one can find two or more stages of the conversion narrative in nearly every poem in Montoya's collection and elaborations of the soma, the intelligent, spiritually ripe physicality, in all. Montoya's collection can be fruitfully read as an artistic soteriology in four parts.

Part 1 of *Ice Worker* is the most political in tone. The speaker is a much maligned figure in the mainstream American imagination, an underserved youth living *la vida loca* on the streets of Fresno, California, but situated within the encumbered project of Aztlán, the birthplace of the Aztec people (Carrasco and Moctezuma 2003), which Latin@/xs have laid claim to since the Chicano Movement of the 1960s. The Movement was successful by many measures but also fell short of its potential, a position called out in the speaker's desperation in *stage two* per the *ordo salutis* and representative of the forlorn in his community. Part 1 draws spaces for spiritual immanence in the pesticide-soaked sports field, the street corner, and the motel room where the speaker receives the sign of salvation per *stage four,* spaces equally ripe for religious revelation. Overall, part 1 establishes the determinants of place, poverty, racism, sexism, and violence to demonstrate the material, and importantly, the *affective* spiritual devastation on his community.

Apocalyptic in tone, part 2 examines the quotidian fallout required in *stage one,* preparatory humiliation of the postulant, and *stage two,* the pain born of his misdeeds, attributable in part to the pressures of racial shaming. In the poems "some days" and "silence," perpetrators act out the hatred and desperation they suffer from harms carried out by the State as well as through Brown-on-Brown violence against kinfolk and in-group members. Part 2 presents a crisis of faith that reflects on evil deeds, dying spirits, and apathy born of resentment. These harms thematize part 3, where the epistolary form swaddles systemic oppression in a tone of private suffering. Actual letters from Montoya to friends vulnerably express regret, hope, and spiritual anticipatory joy that in part 4 will culminate in the language of redemption to complete *stage five* of spiritual vitality promised by the *ordo salutis,* recontextualizing the effect of the cruel world the speaker inhabits and, perversely, enjoys. While poetry cannot take the place of concrete political action (Aldama 2003, 31), Montoya's collection repurposes the didactic intent of the Puritan conversion narrative of old as an unexpected tool that sheds light on the affective and physical harms of racial shaming and offers the experiential prism of the Sophiatic soma for spiritual relief.

Many well-known Puritan sermons were based on written conversion narratives, a pedagogical tool for salvation preferring effusive somatic expression on the journey to conversion (Bercovitch [1975] 2011; Elliott [1975] 2015). From a cognitive neurological lens, our ability to comprehend conversion narratives depends on programming the actions of characters into our bodies so we virtually experience them as argued in chapters 1 and 2. In the conversion narrative, the postulant speaker gains credence by virtue of affectively reporting his or her internal somatic state of shame, self-contempt, disgust, and self-suspicion—note a very similar range of emotional and affective qualities in racial shaming—made socially material through congruent external somatic data (i.e., the postulant *looks* ashamed, self-loathing, repentant, etc.). This somatic and verbal congruence allowed church adjudicators to qualify the postulant in possession of sufficient self-knowledge, which made more credible the postulant's report of the arrival of the divine sign of his or her salvation (Gribben 2008, 18 and 200). The discussion here adds the influence of the Puritan *ordo salutis* in what has become a cultural practice of performing shame and self-contempt for social acceptance. The collection employs *stages* of the Puritan conversion narrative that align with the somatic logic of racializing *steps*. The confluence of the U.S. social logic of shame in these forms purpose scenes of racialization with the added vestige of Puritan narrative affectivity in understanding this U.S. cultural practice.

In *Ice Worker,* Montoya rejoins daily cognition of racial shaming with its surprisingly parallel social and affective paradigm of the conversion's spiritual and social salvation. The reformulation of conversion *stages* into racializing *steps* in scenes of racialization occurs in changing the postulant's subjectivity. I remind readers that intuited evidence of somatic dissonance and contemptuous suspicion leads to disgusted confirmation of one's racialized identity in *steps one* through *three* in scenes of racialization, an affective script that parallels the preparatory humiliation of *stages one* and *two* of the *ordo salutis*. These affective patterns have different aims and destinataries. Instead of the spiritual postulant's assessment of personal shame in *stage one*, the racializer somatically cathects racial shame onto its subject in *step one*, scripting the tone and degree proposed for the humiliated spiritual postulant to pressure the racialized into assuming social wrongness. Additionally, the confrontation in scenes of racialization that seeks to vacate the racialized out of an egalitarian sense of worthy personhood in *steps one* through *four* similarly "hollows out" the racialized as prescribed to the Puritan postulant in *stages one* and *two*. And once racial shaming somatically confirms the racialized's abeyance in *step four*, the somatic expression of the racializer expresses a certain satisfaction analogous to the social power bequeathed to the postulant at the arrival of the sign in *stage five*.

The entrenched habit of affective somatic patterns of oppression circle back to the palpable presence of Puritanism and the conversion narrative. The Puritan backdrop patterns the social power donned by the convert to the racializer who affectively carries that religiously imbued social prestige as an entitlement leading to an obligation to socially marginalize and somatically withdraw peer-to-peer relations from the intersectionally racialized. By comparing the *stages* in the *ordo salutis* to the *steps* in *scenes of racialization*, I point to the cognitive affective patterning common to shaming and shamed somas, legacies from Puritan practices in appreciation of Puritan influence in U.S. culture. This framework tracks the way Montoya's speaker voices the influence of racializing shame on the Sophiatic soma of the earthly divine in *Ice Worker*.

THE PRESENTATION OF RACIAL SHAME AND THE ARRIVAL OF THE SPIRITUAL SIGN

In American letters, lest we forget, U.S. literature includes Latin@/x poetry, though a conversion written in verse is somewhat unusual. Indeed, the first three poems in *Ice Worker* read of hostile conquest rather than conversion. The first poem, "in search of aztlán," calls into awareness a competing cultural and political genealogy of Greater Mexico in the era of late capitalism—itself, a rival descriptor defining the Southwest United States and Mexico, a single region of study. Taken over by concomitant forms of neocolonialism, the region's Mexican population, culture, and history remain unrecognized or occluded in town names like "fresno parlier earlimart" (line 4) and outside of the United States' troubled fulfillment of obligations to honor property holdings—via the recognition of Spanish—and other forms of full citizenship per the 1848 Treaty of Guadalupe Hidalgo. Two centuries later, Mexicans, Chicanos, nuevos mexicanos, tejanos, Latin Americans, and those in Arizona and Colorado and throughout the region who sometimes refer to themselves as hispanos are underrecognized when not "out of sight," the title of Montoya's second poem. In the second poem, the human sensorium is the primary vehicle of sociopolitical insight and expression for the continuing political acrimony in the postwar era established in the poem "in search of aztlán."

In "sight," the speaker observes the quiet indignation somatically expressed through Felix, a Latino bystander, as Felix witnesses the all-too-common scene of an apathetic police officer examining an unidentified Brown body. The speaker provides three plausible accounts of the circumstances leading to the man's murder but none of these are corroborated, suggesting the lack of interest or concern of the investigating officer who probes and prods the cadaver that is representative of the ubiquitous and indiscriminate death of Latin@/x men in his neighborhood (lines 8–10). But onlooker Felix sees the mimetic communication of somas and understands the bitterness in the lifeless man's pose, somatically glaring back with "the sick / smile / of blood / and flesh" (lines 6–9) even, or perhaps finally, in death (lines 52–56).

The opening poem "in search of aztlán" functions as an epigraph for the collection asking Chican@/x readers to fulfill the promises of the Chicano Movement as he questions the possibilities for activism in the post-Movement era. The second poem "sight" despairingly answers these questions with sense data—the poem remarks upon the habitual physical posture of stifled resentment in bystanders like Felix as well as the somatic expression conveyed by the dead Brown man. As Felix considers the scene and the final affect of the dead man, the speaker observes Felix. All three Latin@/x men are in the visual field of the others. The speaker's relative distance between the cadaver and Felix slowly draws visual focus to appreciate how the speaker observes the felt sense experience of Felix, who appears visually attuned to the individual's last suffering and somatic rage, the State's deprecation of Brown life. Thus, the collection's opening political laments are described in later descriptions of Sophiatic somas filled with the spiritual immanence of political protest in the midst of horror and rage in some poems and delight in others, such as in the third poem "the ice worker sings."

In the third poem, ice-stacking affords the speaker relief from the Fresno violence, heat, and solitude; and he, away from the mad-dog eyes of street characters and freed from the pressures of his struggling family, finds himself singing, exploring tonalities and vocal ranges in themes (seemingly) previously unknown to him. At the conclusion of the second stanza, his breath becomes a visual cue to hearing himself produce sound: "He enjoyed seeing song / spring from between his lips / in the white breath of the cold room" (lines 26–28). The speaker's perception of his soma establishes a confluence of senses where the speaker both hears and feels his voice externally and perhaps internally in a cold room filling with his visible warm breath. He displaces the primacy of sound and the meaning of lyrics one normally values in song for the pleasure of witnessing his own body's utterance of breath while he sings, invoking breath and song, classic elements attributed to divine Sophia.

In poems that follow, the speaker's gratification will meet with heartbreak, fear, and abject violence. In these moments, too, divine Sophia's force builds, permeating the speaker's experience and ultimately anointing him with the sign of spiritual conversion in "the ice worker in love" (hereafter "in love"):

In this poem, Sophia presents as "sofía," the sex worker:

> he is in love.
> friday nights before work
> he sees his woman.
> they are not married
> and she doesn't know
> that he loves her.
>
> he tells her
> her hair is like water
> and her skin smells of dew.
> and she tells him
> it'll still cost the eighty bucks
> for the three hours
> in the crusty motel
> that smells of smoke.
> (lines 1–14)

Perhaps it is not surprising the speaker tropes love with aqueous adjectives like "dew" (line 9) and "water" (line 8). The descriptive fluidity of the second stanza combines with images of liquids turned solid, whereas sex work contributes to the physical ambiance described as crusty and smoky (lines 13–14), alluding to a hardening of body fluids and spilled alcohol that, like the ice the speaker of the title stacks, suggests an analogy to masculinity. Texture becomes a modality for describing gender, hard versus soft, solid versus malleable, but most importantly, the woman he believes "sofía" represents, the soft and physically yielding "good news," providing a cognitive alternative to knowing God beyond the firm and unyielding Christian doctrine declaimed by many American religious traditions. The full physical context of this exchange heralds the speaker's conversion through the soma. But different from the soma's message in analyses argued in other chapters of *Shaming into Brown*, the soma in *Ice Worker* exists with the presence of divine Sophia and transfers wisdom to "sofía" through their sexual union in the poem "in love."

The speaker prepares for the arrival of the sign in the third stanza where we enter the speaker's fantasy of intimacy, professing to love this woman although he does not even "know her real name" (line 15). The poem's present tense stops suddenly in "one day" (line 17) when she tells him her name is not "sofía," but "alexandra" (line 18). This clarification challenges the speaker's fantasy of love and romance with the reality of sex commerce. And yet, the reality of sex work posits the everyday feeling of love and our common human desire. Our primal need for human connection points to the possibility for readers to encounter Sophia and to consider the cognitive paradigm she offers in a practice that powerfully contests the spiritual impact of intersectional racialization.

FINDING SOPHIA AND THE ARRIVAL OF THE SIGN

> For she is a breath of the power of God, and a pure emanation of the glory of the Almighty; there nothing defiled gains entrance into her.
> —WISDOM 7:25

Theologians argue Sophia is Jesus' antecedent and, according to St. Augustine, her attributes are copresent in Jesus: "Sophia must be understood as God's Logos. . . . Whatever we have said about Sapientia is also true of the Son of God," confirming their deep affiliation: "This Sapientia is called Only-Begotten because She is Herself the Only-Begotten Son" (quoted in Schipflinger 1998, 68). Sophia and Jesus Christ were tethered for a time in most Christian theologies until she is cast as a threat to the masculinist consecration occurring in many Christian faiths. Sophia is eventually left out of theological discussions, and in various traditions, writing of Sophia's role and power was considered heretical, and her authors, persecuted (68).[13] For some theologians, Sophia "triggers a divine longing in the human person, a divine eros" (Martin 2015, 49). Divided between a heavenly energy and an earthly pulse, Sophia signals Wisdom wrought through the sensual soma in Christian traditions, but she acquires a sociohistorical dimension in accented Spanish. Sofía figures Wisdom in the form of an intersectionally racialized Chicana (perhaps) in a barrio in Fresno, California. Without irony, lying naked next to one another, "sofía" ripens the physical contact into an encounter of Sophia, and the Word becomes flesh.

Sex in all its varieties—whether fantasy, business transaction, or an expression of love—begets a physiological act of undeniable somatic communion. Consider line 25, where the pair is described postcoitus as "sweaty and both feeling a little guilty," the two luxuriating in each other's breathing (lines 25–29). Along with the highly sensate exertion of sex and its pleasures, the poetic rendering of internal feeling and the sound and touch of the other's breath elicits tactile, auditory, and olfactory sensations, focusing the reader on the sensory experience of physical proximity through a somatic lens. The sensory knowing of their bodies continuously communicates their somatic states to the poetic speaker for, as art and religious writer and publisher Gregory Wolfe argues, "If God cannot become present in blood, gut, shit, piss, semen, saliva [per Sophia]—He vanishes into ether" (in Martin 2016, 385).

Thus, what seems merely the emotional delusion of love in the first stanza grows into the speaker's first experience of Christ's feminine antecedent identified in stanza 5, an encounter the speaker will read postconversion as the incarnate sign of her spiritual acceptance of him. The declaration preceding the colon at the end of the line "this is why he loves her" (line 32) prepares for the presentation of the *credulo salutis*, the sign of "sofía" as Sophia:

> she reads him stories from the Bible
> . . .
> sometimes she tells him about a man murdered
>
> forgiving everyone, even his own killers.
> this is when she cries, and he feels he too should cry,
> that he must cry for the murdered man who forgives,
> only he doesn't know how yet.
> (lines 33–43)

This "yet" tells so much. The adverb indicates we are reading the story of his conversion from the temporal position of a fait accompli, pointing to the spiritual transcendence Montoya heralds in the midst of evil deeds, a convergence of the erotic, wisdom, and salvation occurring in breaths but also where the soma signifies the wisdom of the Logos.

With her tears, "sofía" returns the reader to the physical body and to the adjectival play of liquids. She is moved to tears by the Christ story; the tears themselves are a Sophiatic somatic expression of physiological and psychological redemption, a bodily acknowledgement of the accepting love and wisdom, and the release of guilt, apathy, resentment, isolation, exclusion, and dejection. With their bodies still in their ambiance of carnal connection, the speaker contrasts his reaction to hers: "he feels he too should cry / . . . / only he doesn't know how, *yet*" (lines 41, 43; emphasis added). Tears provide evidence of entrance into the "spirit" of the Word, the somatization of Logos, the experience of salvation exemplifying the idea in an interesting modification to the Cartesian self: "Theology is the marriage of the Word and flesh, an endless poem about the mystery of the incarnation. Words and flesh make love and the body is born" (Alves 2002). The Sophiatic soma captures the divine song inspired bodies can sing, and with song and tears, arrives the sign of deliverance, the key event in a conversion narrative and a social arbitration of shame for social incorporation.

PUBLIC SHAMING AND CONTEMPORARY U.S. CULTURE

The conversion narrative's requirement of publicly performing the self as shamed sinner builds a communal transaction into the genre itself. As scholar of psychology Charles Lloyd Cohen explains its effect:

> The new birth "took place" within individuals, but conversion was nonetheless a communal process, stimulated, nurtured, and directed by the extended network of Puritan society stretching from the regenerated individual to the wider public and ultimately to heaven. (1986, 21)

Practically speaking, because church adjudicators gave themselves the responsibility of verifying spiritual arrival, conversion could not occur without this kind of display. If approved, converted men became eligible to take the Freemen's Oath, swearing allegiance to the colony and gaining a civic voice, the right to vote, and the privilege to govern (Brown 1954, 868). Locally, the Puritan government had the power to award or revoke full church status that was at once religious, political, economic, and social. Weber remarks the Puritans were adept in conflating cultural mores, social formation, and civic life with church membership in a cultural hegemony in play for over a century (Carpenter 2003, 41–58), which was vital to cultivating the particularities of U.S. capitalism and U.S. culture at large.

Although separation of church and state later became integral to the U.S. political system, Puritan adjudication forged an affective social script that structured U.S. cultural ethos as a modern state. The cultural practice of hegemonic arbitration of individual immorality, shame, repentance, and salvation, historically tied to spiritual conversion, became a platform to mitigate access to civic rights and to privileges on which social membership turns. Furthermore, we can trace the role of the soma in authenticating spiritual remorse as a cornerstone of our contemporary social logic in popular forms of confession and social rehabilitation where, similar to Puritan forbearers, we demand secular postulants provide "unvarnished accounts of personal experience professed before the entire congregation" (Cohen 1986, 21), where in our contemporary moment we imagine an entire nation. Whether in a court of law, a Twelve-Step meeting,[14] a TED talk, published autobiographies, or the public forums I specifically analyze next, we have procured a communal model derived by the Puritan conversion scene where we subjugate and marginalize in somatic social exchanges of shaming.

Contemporary political showdowns and popular television tabloid talk shows provide an affective platform for public shame that gives the audience the role of judge harkening to this colonial form. In 1998 for example, President Bill Clinton's initial attempt to avoid public scrutiny of his extramarital relations was a crucial factor in his impeachment. Clinton's first display of public contrition for his sexual conduct recasts his desire to maintain his privacy in what was deemed a morally contemptuous omission. Later, in a televised confession, he speaks directly of remorse while he somatically performs shame. Footage of his apology on September 11, 1998, shows his somatic expression navigating between the confidence expected of the President of the United States and the abjection of the repentant sinner (Clinton prayer breakfast 1998, 2:34–43).[15] Looking down, biting his bottom lip, he directs his commentary to the camera, his eyes slightly pleading, while he holds his head and neck erect, a somatic posture of the guilt of the powerful, his guilt, giving his words of misdeed credibility. In fact, one of the first sentences in Clinton's address reveals the importance of performing shame: "I agree with those who've said that in my first statement, I was not contrite enough. I don't think there is a fancy way to say that I have sinned" (1:37–51). He continues: "It is important to me that everyone who has been hurt knows the sorrow I feel is genuine" (1:53–59) as he looks down, again bites his lower lip, his vocal tone becomes soft (much softer than in previous self-righteous demands for privacy). His speech cadence slows for effect, publicly enacting the somatic shame necessary to believe him more truly remorseful. He concludes: "I have asked all for their forgiveness" (2:14–18). While he maintains a somatically powerful torso, erect but without the tension of the fearful or the aggressive, a portrayal sufficiently compelling of remorse but also stately, the tide turns, and we are to imagine the nation has forgiven him because his immediate audience has.

Clinton's address, held before a large group of prominent religious figures, restages the Puritan scene in a modern medium. He looks straight into the camera of an imagined nation of jurors,[16] but his confession is actually staged for the consideration of a group of prominent religious leaders. A camera pans Jesse Jackson, among other religious leaders, orchestrating a predisposition of acceptance in the television audience—if these leaders believe Clinton, so should we. His final statement reflects the dual aims of his somatic posture:

"And if my repentance is genuine and sustained, and if I can maintain both a broken spirit and a strong heart, then good can come of this for our country as well as for me and my family," (5:54–6:07) after which Brian Knowlton from the International Herald Tribune of the *New York Times* reported:

> The clergy members interrupted [Clinton] then with 15 seconds of applause. When he concluded his comments, they stood and applauded loudly for nearly a minute. Afterward, some of the 100 ministers, rabbis and other clergy present praised the president for what they said seemed to be heartfelt penance. (1998)

The *Times* article concluded its report with the words of Reverend Fred Davie of the First Presbyterian Church in Brooklyn, New York: "[Clinton] couldn't be more contrite. . . . Anybody who couldn't see that has another agenda altogether"—the last sentence highlighting the prime value of *somatic expression* in a scene replete with resonances from the Puritan conversion scene. Staging his confession before the prominent U.S. religious leaders gave them the authority to judge the credibility of Clinton's shame, thus fore-thwarting the possible backlash or rejection of the national viewing audience to whom the confession was ostensibly directed. The move to publicly confess shows the enduring affective Puritan practice of performing shame for social restitution that was successful in Clinton's case; rallying sufficient positive public opinion, the effort to remove Clinton from office failed.[17]

Given the rise in televised tabloid talk shows, the secularized Puritan scene of conversion continues prominently as a form of entertainment. Since the 1990s, talk shows that publicly expose personal improprieties have drawn their emotional appeal from choice guests who have committed what is generally considered immoral and at the outset, usually feel no remorse. The live audience is staged to represent the response of television audiences (and as somatic models *for* television audiences). Enjoying their situational power not only to judge the misdeed but also to express outrage over the wrongdoer's shamelessness, the camera focuses on the studio audience shouting their disapproval of and contempt for the unrepentant. In this display, audience members communicate their rejection of the shameless as accepted social peer. Conversely, when the confessant does show shame and apologizes to the aggrieved, the camera pans the audience applauding, smiling ear-to-ear, eyes aglow, gesturing approval of the social reintegration of the repentant, and relief that the audience's imagined shared national moral code has been upheld. The Clinton-Lewinsky scandal, like popular tabloid shows, illustrates the enduring cultural paradigm of Puritan public confession of transgressions, one that demands a performance of shame to be judged authentic or inauthentic and where the performance of shame itself constitutes an act of repentance.

More recently, there has been a revival in criminological circles of the value of public shaming. As Suzy Khimm reported on March 9, 2016, high recidivism and overcrowded prisons have cleared the way for the return of the social logic in support of the "public spectacle of ignominy" that she illustrates in the prostitution scandal "Operation Flush the Johns."[18] In 2013, Nassau County District Attorney Kathleen Rice and Police Commissioner Thomas Dale decided to post mug shots of individuals detained for seeking or engaging a sex worker. Khimm reports several of the accused lost their jobs, some, their marriages, and only one at press time was convicted at trial. Considered "a moral enterprise intended to enforce certain social norms" (Khimm 2016), law professor Dan M. Kahan and philosopher Martha Nussbaum concur that shaming is an economically efficient and expedient moral deterrent. Khimm reports, outside of this sting operation, the majority of police detainees are racialized persons of color, such that the prospect of public shaming cannot stand apart from critiques of social location and the unjust mass media representation of colored innocents, let alone the racialized accused. Given the loaded nature of contemporary confession as a continuation of historic social arbitration, we may wonder why Montoya would choose to employ the Puritan conversion narrative in his desire to make a political difference in his poetry.

It might also surprise readers to learn that many colonized people have written conversion prose narratives because of the form's unique exposure of "the underlying tension between the transgressive and the assimilative aspects of conversion [that] erupts most obviously and most dramatically in situations of asymmetry between civil society and religion" (Viswanathan 1998, 87). The rhetorical form allows the postulant to publicly voice tension and objection to social marginalization dimmed in other forms of discourse. The genre has the unique capacity to offer up the postulant's conversion for public scrutiny, giving significant authority to hegemonic sectors, and because the genre stipulates predisposed audience empathy, forgiveness, and social acceptance, the genre is particularly situated to register political dissent. Shameful confession is itself viewed an affective action, a desire for repentance such that the conversion narrative performs a social pact that, as an expression of vulnerability and surrender to God as well as to human authority, suffices to (re)incorporate the postulant into the collective. As is the case in Montoya's *Ice Worker*, the colonized confessor thus can detail dastardly deeds within a strident political critique because no matter how dire, the confessant's wrongful acts make him or her a sinner "equal to all sons of Adam," per the Puritan reception (Rivett 2011, 101). Christian conversion has historically argued that God, not humans, grants forgiveness, relieving church juries and today's lay audiences of punishing the postulant for his misconduct and to instead focus on the sincerity of the conversion *stages* in order to grant social admission.

For marginalized persons living under colonial or postcolonial rule, or in a neoliberal state,[19] the genre affords the audience's ultimate relief in being able to accept the racialized sinner and let God forgive and/or punish him. It provides a unique social vehicle that accords social permission for hegemonic subjects to hear othered voices, their social critiques, and self-disclosure without penalty, and instead, with empathy. In the remainder of this chapter, I analyze the prominent role of the of the soma since Christianity's proverbial beginning to then trace shame in the Puritan conversion narrative stages as they appear in Montoya's expression of racial shaming. I argue Montoya's Sophiatic soma ingeniously reworks ostracizing racial shame into a political contest that pressures social acceptance bartered by the conversion narrative.

WHO BROWNS AMERICA?

The social politics of the spiritual conversion belie the modern practice of racialized social exclusion. Interestingly, to hide its antisocial and immoral aims, racial shaming is often (mis)presented in the ethical terms of defending racialized nationalistic righteousness wrought in terms of a desired sensorial conformity (see chapter 2)—conditions offered toward normalizing intersectionally racialized notions of beauty and good taste that historically have affected the rule of law (see chapter 4). The harm of racialization is most socially legible in somatic expression, and yet the somatic response as discussed throughout *Shaming into Brown* makes it difficult to pin down the harm, to call it out, and demand redress.

While the press in concert with the law trains us to appreciate harm in gross form, in the following exchange in the poem "in brown america," readers learn of the pain caused in more veiled scenes of racialization.[20] The line "don't make this a race thing" (5) begins the poem: a common one-liner darkly tools this American social praxis intended to disempower the racialized from speaking to intersectional racialization and racism:

> don't make this a race thing they
> keep telling me.
> whi te on br own bro wn on wh ite
> (lines 5–7)

The staccato presentation of ethnic identifiers distinguishes and dismantles the politics of such descriptors where racialized social locations of the speaker and the server condense in sounds: "whi" "te" and "wh" "ite," "br" "own" and "bro" "wn." Montoya graphically and thus aurally fragments these socially potent terms—stylizing their assigned assembly in letters that sound asymmetrical—and simultaneously conditions a disjointed life for both groups. Verbs are superfluous, as the phrasing "whi te on br own" succinctly invokes the complex politics reducing people to made-up categories; their equal graphic dismantling linked with a preposition exposes their emptiness as signs at the same time they call us to appreciate the hate and contempt they invoke.

Unlike Ceci's meaning-rich somatic "grh" in chapter 4's analysis of the play *Lydia*, "whi" "te" and "bro" "wn" underline the terms' socially constructed power that, when spoken aloud, forces the reader into the contraction of breath. The bilabial stop of "te" like the nasal stop of "wn" negate Sophia's song, the graphic presentation visually displacing the vicious social categorization of these words in the stuttering dull of nonsensical sounds. The breakdown of these categories in this poetic rendering introduces the possibility of Sophia's breath and with it, the spiritual transcendence we read of in the conversion poem "in love." But the poem "in brown america" appears early in the collection, such that the quotidian banality of this scene of racialization easily disintegrates the national overture of a democratic, postracial United States in Montoya's aural somatic aesthetic for the fraught affective life conditioned under intersectional racialization for Latin@/xs and others.

What follows is an exchange with a White, female restaurant server, who believes the poetic speaker, her customer, is White, and so speaks to him about race:

> let's just get along,
> said a white waitress at denny's who
> laughed and said,
> besides, they can kiss my racist white booty,
> because she thought i was one of her.
> (lines 8–12)

In line 8, the server in the poem makes the Rodney King beating and subsequent riots a cliché. Without cause, Rodney King was beaten senseless by Los Angeles police officers in 1991, and after officers were found not guilty of excessive force, nor were they found guilty of a hate crime, and despite his suffering, King still cried out for peaceful relations. The server puts herself in the place of King with "let's just get along," allowing her to circumvent her own racism. The poem's funneling of collective hegemony through the Denny's restaurant server points to a popular neoliberal script in such everyday interactions and speech acts that thinly mask the virulence of racial contempt with an insincere desire for racial harmony.

The server repeats more than speaks the bastardized cliché "let's just get along." She (and we) may believe her adopted racializing script instantiates her individual subjectivity and power, but Montoya lifts quotation marks, creating a fluidity suggestive of an entrained social dynamic rather than an indication of the particular conduct of an individual. In line with social scripts, she manipulates the discourse of ethnic and racial tolerance three lines later in her trite remark "besides, they can kiss my racist white booty"; the Denny's waitress follows the hollow of racism, numb to the horror of daily cultural violence. Much like the 2012 killing of Trayvon Martin, the 2014 killing of Michael Brown, and the 2016 killings of Pedro Villanueva and Melissa Ventura, the server's shorthand for the Rodney King beating emblematizes how hegemonic culture bypasses the opportunity for deep reflection and prosocial shame to motivate systemic change. In reality, her employ of King's words seeks to encourage, in this case "Mexicans" (i.e., Chican@xs, Latin@/xs, and Latin Americans), to accept their social station, parroting a social logic guised as liberating and egalitarian to which the speaker's soma responds:

>   my pale skin becoming red with
> anger
>   and
>   embarrassment.
> (lines 13–16)

Made a phenotypic impostor, the speaker does not yield his racial identity in the interaction, but it is nevertheless revealed to the reader by the flush of shame graphically emphasizing his "pale skin becoming red" that somatically authenticates his feelings of "anger / and / embarrassment." His soma portrays the effects of racial shaming—effects moving through him individually but also signifying beyond him, beyond phenotype, and into the collective practice of multisensory racial shaming.

The reader may imagine the poetic voice is that of Montoya himself and, because of his Spanish name, racialize him Chicano. The title of this poem insinuates that the speaker is likely a member of "brown america," a national but truly hemispheric physical codifier of the Global South that is browning the United States. Yet, according to writer and journalist Richard Rodriguez, the Brownness imagined and attributed to Latin@/xs is beginning to include

East Indians, Native Americans, Middle Easterners, and some Asians living in the United States (2003). Similar to the situation voiced in "in brown America" and as argued in chapter 2, all variety of physicality, sense emissions, and naming practices of Greater Mexico mark the relative instability of sensory data for racializing, but more importantly here, the poem indicates the deep habituation of racializing sensory perception.

Mistaken for a White man, the speaker "in brown america" asserts the historicity of racialized perception that deems those who are Brown to be unsavory and thus marginalized social members. The multisensory social construction of "Mexicans" is systemic, entrained, and lives somewhere between rote behavior and conscious awareness, a hegemonic pathology generating a "brown america" to then fear and loath. The speaker thus, mistaken for White, responds with shame. In inadvertent racial passing, he is assumed an ally in racial shaming in this nationalistic practice. While suffering most of his life under intersectional racialization, the speaker's shame also expresses the ambiguity of racialization and its deleterious consequences, demystifying his despair in a common reaction of shame and quiet anger embedded in U.S. intersectional racial hierarchies.

Montoya stated the importance of his placement of poems in a collection, stating otherwise "the whole thing will just be noise" (Chacón 2008, 100). As such, the specific aesthetic in his poem "in brown america" of somatic shame revealed in graphemes and clichés disrupts the reader's complicity in naturalizing racialization and racism, the social sin masked in the server's righteous "white booty" of a nation. In *Ice Worker*'s most marked discussion of racism, "in brown america," somatic contempt, shaming, and shame underline clichés and stammering empty signs of Brown and White, exposing the layered, intertextual, nonplussed, everyday forfeiture of our respective humanity.

THE BIBLICAL SOMA

> If your right eye causes you to sin, pluck it out and cast it from you;
> for it is more profitable for you that one of your members perish,
> than for your whole soma to be cast into Gehenna.
> —MATTHEW 5:29

The frequency and the breadth of the meaning of *soma* is met with its depth of meaning when set against the term *sarx* in biblical texts. Found over one hundred times in the New Testament, the term *soma* takes form in the exterior physical body but signifies "the whole person," evidencing one's spiritually transcendent state according to theologian Rudolf Bultmann ([1951] 2007, 192). The soma is often juxtaposed with the *sarx,* the weak bodily self, described in the Old Testament as the material state of physicality bereft of the Holy Spirit (Cohen 1986, 33). Both Greek terms, the sarx identifies the material body with needs and drives, ending in the body's death and decay. Humans are unclean in the state of unmitigated sarx and "sown in dishonor." Suffering original sin, Christians are advised to make their way out of the sarx state for the transcendence possible per the soma. When left unchecked, those who operate from the sarx forego the life of the soma, the latter described as the material body "raised in glory" (1 Cor. 15:43), "a new creation" according to the gospel of Paul (Sproul [1973] 2015, 11) that will enter the Kingdom of Heaven while the sarx will remain earthbound. The soma and the sarx exist more on a continuum rather than as static states of deliverance. One can begin an action in a sarx state and, with Sophia's influence, flow into a somatic state, but the reverse is also possible. However, some scholars read passages such as Romans 1:24: "God also gave [humans] over to their sinful desires of their hearts to sexual impurity for the degrading of their bodies with one another" and argue their stark divide. Theologically, Sophia intercedes between the sarx and the biblical soma as she "defines the connection between believers and Christ" argues Cohen (1986, 34). As such, those thus blessed, live their complex sinning lives through a soma Sophiatically imbued.

Early theologies write of the agency and transcendence of the Sophiatic soma while the sarx is mired in base desires. The two types of somas work through particular forces. Beginning in the Old Testament, the *pneuma* or spirit of the Sophiatic soma is carried out often in *ruach,* described as breath and a primary mode of Sophia. Conversely, *nephesh* or the lower spiritual level of physical being (Gaskell [1923] 2015), describes the spiritual lack evident in the expression of the sarx, animal-like, mindlessly fulfilling its organic needs. The view of the soma as the expression of enlivened Sophia concerns itself with the material being of humans as integral and interrelated to their spiritual being. Such that, even when one partakes in gluttony, sloth, or other physically expressed states of nephesh (thus leading to a life lived through the sarx), through Sophia, they become the precise circumstance through which Sophia enlivens the sarx into soma—a point largely lost to discussions of the decorporealized soul and of the condemnation of sins of the flesh in contemporary Christian thought and practice.

By the seventeenth century, the eschatological possibility of sin as transcendent can be argued operative in the Puritan conversion scene in positioning the sinning body as capable of spiritual intelligence. Although I did not find direct mention of Sophia in this literature, per *stage one* of the *ordo salutis,* the Puritan postulant who sought spiritual delivery and social acceptance was to first detail her sins, for "the experience of conversion would be meaningless to Puritans bereft of its emotional concomitants" (Cohen 1986, 119). Thus, the postulant was to describe in words and somatically emote how deeply her decrepitude had affected her being—a bridge of sorts between the acting out of the sarx, if you will, leading to the affective performance of repentance as the grounds from which the soma emerges. For church adjudicators, self-loathing was critical to adjudicating the veracity of one's repentance: "Unwilling to defend themselves, the godly also acquiesced in the total humiliation of their fleshly self-esteem" (207). This humiliation is described in somatic terms of "terrors and frenzies," sufficiently discomfiting at times as to lead to thoughts of "the ultimate self-degradation" of suicide (207). This depth of self-loathing was believed to prime relinquishing the self, a state that should lead to the "emptying out of all private feelings and ideas about individual autonomy" and a "melting down the tarnished inner self" so the regenerate "[saw] himself a hollow cast of Adam" (Rivett 2011, 101).

In the conversion practice, the performance of shame is an affective means of professing spiritual redemption, but its design effectively wills the postulant's social subjugation. In fact, as Rivett argues, the state of shame in the Puritan scene could not be conceived of or communicated in intellectual terms because it was "an entirely sensory encounter of hearing and feeling" over which "the convert ha[d] no control" (Rivett 2011, 102). The words used in the Puritan conversion performance and written narrative set out to express the postulant's somatic state, while at the same time, in oral performances, the postulant somatically demonstrated their felt experience as lowly, lost sinners.

Building on my discussion of the internal expression of the soma in chapter 3, in *Ice Worker,* the Bible gives the soma legibility as a subjective force via specific various organs and internal processes. In the New Testament, intestines respond in sympathy, the heart seats not only the intellect, but also the will, feelings, and emotions, serving as a organistic "metonym for the whole personality" (Cohen 1986, 33). However, Montoya's biblical use of the body heeds closer to Old Testament descriptions where the interpenetration of body sensation, parts, and feelings lead kidneys to "rejoice (Prov. 23:16), bones shake with fear (Job 4:14), bowels sound like harps (Is. 16:11)" and where "blood cries out (Gen. 4:10)" (quoted in Cohen 1986, 31). These passages employ a belief in the subjective expressivity of the human body as a "psychophysical entity with no single supreme faculty" (34). From the innards and along the soma-sarx continuum, theological texts present an integrated affectivity that links Montoya's descriptions of the expressive materiality of the body with these biblical antecedents that seem to philosophically inform Puritan conversion narrative discourse. Next, I argue the social sin of racialization and racism elicits the speaker's somatic shame. As such, Montoya describes emotional states through the expressions of bodies, but where the conversion narrative demands detail of the speaker's misdeeds, the poetic speaker declares, no confession is necessary.

WHEN WORDS ARE NOT ALLOWED

Accepting the shortened life expectancy for Latin@/xs tops off the chastening life conditions under racialization (Gilmore 2007, 28), the ice worker does not confess; in fact, he refuses to do so: "i will make no confessions here. / can't you see i've been bathing in blood?" read the opening lines of "the ice worker considers mercy and grace" (lines 1–2). The motif of blood in lieu of shame marks the corporeal experience of pain and life-drain denoted with bleeding as symbol of the humiliation the speaker suffers and to which he subjects others. The closer the speaker comes to detailing his treachery, the more obtuse his expression becomes. In the poem "1981," the speaker distances himself from the "i" of most of the collection, instead using a second-person singular address, where "you" prepares a blood bath in retaliation for the death of gang brother Efraín (line 2). But the speaker gives blood the simultaneous power to baptize, a Sophiatic presence that registers the rage of discrimination as catalyst to spiritual enlivening. Blood spills birth amid his damnation for sins he will admit but not confess. He explains his stance against the requisite detailing of sin:

> but i will not give you, here, the
> address of my sins,
> i won't give you the phone number on a
> piece of paper folded
> for you to slip neatly in your wallet.
> (lines 26–30)

In a world where hurting, killing, and dying are part of everyday life, blood works as a sign of abject violence but also as a letting, a biosocial signing of one's impotency, a physical demonstration of the power others have over one, illness, death, and subject of violence sources of social rejection affectively shamed. Blood is often read as a sign of the defenselessness of the sufferer that stands in relation with the exposure of confessing. Shame marks both bleeding and confession as states that can described by Jean-Paul Sartre's notion of shame of "recognizing myself in this degraded, fixed, and dependent being which I am for the Other" (quoted in Zahavi 2014, 213). In *Ice Worker*, the intersectional racializing humiliation of bleeding takes the place of moral shame that is present when confessing. The bath in blood repeated in different ways in the collection expands through a Sophiatic lens to ritualize the speaker's birth into degrading racializing schemes. From the bowels of social havoc, the speaker enters into the possibility of spiritual transcendence. Bathing in the blood of violence, whether inflicted or received, potentiates a different system of cognition as a kind of baptism into Sophia. The Christological inference of baptism by blood obfuscates the reader's default assignment of villainy. In its place, the numerous references to blood baths embeds such violence with the possibility of spiritual renewal.

The handgun the speaker carries in "1981" marks the physical and emotional weight of blood baptism, somatically connecting physical and sociological violence, poetically expressed in material poverty, affective sorrow and outrage, and State apathy. Variably expressed throughout the collection, the pressures of the threat of dying, witnessing death, preparing to deliver death, and perceiving the approach of another's death in police sirens and gunshots figure in the blood bath somatized in the permanent limp of his leg that he speaks of at various points throughout the collection. The lowercase "i" confers diminishment of the intersectionally shamed, racialized self, flowing in and out of humiliating incidents, many caused by State agents but also by his own hand.

Montoya's "i" graphically concretizes the unending, unavoidable humiliation he and his community suffer, to which he responds: "This is how it was meant to be: death in my pocket and insanity / the limp that keeps dragging me down. a tattoo teardrop falling from / my eyes" ("locura," lines 16–18). As argued in chapters 1 and 2, I remind readers that shame infers the individual's *internalization* of social defectiveness while humiliation in Tomkins affective continuum implicates external forces *upon one*. The frames of shame grow more paradigmatic with the employ of the poem's continuous present tense, marking an unrelenting psychosocial field where shame "fix[es] the self in a sense of *unending present* where its past and future are forgotten" (Goldberg 1991, 215). Montoya incorporates the social eye in the use of the lowercase "i" throughout *Ice Worker*, graphically marking his guilt, and clarifies not only his sense of angry shamed diminishment, but also his prosocial humility. Ultimately, the speaker implies, we, as a society, are all implicated, perhaps the reason Montoya's poetic subject refuses to confess. A conversion narrative using blood-letting and the employ of lowercase "i" for the speaker may itself seek to portray a diminished or conflicted soma in lieu of moral shame while he refuses to confess. His innovation may seem almost disingenuous to the endeavor, but Montoya is in good company in guarding his speaker's sins.

CONVERSION NARRATIVE SECRETS

St. Augustine, who made the transformative process of conversion a subject of narrative, defined this discursive space to document a powerful yet very personal experience to serve as a model of redemption for the greater good. Despite founding the genre, Augustine elides inventory of his sins. As literary scholar Patrick Riley (2004) points out, Augustine prepares the reader to hear a detailed account of his salacious offenses but never quite confesses his misdeeds, perhaps not wishing to provoke prurient thoughts in his reader. In contrast, Jean-Jacques Rousseau ([1781] 2010) accounts his moral failings in affective company of guilt and shame even though his is not a spiritual quest but an examination of the quality of experience that in his confession informs his sense of individuality as he shifts the teleology of Christian contrition in his search for humanistic certitude. Both foundational Western confessions avoid fully disclosing the why of their shame, but they do so in different ways: St. Augustine claims to feel ashamed yet avoids the humiliation of detailing his immoralities so important to the later Puritans, while Rousseau subverts the religious aim for secular self-knowledge and social critique, and thus shame becomes less prescient (Dorsey 1993, 47).

Perhaps in response to these antecedents, in the poem "the ice worker considers mercy and grace," the speaker implies he need not detail his baleful acts to us, for he has already confessed his sins to a barrio poet who condemns the speaker to hell (line 34), to which the speaker responds:

and it was true. i deserved to die.
i deserved to burn. so i do not desire
the complicity of poets or the humble trumpet of
    my pride.
(lines 37–40)

The speaker uses this incident to justify his opposition to ego trappings of the confessor, limitations of human judgment, but he also points a finger at the ironized earnestness of poetry itself. Nevertheless, the speaker admits his culpability in arrogance: "once, i became proud of my sins," carved into his flesh, each scar, a story the "i" believes he should feel regret, but "each time, / in each story, though evil i was, / somehow i became the hero" (lines 18–25).

The speaker does not clearly detail his wrongdoings, and in lieu of naming shame, he accepts what should be his damnation, but he does so in terms suggestive of his nephesh-driven sarx, for which he expresses a sense of guilt, morose, and self-disgust at feeling little guilt, morose, or self-disgust at the time. His guilt instead expresses in his limp, a somatic lament for his sins, and his poem "brittle green teeth" perch in a sardonic smile that wants to feel something better. Somatizing *stages one* through *three* of the *ordo salutis*, when the speaker will not come forth in words, the body will speak desires, express its moral compass, mark its sins and remorse (and lack thereof) in somatic expression.

Montoya clearly describes the experience and effect of intersectional racial shaming, rendering the line hazy between the social project of racialization and recounting regrettable acts in his oblique spiritual confession. Shame is an experience generally left unvoiced in everyday speech (Pattison 2000, 74), which perhaps explains how little shame is discussed in public discourse. The tension between feeling possible prosocial shame of our misdeeds against the disempowering shame of racial inscription could explain why the word *shame* only appears twice in the collection. In psychological terms, shame theory could code Montoya's deliberate moral bypassing, an effort to sidestep the shame of racial shame put upon the speaker (74), and/or an effort to avoid shame's collusion that would remove his misdeeds from their sociopolitical context.

Montoya's conversion narrative is a socially recuperative project seen through a glass darkly, where shame and shaming highlight fundamental effects on the racialized. As thus far argued, the speaker tacitly and somatically admits to sins but he carefully avoids capitulating to shame, a sense that should intensify when detailing sins in preparatory somatic humiliation per *stage one* of the *ordo salutis* and where, in *stage two*, the postulant is lost and despairing but also desiring divine salvation. Likewise, through managing his body image, while toting guns or after committing a brutal act (see chapter 4), he, in his gesture of confession, maintains a somatic attitude of indifference, hostility, and/or arrogance—anything but intersectional inferiority—while his long-standing somatic experience in his limp, like his green and brittle teeth, likely records the effects and stance against physical pain resulting from those acts against him but also the moral devastation he suffers by committing treachery. Recalling shame "marks us as both inside and outside the community," shame collapses the self as experiencer to a loathed object of one's awareness (Bewes 2011, 22), a devastating mental state turning a critical social eye onto the self (K. F. Morrison 1992, 7, 12–13) easily projected onto another.

The innocent man in the poem "the ice worker sings of mercy and grace" figures Christ to the speaker's Judas, where divine Sophia reenergizes the humiliation of this violence, death, and physical pain into the sentient immersion of bathing and baptism, and physical bloodshed becomes the means for spiritual immanence, the hermeneutic for explicating the speaker's spiritual converted experience of barrio life. In this poem, the speaker and his crew carry a nameless and ostensibly innocent victim about on a garbage can, thrusting a beanie of thorns that pierce his head:

> my friends, the preachers and cops said,
> "nail him! nail him!"
>   so we yanked off his beard.
> the whole city came to look
>   so we set him on the alley's
>   trash-can throne.
> all of us applauded, even you.
> (lines 49–55)

Instead of admitting he feels ashamed or that others consider his actions shameful, the speaker takes a defiant stance of aggressive rage that, in figuring the victim "Christ" (line 42), expands his abhorrent behavior with retrospective spiritual humility. The speaker names the trash can, the Jesus-figure, the Christ, the victim and the martyr all for our collective sins, but it is the Sophiatic soma that renders the man Christ-like, passive in the face of such violence where his silent relinquish frustrates our sadistic pleasure:

> this is the naked truth:
> Christ came walking up blackstone avenue and
> i dragged him into an alley
> and spit in his face. he didn't say
>   anything and it pissed me off.
> (lines 41–45)

In lieu of a direct confession per *stages one* and *two*, he states: "This is the naked truth:"—the colon strengthens our belief in his claim to come clean at the same time he forgoes positioning his truth as the direct result of his individual conduct in critique of our daily collective practice and tolerance of violence. With relish, the speaker solidifies his situational authority, calling on others (later, including the reader) to join in the macabre scene:

> we laughed and his blood kept dripping from
> his hands and feet and side and head onto our

> heads, but instead of shame
> we played craps for his sweatshirt.
> (lines 62–65)

Redesigning biblical somatic affect more than rewriting biblical events, the scene establishes the sociopolitical context for socially sanctioned, gratuitous violence. He addresses *stage one* in vibrant details, admitting to his and our collective enjoyment of committing random acts of violence, and while he does not directly express himself forlorn per *stage two*, only in negative relief do we perceive in this violence his search for redemption.

The rhetorical strategy is not comparative for, in this moment, the man *is* the Christ, the catalyst for the speaker's conversion in his theology; to his sins, he layers the wisdom of Sophia in retrospect. In Montoya's frame, Sophia's presence does not change the speaker's living conditions nor their effect on his life, but instead offers the possibility for using his humiliation and cruelty to encounter the Sophiatic soma. The value of this first appearance of the word *shame* of two poems in the collection points to our universal and individual shamelessness in accepting, and oftentimes promoting, violence, including our socially sanctioned shaming practices.

His treachery continues in "a letter to kb," where the word *shame* appears for the second time, postconversion to perceive underlying spiritual communion in the dim of circumstances. In accordance with *stages one* and *two* where the speaker-postulant confesses his sins and shame as the moral free-for-all, leaving him spiritually lost, the "i" recasts himself as Judas in another Christological adaptation where he betrays his brother in death as the speaker had in life. These betrayals of the speaker's fists and turned back (lines 47–49) portray in somatic terms the lack of regard, affection, or intimacy between the two brothers. The speaker's callous treatment of his brother reveals disgust and contempt for he who lies dead by his own hand—suicide, the act of ultimate spiritual depravation in many cultures and times, and so in the Puritan tradition (Como 2004, 350). His dead brother inspires self-hatred in the speaker for his shared sense of failed manhood, which he sees mirrored in his dead brother's corpse. Written postconversion from a Sophiatic cognitive filter of the soma, the speaker recognizes his own self-absorption per *stage four*, ridding himself of ego and his embroilment in biblical terms in the sarx, when, in recollection, he perceives not the cadaver of his weak, effeminate brother but the Sophiatic soma in an intimate instantiation of the crucified Christ lying atop a pile of dirty laundry:

> i found my brother, one day, behind a door, arms spread wide like
> Christ on the cross, laid out on the floor over a pile of colorful clothes

ready for wash, the sad slashes at his wrists weeping
into the stench of stale cigarette smoke and poverty that held captive
that room, his eyes deep dark wells wet and begging for the logic of death.
(lines 16–20)

The wrist wounds reveal sadness and blood shed, tears complementing the frantic search for relief in his dead brother's eyes now perceivable through Sophia. Characterizing the shame of his brother's act as Christ's martyrdom generates social critique of the causes that motivated his suicide, and the blood let becomes a bath of baptism in a living theology, and he sees himself a reforming Judas.

His change from the life of the sarx to the somatic perspective of Sophia brings the speaker to utter his shame:

i was ashamed. what a fool i was. what a scared little boy
i was. he was Christ that day and i held a hammer.
(lines 53–54)

The speaker writes of his allegorical Romanesque posture, "i held the hammer" following the biblical invocation "nail him! nail him!" found in the poem "the ice worker sings of mercy and grace" in critique of a twisted sense of socially promoted toxic manhood for which he feels "ashamed." Tucked into long paragraph-style stanzas of an epistolary poem, the speaker calls out and admits feeling shame for his sarx-led aggression where instead of evidencing virile manhood, he made himself childlike and a "fool."

The paucity of Montoya's use of the word *shame* and its somewhat obscured placements parallels the collection's scarce employ of terms like *evil*, *devil*, and *sin* prevalent in the conversion narrative in the Puritan tradition. Had Montoya used these latter terms, he would have run the risk of reifying racist notions of the speaker and his community. Instead, the speaker owns his misdeeds, tethered as they are to social circumstance. Their contextualization outside of shame but also within his living theology pushes readers to reflect on the spirituality still available in violence, contempt, rage, and wanton sex, bridging into the Sophiatic somatic expression of baptism, breath, sex, tears, song, and blood.

In lyricizing this form of the Puritan conversion narrative, the collection plays out dark feelings to convey the felt sense of shame, but importantly, instead of church jurors per the Puritan tradition or their contemporary modern proxy, the Sophiatic soma provides the cognitive frame for the speaker to witness the immanence of the divine in himself as regenerate, through which he has spiritually transcended. In Montoya's poetry, Sophia effectively elides the breach between sinner and redeemer, the humanness of amoral actions and the seed of salvation contained within the commonplace of sin. Montoya presents the speaker's living theology through Biblical paradigms and formal devices in *stage one* of the conversion narrative, where the confession of sins structured in the *ordo salutis* combines the rhetorical pull of Puritanism at the base of U.S. cultural practices to instead critique U.S. rhetoric of White superiority over those racialized of color. At the same time, the Chicano speaker turns the notion of shame for his sins and those of his community into a collective state of sinning and violence resulting from these cultural practices and beliefs. Sophia's atemporal somatic force offers the prism of spiritual immanence amid our crooked American humanity.

VIOLENCE SHAMES TO SILENCE

As in the poems "sight," "a letter to kb," and "mercy and grace," cadavers speak in nine other poems in the collection. In his employ of shame and lack thereof, Montoya discursively and theologically counters State suppression where cadavers somatically denounce social injustices and where the community falls silent. Of these, I point to the poems "locura" and "silence" and end with an analysis of "fresno night," the final poem of the collection, where the speaker verbally stumbles instead of sings, desirous to hear or speak no more.

The first two stanzas of "locura" pick up the concerns of the collection's first poem, "in search of aztlán":

> *and where, raza, are our heroes?*
>   *the heroes of aztlán?*
> *what became of that great nation we were going to build?*
> *where did all the warriors go with their sharpened knives*
>   *and loaded rifles?*
>
> ("locura," lines 1–5)

The italics give an emotional texture to the words of the speaker's wistful, dejected state. In these few lines, the employ of militaristic means to rectify the pressures of intersectional racialized life jars customary cultural obfuscations to recognizing the continued presence and prominence of the peoples of Greater Mexico and Aztlán in Fresno, California, and throughout the Southwest. This italicized preamble demonstrates a longing for an assertive Chican@/x cultural nationalism followed by sparse, imagistic confessions characterizing Montoya's verse throughout the collection, a lament the speaker delivers in breath and song, the Sophiatic soma lapsing into the state of the unconverted:

> i can't sing anymore.
>   no whistle pushes forth
>   from between my lips.
> (lines 19–21)

The lowercase "i" in this case suggests in addition to humility, social smallness, the poetic "I"'s spiritual despair, overwhelmed by the continuing effects of pervasive intersectional racialization on his mind, body, and spirit. He does not find Sophia in his breath, tears, in blood, or through song: "it wounds me, this silence, / even the tears have been abandoned" ("silence," lines 1–2). Sophia is blocked, falling into "silence," the poem which describes the shameful physical and psychological beat down by racial shaming:

> i keep waiting for the screams.
> screams for the dead, the dying, the decayed.
> but there is only the mute moth eating away at everything.
> (lines 23–25)

Are his neighbors silent out of apathy, fear, or numbness? Is their political withdraw a way of securing their safety, or a method of simply coping with disempowerment? The screams silenced in response to the killing and untimely deaths of several Latin@/xs are redeemed only in the somatic song of the dead:

> you see,
>
> this is the silence of the dead man dancing
> singing forth the crimes of the rich.
>
> but who hears you dead man? who listens
>
> to the truth falling muffled from your mouth?
> (lines 30–34)

Depicted as a cultural sin, intersectional racialization and racism animate the somatically responsive cadaver to speak his righteousness, likely a truth he did not dare make public during his life. Although his message is "muffled" and the crowd silent, his cadaver's soma speaks for the stifled crowd. While we read of the speaker's perception of the dead man's affect, in the next stanza, the police from their racializing view, mistake this instantiation of Christ "for a gangster / or thug or just another mojado moving / in on the precious property of 'providence'" (lines 38–40). The word *providence* set in single quotation marks mocks the doctrine and legacy of colonial Puritanism (and other reformist colonizers) that held racism righteous in the sociopolitical concept of Manifest Destiny, giving Puritans and others the moral right to take over indigenous lands and the jeremiad for which righteous genocide was committed against native peoples.

Employing the term *providence* recalls the history of Whites squatting on the lands of Mexicans and other trickery that disempowered Mexicans, the ancestors of the speaker's community, who are today blamelessly shot dead if found trespassing on land and properties that historically pertained to Greater Mexico and in the rhetoric of Chicano cultural nationalism, the current community can lay claim to. The violence of death shames the dead Christ/thug/gangster/mojado of the poem into anonymity, "beaten blue / and black" (lines 36–37), whoever he was. The silence of the speaker's community, the ignored message of the liberated yet shamed dead, and the historical dereliction of the 1848 Treaty of Guadalupe de Hidalgo concluding the Mexican-U.S. war, leave the question unanswered of how to identify, rally, and respond more than one hundred years later to the U.S. penchant to shame, hurt, and gag the Chican@/xs community into embittered inaction.

I conclude with an analysis of the poem "fresno night," where the postulant-cum-Elect per the spiritual conversion celebrates his salvation in *stage five* of the *ordo salutis*. The speaker resumes his spiritual cathexis through the Sophiatic soma that arrived while lovemaking in the poem "the ice worker in love" in the collection's final poem "fresno night":

> still savoring the breath of each other's skin.
> in this city i sit waiting for the end the world.
> the neighbors of noah are everywhere
>
> and a strange sky has come staggering in.
> i am not holy or noble or righteous, but i still,
> from my crippled mouth call, "Christ, Christ!
>
> let your blood bathe me and not night's nasty
> glare, let love's power bind peace around the neck
> of my soul."
> (lines 12–20)

Montoya elaborates on the speaker's refusal to confess in the earlier poem "denial" to speak to the difficulty of presenting his personal misconduct, imbricated and burdened as it is with racial shaming: "It isn't easy to ask for forgiveness, / it isn't easy to love justice / and judgment like an ax" (lines 36–38). The conflict between moral shame and racializing shame lives somatically in his "crippled mouth," declaiming physical, spiritual, social, and economic suffering—none transcended but their spiritual effect, redeemed in blood. Again, not shame, but his plea of despair and dejection prepare him for *stage five* of the conversion narrative of religious deliverance:

> here in this city i sit, the trumpet's trembling song
> fading away like an adulterous man, and i am left with car horns
>   and gunshots and shouts and smells of grapes
>
>   just about to rot on the vine, surrounded by wasps
> whispering lies and mothers weeping for children brainwashed
>   with insanity, and i am determined to know nothing
>
>   but Christ and him crucified.
> (lines 29–35)

The speaker confesses through breath and song, and where, like bloodbaths, the presence of Sophia resides in the speaker's somatic expression, deironizing what might be otherwise thought of as poetic flourish in a clear endeavor for spiritual sustenance and meaning. And while his conversion is staged throughout the collection in somatic expression of breath, tears, song, and blood, her force does not alter the psychological weight and the physical, material, and emotional harms of racial shaming and the social asymmetries it engenders.

On a "fresno night," the speaker seeks solace in ridding himself of those sensory inputs, entraining material and psychosocial dejection as if, in this last poem, the Sophiatic soma avails him as he weakens under the sensorial cacophony of shaming poverty, violence, and death that leave his mouth crippled, his teeth green, and his leg limp. In essence, the speaker comes to Sophia through the senses but desires postconversion to know "Christ" beyond the senses.

•

In this chapter, I have argued the conversion narrative to structure the poetic endeavor in Andrés Montoya's *The Ice Worker Sings and Other Poems*, focusing on the social value of moral shame in contrast to the social diminishment of racial shaming. The rhetoric of spiritual shame creates a textual frame for reinterpreting racial shaming from a perspective of social critique, thus refusing the indictment of social inferiority. I argue Montoya's employ of the soma rhetorically bridges these two platforms of shame through the figure of Sophia, the second member of the Holy Trinity in some Christian traditions, antecedent to Jesus Christ, and the Holy Spirit in others. Sophia's presence illuminates earthly forces supporting the evolution of the speaker's conversion through somatic expression. The divine sign arrives in breath and song, tears and blood, such that the Sophiatic soma diverts the need for human adjudication, key to disrupting the effect of U.S. racializing shame and its collateral forms of decontextualized acts of violence and aggression and silent injustice.

The speaker in *The Ice Worker Sings and Other Poems* chooses to lyricize his religious odyssey in the Puritan conversion style, and thus prepares the audience to hear his shameful confession as prosocial, in service to his spiritual salvation but also to pressure his social incorporation while challenging his oppressed life circumstance. Employ of the conversion narrative prefigures his social incorporation while simultaneously exposing the tethering of spiritual shame to racial shame. This flux of shames—racial, spiritual, and moral—calls out the hegemonic social investment in intersectional racialization and racism as relentlessly harming him while moral shame loosens its grip on his soul.

When we consider the cultural work of this poetry, we see the cogent adaptation of the conversion narrative in the Puritan tradition without submitting to its shaming logic. For Montoya, the Puritan conversion narrative provides a structure and rhetorical recourse to deliver a vision of self and community without falling into the trap of self-loathing stipulated by U.S. racial logic. In *The Ice Worker Sings and Other Poems,* the subplot of shame demanded by the conversion narrative and intersectional racialization redefines how and what conversion can mean. In response to the prevailing social construction of the Brown American as shamed subject, Montoya's collection presents a community harmed, flawed, and humbly divine, among the anointed, just as it is.

CONCLUSION

The Soma and Transdisciplinary Beginnings

THROUGH LATIN@/X LITERATURE, I came to appreciate bodies as vibrant somatic beings rather than mere material burdens (even when burdens of delight), which led me to fields like cognitive science and neuroscience (and cognitive neuroscience, cognitive psychology, cognitive narratology, social psychology, social work, acting theory, sociology, and Sophiology). I would not have imagined the provocative possibility of more deeply understanding the breadth and dimension of human subjectivity and the body's communicative role in social relations. Mounting informal, institutional, and governmental racism against Latin@/xs makes unpacking how racialization and racism work necessary and urgent. The literature and our social reality inspired me to tackle this transdisciplinary project, using an open method that is necessarily inductive, where patterns more than conclusions are drawn in *Shaming into Brown: Somatic Transactions of Race in Latina/o Literature*.

I have sought to show how the aegis of the soma in Latin@/xs texts allows us to view the categorizations of racialized identification as signs of the social processes *done unto bodies,* rather than debate what race is. The literature illustrates the deep psychosocial interplay of intersectional racialization and racism, social practices embedded in nationalist discourse that cognitivize sense perception in order to birth the notion they seek to then denigrate and shame. Calling oneself Chican@/x or Latin@/x brings these social psychologies to the forefront of the collective mind, concretizing not race, but the political, social, and economic effects of these paradigms in our time. Ethnic and racial terms continue to be useful for political redress, providing a sign pointing to the continuous hegemonic manufacture of the ontological premise of race. And this sign has nevertheless helped produce important empirical data in studies on unequal pay, labor marginalization, redlining, differential education, and unfair subjection to the law. I would have not expected this transdisciplinary method to lead me to identify sense cognition co-optation and scripting, the range of intention and effect of the soma, its membrane-like function that internally receives and responds but that also externally communicates—an energetic catalogue and pulse on our pains and joys.

U.S. nationalist discourse, whether conservative or liberal in tone, regulates bodies into ethnicities and races, or lack thereof in the case of the assumed blank slate of the Anglo-Euro self. For those designated as Chican@/x or Latin@/x or who, like me, claim these terms, we publicly acknowledge our imbrication in a category of illicit national subjects, one that actively delegitimates public recognition of our inherent self-worth. Racialized terms work partly through ambivalence with respect to physical and somatic markers of difference, but sometimes they are minimized as romanticized existentialist claims of Brown bravado or feigned complaint of the foreign but unexotic—both of these, useful for refocusing on the individual's story and choice while dimming the structural marginalization these terms denote.

Creative writing, however, provides a unique, critical venue for investigating racialization and racism as processes, displacing acceptance of the teleology of biological racial and ethnic bodily markers. Latin@/x texts explore how one comes to know oneself as Brown, a social perception one is seldom able to transform no matter one's social position, beauty, strength, intelligence, or social acumen. Narrating accounts of racialization and racism bring the psychosocial dynamic to the reader's consciousness, a risky venture given some readers will interpret scenes of racialization as affirming the validity of racialization. Helpful for considering the difficulty of writing racialization for Latin@/x authors, Monica Chiu poses the question in a similar context: "Are Asian American authors or critics adhering to a dominant ideology or are they creating narratives of dirt based on other cultural practices and premises that might both merge with and diverge from the majority?" (2004, 170). Many Latin@/x texts do not sufficiently disrupt racial reification, falling into what Frances Aparicio and Susana Chávez-Silverman call "tropicalizations" of their own work (1997). As Brownness gets canned into a seductive commercial package, some Latin@/x texts inject Brownness with just enough flavor to keep their racial inscription tasty. Yet, their reception, desired or not, still reflects less on those writers or texts than on the processes that engender them. Latin@/x writers walk a fine political line, argues Chicano literature scholar Hector A. Torres as "the social act of writing has to pay with a compromised status owing to the fact that all interpretations in a discursive formation reinforce power relations" (2007, 9).

Writing is a social act deeply embedded in established cognitive paradigms of reading and sense-making that we disseminate in patterns of culture. Stories are a predilect human form of sociality, creating a sense of "we"-ness in the assumed mutual intelligibility and value we ascribe to the story (Haven 2007; Gottschall 2012). The artful sharing of communal wisdom instantiates social belonging but becomes the conundrum Richard Rodriguez writes of where, when reading Anglo-Euro literature as a Browned subject, we read and neurologically feel ourselves part of the imagined "we" at the same time we are shamed by our racialized absence and/or ridicule in these same stories. The enterprise of reading asks us to somatically mirror and affirm the social worth of characters who are similar to those in our lived experience who have harmed us and our families. Worse yet, the desire to belong, neurologically structured in our brains, is so strong, we sometimes actually *do* like that character, and we *truly* admire the author. Reading and writing may be solitary endeavors, but neither operates in isolation. Appearances to the contrary, writing and reading take place as a function of intense sociality where affect, perhaps even more than emotions, are its currency. Moreover, mirror neurons create the biological platform for understanding what we read, which in the case of the Latin@/x texts studied, points to racial shaming as a paradigmatic felt sense in relaying how racialization and racism transact.

The problem of the racialized body is at the heart of these Latin@/x texts, as writers deliberately call bodies into the purview of the text: the bodies of the writer, the characters, and the reader. Narrating the experience and communication of the soma, the intelligent body, is a critical technique in this regard. The soma embraces the hyperphysicality to which Latin@/xs are subject and then recaptures the power of bodies to express the experience. Thus, by engaging the soma, these texts engender an intensity of body overlap or density of perception with the reader, generating a heightened sense of reality, one that may be uncomfortable for readers given the soma's demand that we recognize the deleterious consequences of racialization and racism.

Narrating racial shaming bids we change our complicity in racism and racializing Latin@/xs. As a somatic expression of aggression, shaming plays on the power to threaten the individual's connection to society, upsetting the integrity and belief in the self, and too often, the well-being of the body and mind. Such an affect grounds the individual in an assembly of processes, the soma taking in and emitting the individual's constitution as an intelligent organism that is profoundly conditioned by its social reception. Latin@/x literature illustrates how shame forms a consistent current of input through which the Latin@/x subject must organize itself.

Understanding the sociality of shame and other affects prevents the facile reduction of Latin@/x identity to an essentialized self; affect is an open system giving measure to all input with which it is presented moment-by-moment as well as across time (Tomkins [1962–92] 2008). These texts present the agential role of socially scripting affective triggers in organizing individual cognition, not necessarily to control experience, but that efficiently create, justify, and maintain social asymmetries. After all, if you get me to feel ashamed of myself, I will hold *myself* down. In community, under terms *Chican@/x* and *Latin@/x*, we write stories, building a "we" experience among ourselves and allies, where we fortify our neural pathways in common with an imagined readership with which to direct and defend the integrity of the self and the other to take into our lived experience.

The commonality of the experience of shame for all social subjects creates an affective lexicon that, whether racially shamed or not, we can all access. With body semiotics provided by psychoanalytic theorists Silvan S. Tomkins and Alexander Lowen, we can infer multiple meanings conferred through the affective soma, particularly the shamed soma of this study. In addition, the posture and expression of shame narrated in literature expediently acknowledges its application in our lives. The threat of social marginalization motivates us to avoid being shamed in order to secure social legitimacy (at least temporarily). When *brown* connotes categories of feeling such as suspicion, disgust, and contempt, the socially Browned body demarcates a shameful existence from whence there is ultimately, no possibility of real repair. From this abject designation, Rodriguez argues, we come together in sexual love he ties to miscegenation and with it, the hope of some measure of connection (2003). Thus, Brownness, though riddled in shame, evidences desire, passion, and love drawing back and forth in time and across the American continents, engendering more people Brown in the plethora of today's so-called interracial couplings in the United States. Rodriguez effectively accepts but then broadens the affective meanings of Brown in U.S. society in a similar way to Tomkins, who notes disgust (and dissmell) as expressions of the abject mark, the lingering want for what was thought to be a desirable object or person, before rejecting it as Other. Using somatic analysis, Rodriguez inadvertently talks sense perception and cognitive patterning as a way to open the field of Brownness.

Perhaps the most impactful work by Latin@/x cultural workers has been to set the material, spiritual, vibrant body against the irrational, unethical, and hate-filled purview of the nationalist imaginary. Sometimes a plea for social acceptance—See me! I am worthy! As did I, that girl made Brown on the playground and rejected—these texts call for heightening awareness of the role society maintains in organizing sensory cognition to inculcate ideology. Literature scholar Katherine Fishburn notes a similar promise of African American literature in her study, *The Problem of Embodiment in Early African American Narrative* (1997). Because Black people, like Brown people, are forced to live with a differential and primary relationship to their bodies, Latin@/xs and African Americans as well as other marginalized communities have specific knowledges and a relationship to corporeality both painful and yet a source of intelligence and power, as scholars of Latin@/x literature have more recently elaborated (Bost 2010; Minich 2013; Halperin 2015)—an acuity my mother strongly possesses that she shared in story with me and my sister when we were in our early teens.

By that time, like literary characters studied in this book, when socially advantageous for someone, I was referred to as a "beaner." My mother would listen to such stories my sister and I would tell of such insults that set us against the popular girls, always blond and tanned, usually blue-eyed and preppy—the complete opposite of my sister and me. My mother swore we were valuable and lovely in spite of our doubts. I remember showing my mother and sister an image of a pretty blond, a Breck shampoo model, in a mainstream magazine. My mom acknowledged the woman's attractiveness but then told me of how she, the Browned daughter of a gardener and a factory worker, was crowned Homecoming Queen of her mostly White, middle-class senior class in high school. She was chosen over and above the Anglo-Euro classmates, some of whom would later form the famous singing group, the Lennon Sisters. However superficial we find the value of looks, beauty relies on the same criteria that racializes, and, when institutionally recognized at a Catholic school in Los Angeles, California, with a White, middle-class dominant demographic, cultural power on this occasion was given to and received by my Chicana mother. She was noted as lovely, extremely intelligent, modest, and humble in her introduction before she was crowned—a good "Mexican" girl who was situationally rewarded but who, in the end, did not attend college despite her grades and spent her work life underemployed. My mother, like Oscar "Zeta" Acosta, did not fully realize the social benefit derived from the ways she was found acceptable by hegemonic culture—no one is capable of removing social stigma—but she did teach me and my sister to love ourselves through the rough-tender ways we would likely never be seen and appreciated with any consistency by hegemonic culture. She taught us we would need to affirm self in a community of allied women and men; to respect female friendship before love, lust, or ambition; to not take ourselves too seriously; to respect ourselves and others, but, like Acosta's realization, to let go of fantasies of full social acceptance. She knew that regardless of our ability, we would likely have to fight to be recognized and might not succeed. It occurs to me, for whatever discomfort readers may feel when recognizing their role in maintaining racism, some Latin@/x readers could find my argument difficult to accept. It is not easy to give up on the promise of U.S. meritocracy.

Mom did not use these terms, but she knew to teach us to look to community to make a reasonably satisfying life, to caution us that isolation is the social technology of successful oppressive ideologies, and she worked to actively entrain our senses to appreciate what made us bad-because-Brown as our badass Brownness. She gave us this advice and her somatic tone expressed the seriousness of intersectional racializing social intercourse with a tinge of irony in expressing the vacuity of its claims. Latin@/x literature is not, however, bleak or joyless; in most texts, pleasure, agency, calm, and success are had in different forms and measures, some of which may actually compound hegemonic racism against Latin@/xs (here, I am thinking of Elaine Scarry's notion of beauty, the good life, and pleasure as critical to how we conceive of ourselves in community such that, those who hold different notions of joy, pleasure, or beauty become out-group members [2001]).

As we continue to recover from the sway of Descartes's conception of a mind/body split, the texts studied in *Shaming into Brown* elucidate an ontology that squarely considers the soma. The notion of the split subject organizing the Western tradition since the Enlightenment discounts what premodern and preindustrial societies have always known: the interconnections between mind, body, affect, and the social mutually inform how we stand with and/or against social scripts and thinly masked oppressive ideologies. If we believe we can separate out sense-making and sensation, we divorce facts and feelings from their integration throughout the many levels of self we experience with and among others.

Latin@/x letters move into a new moment of cultural production and circulation where, given findings in scientific research, these issues are becoming more knowable, on the one hand, while at the same time, Brownness becomes politically more intensely polemical. While a writer might not choose to write of the Brown person's burden, nor can a writer simply ignore her role in its interplay. Somatic analysis allows us to listen to the intersectional, racially shamed somatic body as it speaks from within and against sense scripts serving a national symbolic imaginary, a mode of analysis underlining the value of literature as a rich site for research across disciplines.

NOTES

NOTES TO THE PREFACE

1. Psychological researchers Silvan Tomkins, Alexander Lowen, and Paul Ekman have argued since the 1960s for the universality of a set of feelings (not their causes but as human affects) evidenced in facial expressions and body postures.
2. In appreciation of the conscious evolution of terms, I move from the pan-ethnic term *Latina/o* of the title and employ *Chican@/x* and *Latin@/x,* the @ indicating the importance of gender identity and historic struggles for gender equity within Chican@ and Latin@ communities. The suffix *x* is rising within Latin@/x studies in recognition of gender fluidity and nonconforming sexual identities. I also occasionally use the term *Other* to indicate when a person functions as an out-group member; I use *other* on all occasions to reassert that we *are* peers, whether we are treated as such or not.
3. Princess Elisabeth of Bohemia has been noted as "the first person to note the mind-body problem" in European letters (Shapiro 2007, 23).
4. A partial bibliography of work on Latin@/x identity and debates on *latinidad* for the interested reader: Felix M. Padilla, *Latino Ethnic Consciousness: The Case of Mexican Americans and Puerto Ricans in Chicago,* 1st ed. (Notre Dame, IN: University of Notre Dame Press, 1985); Arlene M. Dávila, *Latinos, Inc.: The Marketing and Making of a People,* (Berkeley: University of California Press, 2001), and *Latino Spin: Public Image and the Whitewashing of Race,* (New York: NYU Press, 2008); David Román and Alberto Sandoval, "Caught in the Web: Latinidad, AIDS, and Allegory in Kiss of the Spider Woman, the Musical," *American Literature* 67, no. 3 (September 1, 1995): 553–85; Juana María Rodríguez, *Queer Latinidad: Identity Practices, Discursive Spaces* (New York: NYU Press, 2003); Juan Flores, *The Diaspora Strikes Back* (New York: Routledge, 2009); Lisa Penaloza, "Latinidad and Consumer Culture" (Hoboken, NJ: Blackwell Encyclopedia of Sociology, 2007); Marta Caminero-Santangelo, *On Latinidad: U.S. Latino Literature and the Construction of Ethnicity* (Gainesville: University Press of Florida. 2007); Richard Delgado and Jean Stefancic,

eds., *The Latino/a Condition: A Critical Reader*, 2nd ed. (New York: New York University Press, 2011); Jorge J. E. Gracia, *Hispanic/Latino Identity: A Philosophical Perspective* (Malden, MA: Blackwell, 2000); Suzanne Oboler and Deena J. González, eds. *The Oxford Encyclopedia of Latinos and Latinas in the United States*, 4 vols. (New York and Oxford: Oxford University Press, 2005); Ilan Stavans, *The Hispanic Condition: Reflections on Culture and Identity in America* (New York: HarperCollins, [1995] 2001); Marcelo M. Suárez-Orozco and Mariela M. Páez, eds., *Latinos: Remaking America*, rev. ed. (Berkeley: University of California Press, 2009).

5. Like many interdisciplinary projects, part of this kind of endeavor requires accepting necessary limitations of depth of disciplinary study. I make no claim to disciplines outside of literary analysis but engage research and theories that help flesh out the shamed soma critical to uncovering how exactly we come to understand why we are marginally located. This work might be better described as transdisciplinary, as nineteenth-century Latin American scholar Alicia Ríos has suggested to me—an approach to scholarship where, rather than adhering to disciplinary methods, I cull from multiple sources to present a more nuanced and contextualized understanding of racial shaming. As such, it is not my intent to provide an exhaustive engagement of these disciplines.

NOTES TO CHAPTER 1

1. For those readers who have not read the Preface, in appreciation of the conscious evolution of terms, I move from the pan-ethnic term *Latina/o* of the title and employ *Chican@/x* and *Latin@/x*, the @ indicating the importance of gender identity and historic struggles for gender equity within Chican@ and Latin@ communities. The suffix *x* is rising within Latin@/x studies in recognition of gender fluidity and nonconforming sexual identities, but to my mind, obscures the work accomplished under gendered forms present in the suffix @. I also occasionally use the term *Other* to indicate when a person functions as an out-group member; I use *other* on all occasions to reassert that we *are* peers, whether we are treated as such or not.

2. Written almost in anticipation of Brown Power, which are civil rights movements where today's Latinos declare racialized Brown, beautiful, *Down These Mean Streets* interrogates the subjacent politic of such revalorizations of *mestizaje* as a discursive move that various approaches in critical scholarship argue minimizes the social functioning of racial logic later argued by Kimberlé Crenshaw (2012), Derrick Bell ([1992] 2008), Martha Menchaca (2010), Juan Flores and Renato Rosaldo (2007), Miriam Jiménez Román (2007), and Miriam Jiménez Román and Juan Flores (2010), among others.

3. Here, I employ "Black Latino" to describe how Piri is seen by hegemonic interlocutors in contrast to "Afro-Latino," an affirming cultural and physical descriptor one attributes to oneself.

4. Here, I refer to the excessive incarceration rate of Latin@/xs, relative dollars earned based on gendered racial categories, police and border patrol violence, hate crimes, anti-immigration policy and organizations, and interpersonal harm against Latin@s/ as some of the ramifications of intersectional racialization and racism.

5. As with Blackness, ascribing hypervisibility to Brownness motivates extreme surveillance yet justifies socially marginalizing Latin@/xs.

6. Like *Chican@/x*, *boricua* is a powerful discursive strategy to collectively recuperate dignity from racial shaming.

7. It is as if the dimmed but ever-present body that philosophers believe contains the mind suddenly and consistently disappears in embodied mind discourse. The embodied aspect of the embodied mind tends to delimit the information produced for and by the mind,

but that still carries traces of the Cartesian split self. Elizabeth Grosz recuperates this presence/absence in mind/body debates in the metaphor of the Mobius strip, giving us a visual image to appreciate the mutual influence of the mind on the body and the body on the mind, itself, an instantiation of the contribution of the body (apprehending the visual image) to mind knowledge (1994, xii).
8. Scenes of racialization are not unique in social orchestrations of shame but extend from a culture wed to shaming as good law but also "good fun." Sociologist Harold Garfinkel (1956) was among the first to note that, for example, U.S. degradation ceremonies seek to materialize deviance and thus to convey stigma while simultaneously legitimating social norms.
9. Far afield from the historic Anglo ideal, which is a transcendent postracial scheme, or multicultural society thought possible yesteryear, writer and journalist Richard Rodriguez anticipates a numerically dominant, stigmatized phenotype that includes many ethnicities, appearances, and countries of origin. Underlying his forecast is this unnamed cognitive practice of scripting Mexican Brownness for pan-Brownness.
10. The Pew Center for Social and Demographic Trends outlines the use of the term *Hispanic* in census reports from 1970 to 2010. Even when including the terms *Latino* and *Spanish*, and despite the controversy of delimiting ties to Spain that eclipse indigenous, African, and other European roots characterizing the diversity of Latin@/xs, the Pew Center like many other U.S. institutions still employs *Hispanic* as the default designator for racialized Brownness (http://www.pewsocialtrends.org/2010/03/03/census-history-counting-hispanics-2/).
11. In a separate article, Muñoz (2006) describes *feeling brown* as a depressive state of *feeling down,* a pained, angry, despairing feeling that is often somatically registered as a psychophysical countenance of the racially shamed. Feeling Brown is also productive as an affective source to *disidentify,* Muñoz's (1999) concept of registering acknowledgment of a hegemonic social norm while subverting the norm in various ways.
12. See David R. Roediger's *Wages of Whiteness: Race and the Making of the American Working Class* (Revised edition [1999] 2003) for discussion of relative Whiteness and social incorporation.
13. Apologist J. D. Vance uncovers the suffering of White working-class shaming of poor and/or rural Whites evident in terms like "crackers," "white trash," "rednecks" in *Hillbilly Elegy: A Memoir of a Family and a Culture in Crisis* (2016), "a special source of shame" reports Joshua Rothman in "The Lives of Poor White People" (*The New Yorker,* September 12, 2016, http://www.newyorker.com/culture/cultural-comment/the-lives-of-poor-white-people). Surely accompanied by somatic expression, in-group shamers exist even among politically progressive groups. In-group shamers carry out political discipline as a tool of social control that I have seen operate among many organizations, including, on occasion, Latin@/x activists and scholars.
14. Linda Martín Alcoff's important philosophical study on Whiteness overlooks the affect of shame when she states: "There is no single emotion that might serve to unify the field of reactions between disdain, fear, distrust, indifference, and disregard" (2015, 123) that attend racism.
15. Goffman ([1963] 2009) explains that the stigmatized should not attempt to completely pass, she should (somehow) accept, but not fully accept, negative attitudes toward her, and she should never perform or enact the full range of stereotypes imputed to her. In this way, the racializer does not have to take the racializer's racializing too seriously. The racialized should act as if her racialized stigma does not really affect her, engaging the myth of the rugged individual, so that the racializer can pretend racism does not really exist. The stigmatized should work toward a demeanor of "gentlemen deviant" (110), embracing nationalistic ideals of gendered personhood; the stigmatized person should appear to earnestly

entertain the racializer's advice on how to survive and thrive as a racialized person, and, in conversation, pause instead of responding to allow time to recover from the racializer's insensitivity.
16. Through the book, I will use "feeling" interchangeably with "affect." However, following Silvan Tomkins's use, emotion signifies mentally deliberated affect.
17. Dissmell is a term Tomkins proposed to describe how the affect of disgust arises when, in desiring contact with something or someone, one enters in close proximity with the object/person, and smelling something other than what one expected, one violently rejects the object/person.
18. The Sandra Bland bill was passed into law in the state of Texas in May of 2017. The bill was gutted of language restricting unwarranted "stop and frisk" actions by police and grounds for arrest. The Sandra Bland bill now mandates the responsibility of jailers to attend to the mental health of detainees and prisoners (https://www.texasobserver.org/sandra-bland-act-passes-senate-unanimously-key-provisions-dropped/).
19. Society sees one as shameful and expects the shamed to act ashamed. An example of this expectation to act ashamed appears in Hawthorne's *The Scarlet Letter* (Mineola, NY: Dover Publications [1850] 2009) when Hester Prynne admits her guilt of sleeping with Arthur Dimmsedale but refuses to feel ashamed of her adultery. She expresses this refusal both verbally and somatically, which leads the town to require she wear the scarlet "A." The "A" signals a social label to indicate the shame Hester refuses to feel.
20. Although eventually we all experience traumatic events (e.g., divorce, death, losing a job, car accidents), as Vaheed Ramazani (2007) notes, social marginalization compounds such trauma and is itself, often traumatic.
21. Mirroring is also effective in emotional repair. Therapeutically, Helen Block Lewis says, "the use of empathetic mirroring [by the therapist] to signify acceptance of the patient's self, can readily be understood as techniques that are needed to help patients cope with their shame experiences" (1987b, 94).
22. This quote paraphrases a study done by Hart, et al. (2000). The quote itself has been cited in several articles, including "The Science of Your Racist Brain: Neuroscientist David Amodio on Subconscious Racial Prejudice and Why We're Still Responsible for Our Actions" (Mooney and Viskontas, 2014) and "The Neuroscience of Conditioned Racism" (Bosman 2012).
23. To distinguish between colors and racialization, I capitalize Brown, Black, and White to indicate the social practice of racializing phenotype and ethnicity categories.
24. By *racializing shame,* I refer to the social technology of shaming into race, and specifically for my interests, shaming into brown. For variety and stylistic reasons, I will limit myself to racializing shame and racial shaming synonymously for this process.
25. The potential for far-reaching control over groups seems to make shame a more interesting problem than guilt for sociologists. Scheff (2003), in his literature review, notes that the initial piecemeal addressing of shame came through psychology, and that although shame appears implicit in the work of several prominent sociologists, it did not become a central concern until the work of Helen Lynd ([1958] 1999) and Helen Block Lewis (1971). Ultimately, the distinction between guilt and shame lies in the idea that guilt services social containment and conformity, while shame socially marginalizes and excludes.
26. Sociologists Simmel (1957), Elias [1939, 1994] 2000), and Goffman ([1963] 2009) each have argued the way threats and experiences of shame interpolate everyday life. I refer the interested reader to their work cited in the bibliography relevant to this question. Here, I note general consensus on the deeply disturbing effect of shame on one's sense of belonging and self-possession, and while these studies consider the specificity of social contexts operating in shame, they tend to maintain the disciplinary perspective of the unaffected observer documenting and theorizing social surfaces (be they physical or verbal) and leaving out

the depth of prescient emotional practices influencing human life evident in intersectional racial shaming in scenes of racialization.
27. Shame is much more frequent an emotion than we may think. As psychoanalyst and researcher Helen Block Lewis (1971) argues, anger often encodes shame, taking shame underground and presenting, in Lowen's assessment, a secondary defensive somatic expression. While anger at feeling ashamed is often an additional source of shame, Lewis, in a longitudinal study, argues, first, that feelings of shame were much more frequent than test subjects were aware; and, second, that the recalling of shame intercalated with feelings of anger, a second source of shame. Interviewees would speak of anger and then admit that anger masked feelings of shame, which would inspire more anger (that often became a secondary source of shame) in a social emotional circuit of shame-anger-shame-anger.
28. When we bring together the strengths of discipline-specific studies to understand problems, we challenge the disciplinary tendency to reify the issue through the terms stipulated in a single approach. Insisting on traditional conceptual frames delimits the object of inquiry as well as our ability to come up with solutions (de Freitas, Morin, and Nicolescu, 1994).
29. Adopted at the First World Congress on Transdisciplinarity (1994), this transdisciplinary manifesto makes no pretense to holistic knowledge. Rather, proponents insist that transdisciplinary knowledge, like knowledge in general, is necessarily partial and contingent but critical to more effective problem-solving. For recent arguments for transdisciplinarity, see Basarab Nicolescu's published *Manifesto of Transdisciplinarity* (2002), his edited collection *Transdisciplinarity: Theory and Practice* (2008), Margaret A. Somerville and David J. Rapport's *Transdisciplinarity: Creating Integrated Knowledge* (2002), and Patricia Leavy's *Essentials of Transdisciplinary Research: Using Problem-Centered Methodologies* (2011).

NOTES TO CHAPTER 2

1. Instant association tested the subject's moral valuing of others based on perceptions of race. The study found implicit racial bias (Hugenberg and Bodenhausen 2003; McConnell and Liebold 2001; Phelps et al. 2000; Richeson et al. 2003).
2. Maurice Merleau-Ponty builds on Edmund Husserl's notion of the body to argue against Descartes's *cogito* and to valorize the body as the primary organism that interprets the world and crafts our sense of ourselves and our notion of reality. Merleau-Ponty focuses on the experience of the body in the world to make his argument but does not look steadily enough at what the body tells—the subject of my project. I hope to further the importance of the lived body by drawing attention to the way the soma communicates what is happening to us in a given moment but also as a register of what we have withstood over the course of our lives.
3. Interestingly, studies of the visually impaired show that sight is not necessary to learn how to racialize (Obasogie 2013).
4. Islam has become a code word to set off an imaginary that is visual, acoustic, and persistently tied to violence such that "Mooslims" provokes a broader and broader threat against "Americans" who ostensibly are not Muslim.
5. See http://www.cnn.com/2017/05/08/politics/trump-muslim-ban-campaign-website/.
6. Paul Ekman, perhaps the most widely known student of Silvan Tomkins, has successfully mapped out the meaning of the very minute facial expression to detect honesty and deceit for organizations like the Central Intelligence Agency and the Federal Bureau of Investigation, while businesses may use these discernments to register market reception to products.

7. Far from making an essentialist or holistic claim to knowledge, the current spate of studies on the body, emotion, and the brain synthesizes the connections between cognitive processes, bodily feeling reactions, and evaluative perceptions. These findings further consider the soma a psychophysical agent and social actor.
8. Social scientists have for some time remarked on the surprising amount of comprehension we surmise from nonverbal communication. In 1972, Albert Mehrabian reported that up to ninety percent of communication was communicated via our bodies. While that statistic has since been revised, it still accounts for about fifty-five percent of what we understand when we interact with another. With its popular culture dissemination, the phrase overlays the powerful substantive work of the soma reflected in a growing body of scientific studies, philosophical writings, and, in my discernment, creative literature. Nevertheless, body language studies and dictionaries inadvertently argue that somatic expression is a feature of normative humanity.
9. I will not delve into their well-known and extensively studied arguments because I bring to question complementary information and arguments from other fields that enriches the topic and the possibility of deeper understandings.
10. Lisa Zunshine (2010) argues the unreliability of the body and refers specifically to body language and its misreading in the examples of amorous intrigue like Eliza Haywood's 1719 *Love in Excess* or *Clarissa* by Samuel Richardson (1748). She discerns the expectation that one accurately reads an interlocutor's body language and reacts but rightfully notes that one reaction cannot be predicted either by the self or by the interlocutor and may not refer to the given interaction directly. One could emit body language about an unrelated memory while in conversation with another in literature and in life. While reaction to a memory when in front of another may confuse the origin of one's somatic expression, it does not obviate the fact that one is still somatically expressing, be it misdirected longing, disinterest in the current conversation, or another emotion. Further, Zunshine has identified body language confusion as a central source of narrative tension in English literature, but she may not take into consideration the possibility that love games between nineteenth-century hegemonic subjects may work through the body quite differently than the way the body instantiates the notion of race and commits acts of racism. In the literature I study, there is no confusion and little nuance as to the intent of somatic expression of the racializer or the demanded somatic expression of shame in the racialized. And while body language is critical to communication, somatic analysis marks the importance of internal physical responses, oftentimes outside of public purview. Quite different than body language as extended expression of mental thoughts or beliefs, the soma demonstrates the body's intelligence as a register of subjectivity. In addition to and beyond the reactive soma, I argue for the *intentionality* of the soma, in the case of Latin@/xs and other marginalized groups, to harm via somatic expression. Unlike simple body language, the harm caused creates the psychosocial conditions to materially subjugate others.
11. I thank my generous colleague Dan A. Weiskopf for directing me to studies that confirm that although there is no region of the brain that recognizes race, there are areas in the brain, such as the fusiform area, that are affected by this nebulous category, evident as well as threated in amygdala activity (See Ito and Bartholow 2009; Liu, Wang, Feng, Li, Tian, and Lee, 2015).
12. As a strategy used in various cultures to force assimilation, "Renouncing Personal Names: An Empirical Examination of Surname Change and Earnings" by Mahmood Arai and Peter Skogman Thoursie (2009) shows the economic benefit of immigrant name change in Sweden to a more Swedish sounding name or a more ethnically neutral-sounding name. They found that workers earned up to two times as much money after changing their names in this way. Women benefitted even more. Arai and Thoursie note that name changes most often take place for women if they adopt their husband's last name. The

researchers note the cultural logic that assumes these immigrant women have married Swedes thus increasing their perception of the women's assimilation into Swedish society. Although in a different context, the pull to nativize the name, I argue, makes an Other familiar to hegemonic subjects by pressuring (and sometimes forcing) an Other to sonorously produce themselves in the vocalic range of the language of the dominant sector.

13. In Valdez's play, Teacher concludes her usurpation of the sound and meaning signification of Moctezuma's name and Moctezuma by extension when she begins singing "The Marine Hymn," tethering the assertive student Moctezuma to the failed historical figure of the Spanish conquest. Used as a symbol to connote Mexico's loss at The Battle of Chapultepec against the United States, the contemporary hymn casts Mexico as impotent against the United States. In this interaction, Teacher's recourse to "The Marine Hymn" summarizes and subsumes Moctezuma's personhood into Montezuma, a marginalized, failed personhood.

14. Tomkins studies the range of the seven affects he studies as discernible in the soma. Lowen, in contrast, specifically studies trauma thus expressed but also elucidates a somatic expression of joy and reconciliation with one's painful past in his many titles. Both Tomkins and Lowen focus on the visually discernible, while my study includes research on other sense data, specifically smell and audition, that frequently appear in scenes of racialization in Latin@/x texts.

15. Conducting his studies in the mid-1950s to the late 1980s, Tomkins supported his analyses with medical and social psychological studies. Now growing in number, findings from cognitive scientific studies, including cognitive neurological studies, seem to support many of Tomkins's theories.

16. The International Institute for Bioenergetic Analysis was founded in 1956 in New York to train psychotherapists in "body-psychotherapy." There are currently about 1600 active members worldwide (http://www.bioenergetic-therapy.org/index.php/en/the-comunity/the-iiba).

17. These are also the primary questions Piri seeks to answer in *Down These Mean Streets*, which we read in a different form in Richard Rodriguez's *Brown: The Last Discovery of America* (2003) discussed in chapter 1. These texts share Cecilia's internalized racial shame, but where Piri takes a hurt and sometimes aggressive response, Rodriguez voices melancholy—a lost connection to self and to his family as the price of a U.S. education, social acceptance, and ascension.

18. For a fascinating study of smell, see Michael Stoddart's *Adam's Nose and the Making of Humankind* (London: Imperial College, 2015). Also see the Center for Non-verbal Studies. org ("aroma cue").

19. Women are sexually used in racializing powerlessness as a physical experience of color, and whether considered beautiful or not, racializing through sexual use removes the possibility of using the social capital of feminine beauty more available to White women.

20. For cultural histories of smell, see *Aroma: The Cultural History of Smell* by Constance Classen, David Howes, and Anthony Synnott (1994) and *Past Scents: Historical Perspectives on Smell* by Johnathan Reinarz (2014).

21. I have not located neuroscientific studies to further corroborate or challenge Kinzler's findings, but I find Kinzler's conclusion a valuable starting point for understanding the immediacy and predictability of the biosociality of somatic input of accent (of pitch, cadence, modification of letter sounds) in relation to social marginalization.

22. In fact, Kinzler's study of children further showed that "the children chose to be friends with native speakers of their native language rather than children with foreign accents . . . not due to the verbal intelligibility of the foreign speakers' speech. . . . [but] based on paralinguistic cues . . . children use accent more than race as a criterion in choosing friends" (in Neuliep 2014, 300).

NOTES TO CHAPTER 3

1. I want to thank the editorial board of *Transmodernity: Journal of Peripheral Cultural Production of the Luso-Hispanic World* for allowing me to reprint an earlier version of this chapter that was published in article form in 2016, issue 6:1, pages 88–109.
2. Acosta is frequently referred to as the Gonzo alter-ego of Hunter S. Thompson, a charge Acosta strongly contested. Indeed, Acosta made legal entreaty for recognition of his cocreation of the endeavor and style (Stavans [1995] 2003, 96–104).
3. Utsey et al.: "Race-related stress was a significantly more powerful risk factor than stressful life events for psychological distress" (2008, 49). See Mangold, Wand, Javors, and Mintz's 2010 study "Acculturation, Childhood Trauma and the Cortisol Awakening Response in Mexican American Adults" for related findings of early trauma and acculturation in subjects the study refers to as Hispanic.
4. Juan Bruce-Novoa (1979) argued against understanding *Brown Buffalo* as chaotic; Bruce-Novoa argues "that Gonzo fiction becomes a metaphor for the chaos of the American Dream" (43) and that Acosta writes with typical irony and vivid narrative "but not chaotically" (45).
5. Oscar's only rule: no map, no set destination (103).
6. A similar argument could have been made about the respiratory system. The nose and lungs comprise an organ that also ingests, responds, and expels in a very responsive fashion. The respiratory system has been shown to be one of a human's strongest indicators of harm, as breathing reacts quickly in somatic fashion to internal and external stressors. Because oxygen is more critical to human life than food, it would seem the respiratory system would have had a bigger role in the development of biology.
7. Jay Pasricha, MD, director of the Johns Hopkins Center for Neurogastroenterology, whose research on the enteric nervous system has garnered international attention: "The enteric nervous system doesn't seem capable of thought as we know it, but it communicates back and forth with our big brain—with profound results" (Johns Hopkins Medicine n.d.).
8. Ian Miller states, "The complexities and debates surrounding the stomach remain with us today" ([2011] 2016, 2). For further information, see Selye's 1950 article, "Stress and General Adaptation Syndrome;" (1950a); Chrousos and Gold's 1992 study, "The Concepts of Stress and Stress System Disorders: Overview of Physical and Behavioral Homeostasis;" and Chrousos, Loriaux, and Gold's 1988 article, "The Concept of Stress and Its Historical Development."
9. Calderón presents the dawn of Gonzo, the attribution of Gonzo to Thompson, and its effect on Acosta's publication history in "Oscar Zeta Acosta and Brown Buffalo" in *Narratives of Greater Mexico: Essays on Chicano Literary History, Genre, and Borders* (2004).
10. In evidence, there is much less scholarship on Acosta's *The Revolt of the Cockroach People*.
11. For these and other scholars, *Brown Buffalo* approaches the project and quality of *Gargantua and Pantragruel* by Francois Rabelais but in Chicano@/x frame. Michael Hames-García argues for reading *Brown Buffalo* through the carnivalesque lens where Acosta writes Oscar and his world according to an aesthetic where social orders are upset. See "Dr. Gonzo's Carnival: The Testimonial Satires of Oscar Zeta Acosta" (2000).
12. Interestingly, professor of philosophy Linda Martín Alcoff identifies the Beats' cultural disconnection as "the most famous attempt to escape from whiteness through a self-presentation of sensibilities that they characterized as non-white" (2015, 169). Like in the case of Jack Kerouac, who finds cultural patrons in African American and Mexican culture, the Beats effectuate White double-consciousness where they are aware of (and dissatisfied with) their ascription of Whiteness (136–77).
13. Calderón's work classifies *Brown Buffalo* as a satire where the Gonzo journalistic style effectively "distorts and creates caricature . . . to reject the limitations of novelistic dis-

course and capture a broad sequential representation of social and cultural life in the United States" (2004, 107).
14. Oscar mentions what he believes to be a particularly small penis several times in *Brown Buffalo*. Although it could be factual, this rendering most likely physicalizes his diminished social power in metaphor.
15. Silvan Tomkins's dissmell affect warns of the social prohibition against bad smells as prohibiting toxic ingestion. However, Tomkins argues dissmell as an affect that develops into schema where triggers set off the impression of dissmell even when the smell is not a threat. I argue the primary function of smell in schemes of racialization. For further detail, see chapter 1.
16. These long-term effects of the organism's accommodation to certain types of stress have been referred to as allostatic load (McEwen 1998), the "wear and tear" resulting from chronic overactivity or underactivity of physiological stress response systems. Stressors associated with such maladaptive consequences, both acute and chronic, are referred to in this review as pathological stressors. The outcome of pathological stress on the patient is determined not only by the duration, severity, and type of stressor, but also by other factors, such as genetics, early life experiences, cognitive factors, and environmental support.
17. For example, see "Interpersonal Discrimination and Depressive Symptomatology: Examination of Several Personality-related Characteristics as Potential Confounders in a Racial/Ethnic Heterogeneous Adult Sample" by Hunte, et al. (2013).
18. Studies repeatedly illustrate links between stress and trauma affecting the stomach in developing conditions like ulcers, gastrointestinal disorders, and other digestive maladies (Stamm, Akkermans, and Wiegant 1997, 704–9).
19. For a more in-depth analysis, see Eley and Plomin's 1997 study "Genetic Analysis of Emotionality." See Ladd, Huot, and Thrivikraman's article "Long-Term Behavioral and Neuroendocrine Adaptations to Adverse Early Experience" (2000).
20. The delicacy of the stomach also seems to be a mark of good character, a finer sensibility of the righteous. Voltaire remarks on the gluttony of the upper class where excess is the sought-after experience that foregoes the exquisiteness of taste. Voltaire considers gluttony when coupled with linguistic barb equally vapid. Voltaire surmises the upper class either doesn't care how their conduct affects their stomachs, or, because they are of an inferior category of human being, their stomachs do not register the excess or the lack of character as it does for Voltaire (Forth and Carden-Coyn 2005, 96–98).
21. Acosta may have been affected by the counterculture literary scene in Mexico circa 1960s and '70s influencing other prominent Chicano writers. Dramaturge Luis Valdez and Teatro Campesino were performing in Mexico while Chicano novelists Alejandro Morales, Miguel Méndez, and Rolando Hinojosa-Smith were among an emerging group of Chicano writers published and recognized by Latin American institutions beginning in the early 1970s. Stavans argues that whereas Acosta may have had knowledge of his literary Mexican contemporaries; those writers had no knowledge of Acosta ([1995] 2003).
22. Centering the reader on Oscar's body from the autobiography's first page, first sentence, "I stand naked before the mirror" (11) to nearly the last, "I stand before the mirror. I cry in sobs" (195) effectively exposes the process and effects of racialization in the making of Latin@/xs; however, some readers consider Acosta's fat, flatulent Oscar a testimonial form of Mikhail Bakhtin's grotesque (See Hames-García's well-argued "Dr. Gonzo's Carnival: The Testimonial Satires of Oscar 'Zeta' Acosta" [2000]). I point to the soma as an intelligent, expressive, and responsive entity in the substantive form of human subjectivity. Acosta writes somatic Oscar reflecting the historical subject's numerous health challenges documented in *Oscar "Zeta" Acosta: The Uncollected Works* (Stavans 1996) at the same time the narrated soma serves literary purposes of poking holes in the autobiographical hero.

23. In *The Revolt of the Cockroach People*, Acosta occasionally indicates the state of his stomach and in terms evidencing a Gonzo style; however, the memoir is focused on Oscar's involvement in the Chicano Movement, a different project from his coming-to-politicization of his autobiography *Brown Buffalo*.

NOTES TO CHAPTER 4

1. To date, *Lydia* has been staged at The Denver Center for the Performing Arts, Denver, Colorado, January 2008; Attic Rep, San Antonio, Texas, 2009; The Yale Repertory Theater, February 2009; Marin Theater Company, Mill Valley, California, March 2009; Center Theater Group/Mark Taper Forum, Los Angeles, California, April–May 2009; National Pastime Theater, Chicago, Illinois, October 2013; Napa Valley Conservatory Theater, Napa, California, January–February 2015; Cara Mia Theater Company, Dallas Texas, April 2015; Brown Bag Players, Irvine, California, May 2016; Teatro Milagro, Portland, Oregon, March–April 2017.
2. Perhaps unknown to Solís, after four weeks in a vegetative state, sufferers are classified in a pervasive vegetative state (PVS). Ceci more accurately suffers from pervasive vegetative state rather than semi-permanent vegetative state.
3. Here, I borrow the term *normative* from Rosemarie Garland-Thomson's *Extraordinary Bodies: Figuring Physical Disability in American Culture and Literature* where disability functions to some extent with the notion of race ([1997] 2017).
4. Plays by Cherríe Moraga, Migdalia Cruz, Ricardo Bracho, Luis Valdez, Elaine Romero, Silviana Wood, and Luis Alfaro are examples of Latin@/x dramas that employ the body in ways that explore the somatic self as a primary dramatic means to convey sociopolitical analysis.
5. Variations of Method acting that focus on "somatics" include Frederick Matthias Alexander, Anne Bogart, Michael Chekhov, Moshe Feldenkrais, Jerzy Grotowski, Rudolf von Laban, Jacques Lecoq, Tadashi Suzuki, and Alba Emoting (Barton and Sellers-Young 2017, 57–75).
6. Here, I interject the specific use of the term *theater* against the specific theatricalities of *performance, performance theater, verbatim theater*, and *autobiographical theater* (among others) that craft a different relationship between performance, performers, and the social real.
7. Robinson argues for the complementarity of social dynamics that run through what neuroscientist Antonio Damasio refers to as somatic markers, bodily cues prompted by feelings from which we make decisions (2010); and through the sociopolitical soma Robinson calls *ideosomatics*, where culturally taught, bodily cues form a basis of commonality and stability in human communication (2008).

   In contrast, body image management deliberately confects a way to be seen in character rather than expressing the soma of the actor or the actor in character proper. David V. Mason presents the term *consciousness* to describe whether and how the actor manages her awareness of what she is scripted to do, feel, and respond to, with the express goal of appearing naturally; the need to train an actor in consciousness evidences the default script against which it is exerted: acting takes ordinary and extraordinary actions and words out of their natural expression and through consciousness—the actor learns to perform "as if" the character, an act different from simply being that character. That theater works through make-believe and believing; David V. Mason and Doug Rosson (Rosson 2013) separately argue that it is the audience's absolute assuredness of theater as make-believe that is the condition that makes audience engagement possible. The normative material conditions of theater elicit theater goers' metacognition of make-believe in the purchase of the ticket, in entering the theater house, the special space of the stage, props, lighting, etc. (Mason 2013).

8. Theater scholars Blair and Cook clearly delineate theatrical speech from lived expression. Despite Method acting and its variants, they contend, "The interaction between language and other modalities not only defines theater as a different artistic event, but also changes the language of the play. . . . It is enough to compare a corpus of conversational discourse with any play to see that people commonly speak in a much less coherent way, that the turns in conversations are often shorter, that there are numerous false-starts and sudden changes of tack, etc." (2016, 27).

9. Although microphones are increasingly used to make audible quieter dialogue, intentional loudness or softness conveys the artifice of body image management on the stage, decisions made for the stage that differ from the spontaneous decisions we make in our lives.

10. Douglas Robinson (2008), Barbara Sellers-Young (2002), and Juliet Koss (1997) discuss the necessity of regarding (what I will summarize as) the soma in drama. Sellers-Young and Koss focus on the actor's performance, to which I add here other modalities of acting in creating an internal appearance of sense perception. Externally, physical maneuvers of the stage and on the stage generate a desired awareness of the theatricality of sense perception. Robinson and Ross refer to Brecht's distantiation/estrangement principle to think through theatrical experience as the play between emotional engagement and the distancing of perceptible artifice.

11. In very general terms (and with many exceptions), we can compare theater performance to other kinds of dramatic performances, such as agitprop, testimonies, and stand-up performances where the type of performance stipulates that the performer portrays herself rather than a character.

12. In her article "A Savage Performance: Guillermo Gómez-Peña and Coco Fusco's 'Couple in the Cage,'" Diana Taylor refers to the performance by the title "Two Undiscovered Amerindians visit . . ." (*The Drama Review* 42, no. 2 [1998]: 160–75) while Fusco and Paula Heredia's film on the same is titled *The Couple in the Cage: A Guatinaui Odyssey* (Authentic Documentary Productions, 1993).

13. Ethnic studies are sometimes criticized for employing the language of disability to describe experiences of racialization and other forms of ostracism of people of color (Shakespeare 2010, 266). However, in her study of the social construction of disability during the nineteenth and early twentieth centuries, Thomson's *Extraordinary Bodies: Figuring Physical Disability in American Culture and Literature* ([1997] 2017) compels us to consider the plight of the racialized and the marginalization of gender as historical categories of Otherness in relation to disability.

14. I base my statement on the inaccuracies of Ceci's portrayal that I saw compared to the description of those afflicted with PVS (Royal College of Physicians 2003, 3–4).

15. In fact, this belief has on more than one occasion successfully convinced courts to permit some families to euthanize the PVS-afflicted (Jennett 2003, 127–46).

16. Rosa maintains the position of a somewhat submissive role of wife and mother to Claudio's aggressive patriarchal rule. Eldest son René closets his homosexuality in violent homophobia, while tender-hearted younger son Misha is accused of being less than a real macho for his love of poetry and gentle relating. For Claudio, the father, Ceci-the-body is evidence of his personal failure, a broken flower, and an emblem of familial shame (Minor 2009).

17. Rosa's plastic furniture coverings and her penchant for blue chip stamps and store catalogues provide small practices of U.S. mainstream culture where the goal of working hard and socially ascending is to acquire stuff.

18. This pain of rejection in somatic expression often includes various organs like those of the digestive system, as I have argued in chapter 3. The gut, in particular, demonstrates an intelligence and communicative role to other organs but also to our conscious minds.

Shannon Sullivan might agree with Elspeth Probyn's argument and tie somatic expression into a system of organ affectivity, an evolutionary strategy, Sullivan argues, where organs actively soothe themselves as a matter of survival and wellbeing (2015). Sullivan argues the biological systems of self-soothing in the face of agitation and lend metaphoric value to Ceci's somatic portrayal.

19. In nervous system and gut, the organs and nerves work to stave off trauma and to calm and comfort themselves first, and then, the whole organism. In effect, organs execute a level of intelligence and subjectivity (Bazar, Lee, and Joon, 2004).
20. This device is not without literary antecedents: Connor illustrates buried shame and anger in the work of Sylvia Plath in her poem "Daddy" where she employs "Ich, ich, ich, ich" as a German guttural (2014, 114).
21. This position remains in evidence today. Currently, biological sciences consider the brain itself an organ, which is to say, susceptible to becoming physically damaged. Cognitive difference explained as such leaves the belief in human reason intact, explains Porter (2003, 305–19).
22. For further discussion, I refer my reader to Elaine Scarry, who writes on striving to experience culturally scripted notions of beauty as an overlooked tenet in promoting social asymmetries in the Western world in *On Beauty and Being Just* (2001).
23. I employ Schweik's analytic of ugly in conjunction with Rosemarie Garland-Thomson's rubric of corporeal deviance to argue the overlap in discourse despite the variables of the Ugly Laws, disability discourse, and gender, race, and ethnicity oppressions ([1997] 2017).
24. Today, mental and physical non-normatives continue to be treated with practices stemming from this ontology. We can see this premise underlies modalities of occupational therapy, physical therapy, psychiatry, and much of behavioral therapy that use exercises to prompt the patient or client to respond or react in an imagined normative way; the common goal of these protocols remains working toward normative comportment without considering the conservative politic on which these practices rest.
25. The fashion industry and retailers have on occasion helped redress the public imagination of beauty by featuring (albeit seldom) models in wheelchairs (e.g., Nordstrom's catalogues), and recently, surf wear model Bethany Hamilton, maimed by a shark.
26. Clearly, U.S. popular culture has yet to fully embrace the disabled or those historically racialized as attractive as attested to by the popular television show *Ugly Betty* (2006–10), where a young normative Latina is codified an ugly woman in her work milieu. Such television programming asks us to like Betty; we should consider her endearing and capable, somewhat less than super attractive, yet involved in romantic relationships with several men. Nevertheless, her work colleagues continually treat Betty as intersectionally ugly. Programs like *Ugly Betty* attempt to ameliorate the stigma of the lingering cultural legacy of gendered race, ethnicity, and poverty scripted in the Ugly Laws, while they sometimes simultaneously reinforce the frame they aspire to dismantle.
27. Solís's *Lydia* contrasts with other American plays where, when they present disability, they do so elliptically. Tennessee Williams's *The Glass Menagerie* (1945) and *A Hot Cat on a Tin Roof* (1955), for example, tend to skirt the physiological implications of disability for the psychological profile of their respective characters, while Samuel Beckett's theater distorts the politics of disability through characterological synecdoche. Ceci is not the first mentally or cognitively impaired character Solís has developed in his body of work, but his focus on Ceci in *Lydia* is akin to Peter Nichol's 1967 play *A Day in the Death of Joe Egg*, where disability is similarly staged through the lens of the mundane.
28. Joel Chandler Harris's 1881 *Uncle Remus* paradigmatically inculcates the basis for the figure of the racialized domestic worker into U.S. mass culture, against which plays like Tony Kushner's 2003 *Caroline, or Change*, Tate Taylor's 2011 film *The Help*, the television series

Devious Maids (2013–16), and Matthew Lopez's Pulitzer Prize winning play, *The Whipping Man* (2006) argue.

29. I offer a long quote by Cassandra Mallett to appreciate the depth of the archetype in U.S. culture: "Uncle Remus was the illustration of the 'perfect' Black man in the eyes of White America; however, he was the enemy of Black Americans. Harris borrowed the faithfulness of Uncle Tom from Harriet Beecher Stowe's *Uncle Tom's Cabin* ([1852] 2005) and did away with the harsh masters. He took the minstrel grin and the loving demeanor and created Uncle Remus. Harris took the stories that were told to him in his childhood and brought them to the world. Uncle Remus assured Southern Whites about their greatest fears of Blacks: free Black people would love, not demand retribution. Black people would wait and not protest to earn their equality. At the same time, he assured Northern Whites that they were not failures in moral responsibility when they did not live to their promises of just opportunities. Uncle Remus told that Blacks would turn the other cheek and would continue to love despite all broken promises from America (Hemenway in Harris [1880] 1986, 20). He was an 'old time Negro' that reminded Southerners what was 'good' about slavery (21). He knew his place, never threatened, and helped to heal emotional scars" (22; Mallett 2002, 1540–41).

30. Spike Lee has referred to the Uncle Remus character as a "super-duper magical negro" (2001), a stock character who spends his time and effort helping out White people, often without reward or personal investment. "Magic negro" has been the basis of later critiques such as Rita Kempley's "Too Too Divine; Movies' 'Magic Negro' Saves the Day, but at The Cost of His Soul" (2000); and Nnedi Okorafor's "Stephen King's Super-Duper Magical Negroes" (2004).

31. For an extended analysis of the world of domestic work and disability as a play on presence/absence, see my article "Disability, Domestic Workers, and Disappearance in Octavio Solís's *Lydia*" (2015). For social studies on the situation of *domésticas*, see Alma M. García's seminal 1994 article, "Maids No More: The Transformation of Domestic Work" and her 1994 monograph *Gendered Transitions: Mexican Experiences of Immigration*. Maggie Caldwell's "Invisible Women: The Real History of Domestic Workers in America" (2013) offers a current view on the longstanding, underappreciated situation, as does Moni Basu's report, "The Invisible World of Domestic Work: Report Documents Abuses" (2013).

32. Some sociologists refer to lack of affective complicity as "emotional dissonance" against the demands of employers (Abraham 1999). Studies of this problem cite workers' ability to feign emotions, but at a cost to their wellbeing (Pugh, Groth, and Hennig-Thurau 2011).

33. The connection between cultural production and lived acts of racialization and racism is aptly evident in Sandra Bland's 2015 murder, which shows her mostly mild verbal and somatic resistance to the unfair allegations and treatment by the police officer who pulled her over—resistance that ultimately found her dead in a jail cell (https://www.google.com/search?q=sandra+bland+arrest+video&ie=utf-8&oe=utf-8).

34. One must exercise considerable discipline to attempt to neutralize one's authentic somatic response to racial shaming and simulate a socially acceptable somatic portrayal. As argued in chapter 2, repeated over time and heavily disseminated across social roles, many racialized persons adopt a habituated somatic portrayal to safely manage lived experiences of scenes of racialization. Such patterns begin by utilizing bodily image management, conscious whole-body gesturing toward producing the archetypal effect described here. However, the more pressured they are to so enact and thus perform different than they feel, these expressions can become a habit replacing their somatic expression prior to racialization. As a threshold in a dynamic understanding of soma and subjectivity, somatic portrayal can lead the racialized to adopt the racializer's perception, and intersectional racial shaming can eventually naturalize in the racialized's somatic expression. This bodily habit pattern is operative in archetypal display.

35. Of the Chicano plays featuring maids, there are few protagonized by maids or domestic workers, only Luis Valdez's *I Don't Have to Show You No Stinking Badges!* (1992), and Milcha Sanchez-Scott's *Latina* (2018). *Badges* centers on Hollywood extras Connie and Buddy Villa, who may be successful professionals, but their success lies contingent to their on-screen passive countenance reifying the real-life expectations of domestic workers that Solís depicts through his character Lydia. Sanchez-Scott also peripherally employs the figure of the maid in her play *Latina*. Based on an autobiographical account, the play takes up the story of Sarita, a temporary receptionist in an employment agency specializing in farming out domestic laborers to well-off Anglo-Euro women. As Sanchez-Scott enters the subject of the trials of domestic work via backroom exchanges between worker hopefuls, her *Latina* limits the subject to a topic rather than a fully developed theme. *Badges* and *Latina* plays employ the figure of the Mechicana domestic laborer as a symbol of abject work of a social underclass, gesturing toward but do not directly address the reality of Mechican@ domestic work.

36. From the German, *doppelganger* signifies alter ego but also has a ghostly connotation, in evidence in Ceci's description of Lydia (Merriam-Webster, https://www.merriam-webster.com/dictionary/doppelg%C3%A4nger).

37. I make a distinction between what could be misread as a collapse of Lydia and Ceci into a single character and the telepathic connection where they maintain their individuality, but which affords intimate, spontaneous knowledge of the other in any given moment. The characters as dyad dramatically assert their visibility as full-fledged people while politically, the dyad challenges the atomization of both characters, so deeply inscribed in their diminished intersectional subject positions as to be somehow outside of the social and fettered into silence. The connection reported by social research, which offers the telepathic state as an alternate form of being, disrupts their relationship as purely invented for the understanding of their relationship as plausible and most capable of politically voicing their respective subjugation.

NOTES TO CHAPTER 5

1. Prominent figures in Sophiology and followers of Sophia include twelfth-century Roman Catholic Doctor of the Church, St. Hildegard of Bingen; seventeenth-century theologian Gottfried Arnold, Jacob Boehme's Puritan theology, mystics Lady Jane Lead and Johann Georg Gichtel; eighteenth-century philosopher Louis-Claude de Saint Martin, and theosophist Johann Jacob Wirz; as well as nineteenth-century mystic and visionary Anne Catherine Emmerich.
2. As the body becomes more intimately proven to be related to cognition, I propose cognition as whole body knowing that I term *soma*.
3. Montoya earned a bachelor's degree from California State University, Fresno, and a Master of Fine Arts from University of Oregon.
4. Song of Songs is also referred to as the Song of Solomon.
5. Perhaps the speaker, like most of us, construes his quotidian experience of self as driven by a notion of himself as a mind that uses the body to carry out its will. The body interjects its needs and, at times, we must attend to its needs despite our preferences. Physical needs can be a starting point in recognizing the soma.
6. Sophia is argued "the Mother of the Universe" in the Sophia of Jesus tractate and in the Gospel of Mary (Magdalene) in the Nag Hammadi Codices (respectively, Pearson 200; Evans 2015)

7. His poetry inspired the establishment of the University of Notre Dame biennial Andrés Montoya Poetry Prize as well as a scholarship founded in Montoya's name awarded by California State University, Fresno.
8. The collection has influenced a generation of poets and motivated a special edition of *In the Grove* entitled *An Homage to Andrés Montoya* (Chacón 2008, 10).
9. Interest in Montoya's work motivated the 2017 publication of a posthumous collection of his work entitled *Jury of Trees* edited by Daniel Chacón.
10. As Latin@/x literary scholar Frederick L. Aldama states, poetry may serve to further political gains; however, by itself, poetry nor other forms of creative expression do not constitute political action. Of course, it is important to note a prominent counterexample: Diana Ferrus's poem "I've Come to Take You Home" (1978) inspired the French legislature in March of 2002 to drop the French claim to the remains of Sarah Baartman, more popularly known as the Hottentot Venus. For an analysis of Baartman's cultural circulation written against Baartman's biography see Clifton Crais and Pamela Scully's *Sara Baartman and the Hottentot Venus: A Ghost Story and a Biography* (2010).
11. The temporal paradigm of the conversion narrative establishes that the poetic "I" believes she or he has already converted at the time of writing.
12. Scholarship on Augustine generally elides his fervor for Sophia, omitting her prominence in many traditions throughout the centuries.
13. I cite Romans 8:29–30: "For whom he did foreknow, he also did predestinate to be conformed to the image of his Son, that he might be the firstborn among many brethren. Moreover, whom he did predestinate, them he also called: and whom he called, them he also justified: and whom he justified, them he also glorified" (King George Edition). These verses provide the theological premise inspiring the structure of the conversion narrative. There is little agreement on the number of stages of the *ordo salutis* or their sequencing across Christian faiths. Most traditions emphasize detailing of sins, shame, contrition, and longing for deliverance; the arrival of the sign; and evidence of a converted life. For many, linear chronology is less important than the process of eventually completing each stage. Some postulants report less than obvious signs of their salvation and solicit the counsel of clergymen. All biblical verses cited from New International Version Bible (Colorado Springs, CO: Biblica, [1973] 2011).
14. The influence of the *ordo salutis* is quite palpable in the steps of Twelve-Step programs for addiction. I summarize the steps as follows: step one, admitting one's life has become unmanageable; step two, coming to believe a power greater than oneself can restore one to sanity; step three, deciding to turn one's will over to a higher power; step 4, taking a personal inventory of one's defects and behavior; step 5, admitting to a higher power, oneself, and another person the exact nature of one's wrongs; steps 6 and 7, becoming willing to then ask higher power to remove these shortcomings; steps 8–10 do not have such a strong tie to the *ordo salutis*, but this practice reappears in the form of steps 11 and 12 where, now rehabilitated, one continues to seek connection to higher power via prayer and meditation and then carries the message of recovery to others.
15. See https://www.c-span.org/video/?c4504260/clinton-prayer-breakfast.
16. Here, I build on Benedict Anderson's notion of imagined community and incorporate ethnicity and race as what is imagined as outside of hegemonic national community ([1983] 2006).
17. Clinton was officially impeached, but his removal from office was voted down. Not coincidentally, in Monica Lewinsky's March 2015 TED talk, Lewinsky focuses her remarks on the damning effect of *shame* caused by the scandal that led her at one point to the brink of suicide (https://www.ted.com/talks/monica_lewinsky_the_price_of_shame).

18. Specifically, the article details the use of the internet as the primary vehicle used for publicly shaming people soliciting prostitution, a medium that hardly lends itself to public repentance, let alone deeper levels of spiritual or moral conversion.
19. Michael Dowdy's "broken compass" (2013) is a useful metaphor to explore the consequences of neoliberalism on Latin@/xs in poetic expression that could be extended to consider the broken *social* compass of intersectional racializing shame in Montoya's poetry. Dowdy explores how Latin@/x poetics examine the production of place, space, and nature against a global neoliberal political project that looks to "restore capitalist class power by any means necessary" (ix), both within its borders and beyond. Dowdy's metaphor of broken souths is where "Latino and Latin American gazes" (vii) meet in multiple dimensions of residence, commerce, and orchestrated cultural consolidation. I add hegemony effectively sees, hears, and smells through aims of racialization and racism, such that both terms *Latino* and *Latin American* function almost indiscriminately inscribing both groups as rejected "Mexicans."
20. Montoya introduces the adjective *brown* to describe an/othered reality of Americanness in his Master's Thesis titled *in brown america*, highlighting this particular poem in *Ice Worker*.

BIBLIOGRAPHY

Abbas, Niran. *Mapping Michel Serres*. Ann Arbor: University Press of Michigan, 2005.

Abraham, Rebecca. "The Impact of Emotional Dissonance on Organizational Commitment and Intention to Turnover." *The Journal of Psychology: Interdisciplinary and Applied*, 133, no. 4 (1999): 441–55. Doi: 10.1080/00223989909599754.

Acosta, Oscar "Zeta." *The Autobiography of a Brown Buffalo*. Introduction by Hunter S. Thompson. Afterword by Marco Acosta. San Francisco: Straight Arrow Books, [1972] 1989.

Ahmed, Sara. *The Cultural Politics of Emotion*. New York: Routledge, 2004.

Aho, Tanja, Liat Ben-Moshe, and Leon Hilton. "Mad Futures: Affect/Theory/Violence." *American Quarterly* 69, no. 2 (2017): 291–302. Doi: 10.1353/aq.2017.0023.

Alarcón, Norma. "The Theoretical Subject(s) of *This Bridge Called My Back* and Anglo-American Feminism." In *Making Face, Making Soul/Haciendo Caras: Creative and Critical Perspectives by Feminists of Color*, edited by Gloria Anzaldúa, 356–59. San Francisco: Aunt Lute Books, 1990.

Alcoff, Linda Martín. *The Future of Whiteness*. Cambridge, UK: Polity, 2015.

Aldama, Frederick Luis. *Postethnic Narrative Criticism: Magicorealism in Oscar 'Zeta' Acosta, Ana Castillo, Julie Dash, Hanif Kureishi, and Salman Rushdie*. Austin: University of Texas Press, 2003.

———, ed. *Toward a Cognitive Theory of Narrative Acts*. Austin: University of Texas Press, 2010.

Alves, Rubem. *The Poet, the Warrior, the Prophet*. London: SCM Press, 2002.

American Heart Association. "Hispanics and Heart Disease, Strokes." April 18, 2015. https://www.heart.org/idc/groups/heart-public/@wcm/@sop/@smd/documents/downloadable/ucm_483968.pdf

Americans with Disabilities Act. "The Americans with Disabilities Act of 1990 and Revised ADA Regulations Implementing Title II and Title III." *ADA.gov*, 1990. https://www.ada.gov/2010_regs.htm

Anderson, Benedict. *Imagined Communities: Reflections on the Origin and Spread of Nationalism*. London: Verso, [1983] 2006.

Andrews, James, ed. *Rhetoric, Religion, and the Roots of Identity in British Colonial America*. Vol. 1, *A Rhetorical History of the United States*. East Lansing: Michigan State University Press, 2007.

Anthanasius. *The Incarnation of the Word of God*. Translated and annotated by T. Herbert Bindley. 2nd ed. London: The Religious Tract Society, 1903.

Anzaldúa, Gloria. *Borderlands / La frontera: The New Mestiza*. San Francisco: Aunt Lute Press, 1987.

Aparicio, Frances R., and Susana Chávez-Silverman. *Tropicalizations: Transcultural Representations of Latinidad*. Hanover, NH: Dartmouth College, University Press of New England, 1997.

Arai, Mahmood, and Peter Skogman Thoursie. "Renouncing Personal Names: An Empirical Examination of Surname Change and Earnings." *Journal of Labor Economics* 27, no. 1 (2009): 127–47. Doi: 10.1086/593964.

Avenanti, Alessio, Angela Sirigu, and Salvatore Aglioti. "Racial Bias Reduces Empathic Sensorimotor Resonance with Other-Race Pain." *Current Biology* 20, no. 11 (2010): 2018–22. Doi: 10.1016/j.cub.2010.03.071.

Bailey, Richard A. *Race and Redemption in Puritan New England*. New York: Oxford University Press, 2011.

Bal, P. Matthijs, and Martijn Veltkamp. "How Does Fiction Reading Influence Empathy? An Experimental Investigation on the Role of Emotional Transportation." *PLOS* 1, no. 8 (2013): 1–12.

Barton, Robert, and Barbara Sellers-Young. *Movement Onstage and Off*. New York: Routledge, 2017.

Basu, Moni, "The Invisible World of Domestic Work: Report Documents Abuses." *CNN*, September 29, 2013. http://inamerica.blogs.cnn.com/2012/11/27/the-invisible-world-of-domestic-work-report-documents-abuses/

Bazar, Kimberly, Patrick Lee, and A. Joon Yun. "An 'Eye' in the Gut: The Appendix as a Sentinel Sensory Organ of the Immune Intelligence Network." *Medical Hypotheses* 63, no. 4 (2004): 752–58. Doi: 10.1016/j.mehy.2004.04.008.

Bell, Derrick. *Faces at the Bottom of the Well: The Permanence of Racism*. New York: Basic Books, [1992] 2008.

Benedict, Ruth. *The Chrysanthemum and the Sword: Patterns of Japanese Culture*. Rutland, VT: Charles E. Tuttle Co., [1946] 1954.

Bercovitch, Sacvan. *The Puritan Origins of the American Self*. New Haven, CT: Yale University Press, [1975] 2011.

Bertrand, Marianne, and Sendhil Mullainathan. "Are Emily and Greg More Employable Than Lakisha And Jamal? A Field Experiment on Labor Market Discrimination." *American Economic Review* 94 (2004): 991–1013.

Bewes, Timothy. *The Event of Postcolonial Shame*. Princeton, NJ: Princeton University Press, 2011.

Blair, Rhonda. *The Actor, Image, and Action: Acting and Cognitive Neuroscience*. New York: Routledge Press. 2008.

Blair, Rhonda, and Amy Cook, eds. *Theatre, Performance and Cognition: Languages, Bodies and Ecologies*. London: Bloomsbury Methuen Drama, 2016.

Bonilla-Silva, Eduardo. *Racism without Racists: Color-Blind Racism and the Persistence of Racial Inequality in America*. 4th ed. New York: Rowman and Littlefield, [2006] 2013.

Bosman, Manie. "The Neuroscience of Conditioned Racism." *Strategic Leaders*. August 29, 2012. https://strategicleaders.wordpress.com/2012/08/29/the-neuroscience-of-conditioned-racism/

Bost, Suzanne. *Encarnación: Illness and Body Politics in Chicana Feminist Literature*. Bronx, NY: Fordham University Press, 2010.

———. "Illness." In *The Routledge Companion to Latino/a Literature*, edited by Suzanne Bost and Frances R. Aparicio, 84–94. New York: Routledge, 2013.

Brennan, Teresa. *Transmission of Affect*. Ithaca, NY: Cornell University Press, 2004.

Brown, Katherine B. "Freemanship in Puritan Massachusetts." *American Historical Review* 59, no. 4 (1954): 865–83.

Bruce-Novoa, Juan. "Fear and Loathing on the Buffalo Trail." *Multi-Ethnic Literature of the United States* 6, no. 4 (1979): 39–50.

Brown, Adam, and Danielle Christmas. "When the Holocaust Comes to Harlem: Traumatic Memory, Race, and Economic Injustice in American Holocaust Film." In *Mapping Generations of Traumatic Memory in American Narratives*, edited by Dana Mihăilescu, Roxana Oltean, and Mihaela Precup. Newcastle upon Tyne: Cambridge Scholars Publishing, 2014.

Bryant-Davis, Thelma, and Carlota Ocampo. "Racist Incident-Based Trauma." *The Counseling Psychologist* 33, no. 4 (2005): 479–500. Doi: 10.1177/0011000005276465.

Bullington, Jennifer. *The Expression of the Psychosomatic Body from a Phenomenological Perspective*. New York: Springer, 2013.

Bultmann, Rudolf. *Theology of the New Testament*. Translated by Kendrick Grobel. Waco, TX: Baylor University Press, [1951] 2007.

Bush, George W. "Remarks Accepting the Presidential Nomination at the National Convention in New York City." *The American Presidency Project*. University of California, Santa Barbara. September 2, 2004. http://www.presidency.ucsb.edu/ws/index.php?pid=72727&.

Calderón, Héctor. *Narratives of Greater Mexico: Essays on Chicano Literary History, Genre, and Borders*. Austin: University of Texas Press, 2004.

Caldwell, Maggie. "Invisible Women: The Real History of Domestic Workers in America." *Mother Jones*, February 7, 2013. www.motherjones.com/politics/2013/02/timeline-domestic-workers-invisible-history-america.

Caldwell, Patricia. *The Puritan Conversion Narrative: The Beginnings of American Expression*. Cambridge, UK: Cambridge University Press, [1983] 1985.

Candelario, Ginetta. *Black Behind the Ears: Dominican Identity from Museums to Beauty Shops*. Durham, NC: Duke University Press, 2007.

Carlin-Metz, Elizabeth. "The Neuroscience of Performance Pedagogy." In *Embodied Consciousness: Performance Technologies*, edited by Jade Rosina McCutcheon and Barbara Sellers-Young, 31–45. London: Palgrave, 2013.

Carpenter, John B. "New England's Puritan Century: Three Generations of Continuity in the City upon a Hill." *Fides Et Historia* 30, no. 1 (2003): 41.

Carrasco, Davíd, and Eduardo Moctezuma. *Moctezuma's Mexico: Visions of the Aztec World*. Rev. ed. Boulder: University Press of Colorado, 2003.

Carrasquillo, Marci L. "Oscar 'Zeta' Acosta American Odyssey." *MELUS* 35, no.1 (2010): 77–97.

Carter, Robert T. "Racism and Psychological and Emotional Injury: Recognizing and Assessing Race-Based Traumatic Stress." *The Counseling Psychologist* 35, no. 1 (2007): 13–105. Doi: 10.1177/0011000006292033.

Cervantes, Lorna Dee. *Emplumada*. Pittsburgh, PA: University of Pittsburgh Press, 1981.

Chacón, Daniel. *Pákatelas—In the Grove: An Homage to Andrés Montoya*. Edited by Daniel Chacón, no. 16. Fresno, CA: 2008.

Chiu, Monica. *Filthy Fictions: Asian American Literature by Women*. Walnut Creek, CA: Alta Mira Press, 2004.

Chrousos, George, and Phillip Gold. "The Concepts of Stress and Stress System Disorders: Overview of Physical and Behavioral Homeostasis." *JAMA* 267, no. 9 (1992): 1244–52. Doi: 10.1001/jama.1992.03480090092034.

Classen, Constance, David Howes, and Anthony Synnott. *Aroma: The Cultural History of Smell*. 1st ed. New York: Routledge, 1994.

Clinton, William. "Bill Clinton Admits to Having Inappropriate Relationship with Monica Lewinsky." Filmed September 1998. YouTube video, 00:01:17, posted November 2010. https://www.youtube.com/watch?v=kPxwKS12TXE).

Coates, Te-Nahisi. *Between the World and Me*. New York: Spiegel and Grau, 2015.

Cobas, José A., Jorge Duany, and Joe R. Feagin, eds. *How the United States Racializes Latinos: White Hegemony and Its Consequences*. Boulder, CO: Paradigm Publishers, 2009.

Cohen, Charles Lloyd. *God's Caress: The Psychology of Puritan Religious Experience*. Oxford, UK: Oxford University Press, 1986.

Como, David R. *Blown by the Spirit: Puritanism and the Emergence of an Antinomian Underground in Pre-Civil-War England*. Palo Alto, CA: Stanford University Press, 2004.

Conger, John. "The Body of Shame: Character and Play." *Bioenergetic Analysis* 12, no. 1 (2001): 71–85.

Connor, Steven. *The Book of Skin*. Ithaca, NY: Cornell University Press, 2004.

———. "Michel Serres' *Five Senses*." In *Empire of Senses: The Sensual Culture Reader*, edited by David Howes, 318–34. Oxford, UK: Berg, 2005.

———. *Beyond Words: Sobs, Hums, Stutters and Other Vocalizations*. London: Reaktion Books, 2014.

Cosmides, Leda, John Tooby, and Robert Kurzban. "Can Race be Erased? Coalitional Computation and Social Categorization." In *Proceedings of the National Academy of Sciences*, 15387–92. Washington, DC: National Academy of Science, 2001. Doi: 10.1073/pnas.251541498.

———. "Perceptions of Race." *Trends in Cognitive Sciences* 7, no. 4 (2003): 173–79. Doi: 10.1016/S1364-6613(03)00057-.

Crais, Clifton, and Pamela Scully. *Sara Baartman and the Hottentot Venus: A Ghost Story and a Biography*. Princeton, NJ: Princeton University Press, 2010.

Crenshaw, Kimberlé. *On Intersectionality: The Essential Writings of Kimberlé Crenshaw*. Jackson, TN: Perseus Distribution Services, 2012.

Cvetkovich, Ann. *An Archive of Feelings: Trauma, Sexuality, and Lesbian Public Cultures*. Durham, NC: Duke University Press, 2003.

Damasio, Antonio. *Self Comes to Mind: Constructing the Conscious Brain*. New York: Random House, 2010.

Daubenmire, M. Jean, and Sharon Searles. "A Dyadic Model for the Study of Convergence in Nurse-Patient Interactions." In *Interaction Rhythms: Periodicity in Communicative Behavior*, edited by Martha Davis, 299–318. New York: Human Sciences Press, 1982.

Dávila, Alberto E., Alok K. Bohara, and Rogeli Saenzi. "Accent Penalties and the Earnings of Mexican Americans." *Social Science Quarterly* 74, no. 4 (1993): 902–16.

De Freitas, Lima, Edgar Morin, and Basarab Nicolescu. "Charter of Transdisciplinarity." *The First World Congress of Transdisciplinarity*. Adopted by participants in the Convento da Arrábida, Portugal, November 2–6, 1994. http://basarab-nicolescu.fr/chart.php

Deleuze, Gilles. *Essays Critical and Clinical*. Translated by Daniel W. Smith and Michael A. Greco. Minneapolis: University of Minnesota Press, 1997.

Delgado, Richard, and Jean Stefancic. "Critical Race Theory: An Annotated Bibliography." *Virginia Law Review* 79 (1993): 461–516.

———. *Understanding Words that Wound*. Boulder, CO: Westview Press, 2004.

———. *The Latino/a Condition: A Critical Reader*. 2nd ed. New York: New York University Press, 2011.

Del Valle, Sandra. *Language Rights and the Law in the United States: Finding Our Voice*. Bristol, UK: Multilingual Matters, 2003.

Deonna, Julien A., Raffaele Rodogno, and Fabrice Teroni. *In Defense of Shame: The Faces of Emotion*. Oxford: Oxford University Press, 2012.

Derwing, Tracey M., and Murray J. Munro. *Pronunciation Fundamentals: Evidence-based Perspectives for L2 Teaching and Research*. Amsterdam: John Benjamins, 2015.

Désy, Marie-Christine, and Hugo Théoret. "Modulation of Motor Cortex Excitability by Physical Similarity with an Observed Hand Action." *PLoS One* 10, no. e971 (2007): 1–6. Doi: 10.1371/journal.pone.0000971.

Diaz-Strong, Daysi, Maria Luna-Duarte, Cristina Gómez, and Erica Meiners. "Too Close to the Work/We've Got Nothing Right Now." In *Humanizing Research: Decolonizing Qualitative Inquiry with Youth and Communities*, edited by Django Paris and Maisha T. Winn, 3–18. Los Angeles: Sage Publishers, 2014.

Doleac, Jennifer L., and Luke C. D. Stein. "The Visible Hand: Race and Online Market Outcomes." *The Economic Journal* 123, no. 11, (2013): 1–18.

Dollard, John. *Caste and Class in a Southern Town*. Madison: University of Wisconsin Press, [1937] 1998.

Dorsey, Peter A. *Sacred Estrangement: The Rhetoric of Conversion in Modern American Autobiography*. University Park: Pennsylvania State University Press, 1993.

Dowdy, Michael. *Broken Souths: Latina/o Poetic Responses to Neoliberalism and Globalization*. Tucson: Arizona University Press, 2013.

Drobnick, Jim. Preface to *The Smell Culture Reader*, edited by Jim Drobnick, 13–17. New York: Berg, 2006.

Earle, Sarah. "Disability, Facilitated Sex and the Role of the Nurse." *Journal of Advanced Nursing* 36, no. 3 (2001): 433–40. Doi: 10.1046/j.1365–2648.2001.01991.x.

Elam Jr., Henry J. "We Wear the Mask: Performance, Social Dramas, and Race." *Doing Race: 21 Essays for the 21st Century*, edited by Hazel Rose Markus and Paula M. L. Moya, 545–61. New York: W. W. Norton, 2010.

Elam, Keir. *The Semiotics of Theatre and Drama*. Hove, UK: Psychology Press, [1980] 2002.

Eley, Thalia, and Robert Plomin. "Genetic Analysis of Emotionality." *Current Opinion in Neurobiology* 7, no. 2 (1997): 279–84. Doi: 10.1016/S0959-4388(97)80017-7.

Elias, Norbert. *The Civilizing Process: Sociogenic and Psychogenic Associations*. Oxford: Blackwell, [1939, 1994] 2000.

Elliott, Edward. *Power and the Pulpit in Puritan New England*. Princeton, NJ: Princeton University Press, [1975] 2015.

Encyclopedia Britannica. 2017. "Galen of Pergamum: Greek Physician." http://www.britannica.com/biography/Galen-of-Pergamum

Enders, Giulia. *Gut: The Inside Story of Our Body's Most Under-Rated Organ*. London: Scribe, 2015.

Evans, Erin. *The Books of Jeu and the Pistis Sophia as Handbooks to Eternity: Exploring the Gnostic Mysteries of the Ineffable*. Netherlands: Brill Publishers, 2015.

Fabian, Ann. *The Skull Collectors: Race, Science, and America's Unburied Dead*. Chicago: University of Chicago Press, 2010.

Facio, Elisa, and Irene Lara. *Fleshing the Spirit: Spirituality and Activism in Chicana, Latina, and Indigenous Women's Lives*. Tucson: University of Arizona Press, 2014.

Fanon, Franz. *Black Skin, White Masks*. New York: Grove Press, [1952] 2008.

Feagin, Joe R., and Karyn D. McKinney. *The Many Costs of Racism*. Lanham, MD: Rowman & Littlefield Publishers, Inc., 2003.

Fetta, Stephanie. "Disability, Domestic Workers, and Disappearance in Octavio Solís's *Lydia*." *Chicana/Latina Studies Journal* 14, no. 2 (Spring 2015).

———. "A Bad Attitude and a Bad Stomach: The Soma in Oscar 'Zeta' Acosta's *The Autobiography of a Brown Buffalo*." *Transmodernity: Journal of Peripheral Cultural Production of the Luso-Hispanic World* 6, no.1 (2016): 88–109.

Fishburn, Katherine. *The Problem of Embodiment in Early African American Narrative*. Westport, CT: Greenwood Press, 1997.

Flores, Juan, and Renato Rosaldo, eds. *A Companion to Latina/o Studies*. Hoboken, NJ: Wiley-Blackwell, 2007.

Forth, Christopher E., and Ana Carden-Coyne. *Culture of the Abdomen: Diet, Digestion, and Fat in the Modern World*. New York: Palgrave, 2005.

Foucault, Michel. *Madness and Civilization: A History of Insanity in the Age of Reason*. New York: Vintage Books, [1964] 1988.

———. *The Archeology of Knowledge*. New York: Vintage Books, [1972] 2010.

Freud, Sigmund. *Three Essays on the Theory of Sexuality*. Rev. ed. New York: Basic Books, [1905] 2000.

Gallese, Vittorio, Christian Keysers, and Giacomo Rizzolatti. "A Unifying View of the Basis of Social Cognition." *Trends in Cognitive Science* 8, no. 9 (2004): 396–403.

Ganzel, Barbara, Jason Rarick, and Pamela Morris. "Stress and Emotion: Embodied, in Context, and Across the Lifespan." In *Handbook of Emotions*, edited by Lisa Feldman Barrett, Michael Lewis, and Jeannette M. Haviland-Jones, 709–16. New York: The Guilford Press, 2016.

García, Alma M. "Maids No More: The Transformation of Domestic Work." *Frontiers: A Journal of Women Studies* 14, no. 3 (1994): 171–80. Doi: 10.2307/3346692.

———. *Gendered Transitions: Mexican Experiences of Immigration*. Berkeley: University of California Press, 1994.

Garfinkel, Harold. "Conditions of Successful Degradation Ceremonies." *American Journal of Sociology* 61, no. 5 (1956): 420–24. Doi: 10.1086/221800.

Garland-Thomson, Rosemarie. *Extraordinary Bodies: Figuring Physical Disability in American Culture and Literature*. New York: Columbia University Press, [1997] 2017.

Gaskell, G. A. "Nephesh." In *A Dictionary of the Sacred Language of All Scriptures and Myths*, 529. New York: Routledge Press, [1923] 2015.

Gilmore, Ruth Wilson. *Golden Gulag: Prisons, Surplus, Crisis, and Opposition in Globalizing California*. Berkeley: University of California Press, 2007.

Gilroy, Paul. "Race Ends Here." In T*he Body: A Reader*. Edited and introduced by Mariam Fraser and Monica Greco. New York: Routledge, 2005.

Goffman, Erving. *Stigma: Notes on the Management of Spoiled Identity*. Upper Saddle River, NJ: Prentice-Hall, [1963] 2009.

Goldberg, Carl. *Understanding Shame*. Northvale, NJ: Jason Aronson, 1991.

Gonzalez, Rita. "Boricua Gazing: An Interview with Frances Negrón-Muntaner." *Signs: Journal of Women in Culture and Society* 30, no. 1 (2004): 1345–60.

Gottschall, Jonathan. *The Storytelling Animal: How Stories Make Us Human*. Boston and New York: Houghton, Mifflin, Harcourt, 2012.

Gracia, Jorge J. E. *Race or Ethnicity? On Black and Latino Identity*. Ithaca, NY: Cornell University Press, 2007.

Gregg, Melissa, and Gregory Seigworth, eds. *The Affect Theory Reader*. Raleigh, NC: Duke University Press, 2010.

Gribben, Crawford. *The Puritan Millennium: Literature and Theology, 1550–1682*. Rev. ed. Eugene, OR: Wipf and Stock, 2008.

Grosz, Elizabeth. *Volatile Bodies: Toward a Corporeal Feminism*. Bloomington: Indiana University Press, 1994.

Guajardo, Paul. *Chicano Controversy: Oscar Acosta and Richard Rodriguez*. Bern, Switzerland: Peter Lang, 2002.

Gutsell, Jennifer, and Michael Inzlicht. "Empathy Constrained: Prejudice Predicts Reduced Mental Simulation of Actions During Observation of Outgroups." *Journal of Experimental Social Psychology* 46, no. 5 (2010): 841–45. Doi: 10.1016/j.jesp.2010.03.011.

Hage. Ghassan, ed. *Waiting*. Melbourne: Melbourne Academic Publishing, 2009.

Halperin, Laura. *Intersections of Harm: Narratives of Latina Deviance and Defiance*. American Literatures Initiative. New Brunswick, NJ: Rutgers University Press, 2015.

Hames-García, Michael. "Dr. Gonzo's Carnival: The Testimonial Satires of Oscar Zeta Acosta, Chicano Lawyer." *American Literature* 72, no. 3 (2000): 463–93.

Harcup, Tony. *A Dictionary of Journalism*. Oxford: Oxford University Press, 2014.

Haring, Keith. *Keith Haring Journals*. New York: Penguin Classics, 2010.

Harris, Joel Chandler. *Uncle Remus, His Song and Sayings: The Folklore of the Old Plantation*. North Charleston, SC: BookSurge Classics, [1881] 2002.

———. *Uncle Remus: His Songs, His Saying.* Introduction by Robert Hemenway, 7–32. New York: Penguin, [1880] 1986.

Hart, Allen, J., Paul J. Whalen, Lisa M. Shin, Sean C. McInerney, Hakan Fischer, and Scott L. Rauch. "Differential Response in the Human Amygdala to Racial Outgroup versus Ingroup Face Stimuli." *Neuroreport* 11, no. 11 (2000): 2351–55.

Hartl, Emil M., Edward P. Monnelly, Roland D. Elderkin. *Physique and Delinquent Behavior (A Thirty-Year Follow-Up of William H. Sheldon's Varieties of Delinquent Youth).* New York: Academic Press, 1982.

Haslyn, E. R. Hunte, Katherine King, Margaret Hicken, Hedwig Lee, and Tene T. Lewis. "Interpersonal Discrimination and Depressive Symptomatology: Examination of Several Personality-related Characteristics as Potential Confounders in a Racial/Ethnic Heterogeneous Adult Sample." *BMC Public Health* 13, no. 1084 (2013): 1–10.

Haven, Kendall F. *Story Proof: The Science Behind the Startling Power of Story.* Westport, CT: Libraries Unlimited, 2007.

Hawthorne, Nathaniel. *The Scarlet Letter.* Mineola, NY: Dover Publications, [1850] 2009.

Heimart, Alan, and Andrew Delbanco. *Puritans in America: A Narrative Anthology.* Cambridge, MA: Harvard University Press, [1985] 2001.

Helgadottir, Gerardo. "Racist Seattle Cop Beating a Mexican!!!!!" YouTube video, 00:01:03. Posted May 2010. https://www.youtube.com/watch?v=VUBvtdIpKXg

Hill, Susan. *Eating to Excess: The Meaning of Gluttony and the Fat Body in the Ancient World.* Santa Barbara, CA: Praeger, 2011.

Hogan, Patrick Colm. "The Psychology of Colonialism and Postcolonialism: Cognitive Approaches to Identity and Empathy." In *The Oxford Handbook of Cognitive Literary Studies,* edited by Lisa Sunshine, 329–46. New York: Oxford University Press, 2015.

Hondagneu-Sotelo, Pierrette. *Doméstica: Immigrant Workers Cleaning and Caring in the Shadows of Affluence.* Berkeley: University of California Press, [2001] 2007.

hooks, bell. *Black Looks: Race and Representation.* Boston: South End, 1992.

Houck, Harry. "Sandra Bland was 'Arrogant from the Beginning.'" Filmed July 10, 2105, posted July 22, 2105. https://youtube/cCYfQIgfCQw

Howes, David, ed. *Empire of the Senses: The Sensual Culture Reader.* Oxford: Berg, 2005.

Howson, Alexandra. *The Body in Society: An Introduction.* 2nd ed. Cambridge, UK: Polity Press, 2013.

Hugenberg, Kurt, and Galen Bodenhausen. "Facing Prejudice: Implicit Prejudice and the Perception of Facial Threat." *Psychological Science* 14, no. 6 (2003) 640–43. Doi:10.1046/j.0956-7976.2003.psci_1478.x.

Hunte, Haslyn E. R., Kathryn King, Margaret Hicken, Hedwig Lee, and Tene T. Lewis. "Interpersonal Discrimination and Depressive Symptomatology: Examination of Several Personality-related Characteristics as Potential Confounders in a Racial/Ethnic Heterogeneous Adult Sample." *BMC Public Health* 13, no. 1084 (2013): 1–7.

Hurtado, Aida. *The Color of Privilege: Three Blasphemies on Race and Feminism.* Ann Arbor: University of Michigan Press, 1996.

Huston, Hollis. *The Actor's Instrument Body, Theory, Stage.* Ann Arbor: University of Michigan Press, 1992.

Hyvärinen, Matti, Lars-Christer Hydén, Marja Saarenheimo, and Maria Tamboukou, eds. *Beyond Narrative Coherence.* Amsterdam: John Benjamins, 2010.

Ioanide, Paula. *The Emotional Politics of Racism: How Feelings Trump Facts in an Era of Color-blindness*. Stanford, CA: Stanford University Press, 2015.

Iser, Wolfgang. *The Implied Reader: Patterns of Communication in Prose Fiction from Bunyan to Beckett*. Baltimore, MD: Johns Hopkins University Press, 1974.

Ito, Tiffany A., and Bruce D. Bartholow. "The Neural Correlates of Race." *Trends in Cognitive Science* 13, no.12 (2009): 524–31. Doi: 10.1016/j.tics.2009.10.002.

Jacoby, Mario. *Shame and the Origins of Self-Esteem: A Jungian Approach*. New York: Routledge, [1994] 2015.

Jaggar, Alison M. "Love and Knowledge: Emotion in Feminist Epistemology." *Inquiry* 32, no. 2 (1989): 151–76.

Jennett, Bryan. *The Vegetative State: Medical Facts, Ethical and Legal Dilemmas*. Cambridge, UK: Cambridge University Press, 2003.

Jiménez Román, Miriam. "Looking at the Middle Ground: Racial Mixing as Panacea?" In *A Companion to Latina/o Studies*, edited by Juan Flores and Renato Rosaldo, 225–36. Malden, MA: Blackwell, 2007.

Jiménez Román, Miriam, and Juan Flores, eds. *The Afro-Latin@ Reader: History and Culture in the United States*. Durham, NC: Duke University Press, 2010.

Johns Hopkins Medicine. "Healthy Body. The Brain-Gut Connection." *Johns Hopkins Medicine, Healthy Body*. Accessed February 10, 2015. https://www.hopkinsmedicine.org/health/healthy_aging/healthy_body/the-brain-gut-connection

Johnson, Erica L., and Patricia Moran. *The Female Face of Shame*. Bloomington: Indiana University Press, 2013.

Kalin, Rudolf, and Donald S. Rayko. "Discrimination in Evaluative Judgments Against Foreign-Accented Job Candidates." *Psychological Reports* 43, no. 3 (1978): 1203–9.

Kang, Esther. "For L. A.'s Illegal Street Vendors, Selling Food and Avoiding Police is a Full-Time Job." *Neon Tommy: Annenberg Digital* News. Updated October 26, 2011b. Accessed November 2013. http://www.neontommy.com/news/2011/10/las-illegal-street-vendors-selling-food-and-avoiding-cops-full-time-job

———. "L. A. County Health Regulations Don't Deter Illegal Street Vendors." *Neon Tommy: Annenberg Digital News*. Updated October 26, 2011a. Accessed November 2013. http://www.neontommy.com/news/2011/10/la-county-health-department-regulations-dont-deter-illegal-street-vendors

Kaufman, Gershen. *The Psychology of Shame: Theory and Treatment of Shame-Based Syndromes*. 2nd ed. New York: Springer, [1989] 1996.

Kaufman, Gershen, and Lev Raphael. *Dynamics of Power: Fighting Shame and Building Self-Esteem*. Rochester, NY: Schenkman Books, [1983] 1991.

Kempley, Rita. "Too Too Divine: Movies' 'Magic Negro' Saves the Day, but at the Cost of His Soul." *Washington Post*, June 7, 2000. http://www.washingtonpost.com/wp-dyn/articles/A26850-2003Jun6.html

Kennedy, John F. "The President-Elect: City Upon a Hill." Time, January 20, 1961. ISSN 0040–781X.

Khimm, Suzy. "The Shame Game: The Internet Has Given Us a New Public Square. Now Law Enforcement Is Trying to Harness its Power." *New Republic*. March 9, 2016. https://newrepublic.com/article/130803/shame-game

Kidd, David Comer, and Emanuele Castano. "Reading Literary Fiction Improves Theory of Mind." *Science* 342, no. 6156 (2013): 377–80. Doi: 10.1126/science.1239918.

Knowlton, Brian, and International Herald Tribune. "He Says in Apology That Includes Lewinsky: Clinton Vows He Will Stay and Fight." *The New York Times*. September 12, 1998. http://www.nytimes.com/1998/09/12/news/i-sinned-he-says-in-apology-that-includes-lewinsky-clinton-vows-he-will.html

Koss, Juliet. "Playing Politics with Estranged and Empathetic Audiences: Bertolt Brecht and Georg Fuchs." *The South Atlantic Quarterly* 96, no. 4 (1997): 809–20.

Krieger, Nancy. "Embodiment: A Conceptual Glossary for Epidemiology." *Journal of Epidemiology and Community Health* 59, no. 5 (2005): 350–55.

Ladd, Charlotte, Rebecca Huot, K. V. Thrivikraman, Charles Nemeroff, Michael Meaney, and Paul M. Plotsky. "Long-Term Behavioral and Neuroendocrine Adaptations to Adverse Early Experience." In *Progress in Brain Research*, edited by E. A. Mayer and C. B. Saper, 81–103. Amsterdam: Elsevier, 2000. Doi: 10.1016/S0079-6123(08)62132-9.

La Fountain-Stokes, Lawrence. "Gay Shame, Latina- and Latino-Style: A Critique of White Queer Performativity." In *Gay Latino Studies: A Critical Reader*, edited by Michael Hames-García and Ernesto Javier Martínez, 55–80. Durham, NC: Duke University Press, 2011.

Landrine, Hope, Elizabeth Klonoff, Robert Carter, and Jessica Forsyth. "Race-Based Traumatic Stress." In *Encyclopedia of Trauma: An Interdisciplinary Guide*, edited by Charles R. Figley. Los Angeles: Sage, 2012.

Leavy, Patricia. *Essentials of Transdisciplinary Research: Using Problem-Centered Methodologies*. New York: Routledge, 2011.

LeDoux, Joseph E. "Coming to Terms with Fear." *Proceedings of the National Academy of Sciences* 111, no. 8 (February 2014): 2871–78. Doi: 10.1073/pnas.1400335111.

Lewis, Helen Block. *Shame and Guilt in Neurosis*. New York: International Universities Press, 1971.

———. "Shame: The 'Sleeper' in Psychopathology." In *The Role of Shame in Symptom Formation*, edited by Helen Block Lewis, 1–28. Hillsdale, NJ: Erlbaum, 1987a.

———. "Shame and the Narcissistic Personality." In *The Many Faces of Shame*, edited by Donald Nathanson, 93–132. New York: Guilford Press, 1987b.

———. "The Role of Shame in Depression Over the Lifespan." In *The Role of Shame in Symptom Formation*, edited by Helen Block Lewis, 29–50. Hillsdale, NJ: Erlbaum, 1987c.

Lewis, Michael. *Shame: The Exposed Self*. New York: The Free Press, [1992] 1995.

Leys, Ruth. *Trauma: A Genealogy*. Chicago: University of Chicago Press, 2000.

Lima, Lázaro. *Latino Bodies: Crisis Identities in American and Literary Cultural Memory*. New York: New York University Press, 2007.

Lion's Roar. "Strike! Rise! Dance!—bell hooks & Eve Ensler." *Lion's Roar, Buddhist Wisdom for Our Time*. Posted June 18, 2014. Accessed December 10, 2017. https://www.lionsroar.com/strike-rise-dance-bell-hooks-eve-ensler-march-2014/

Lippi-Green, Rosina. *English with an Accent: Language, Ideology and Discrimination in the United States*. New York: Routledge, [1997] 2012.

Liu, J., Z. Wang, L. Feng, J. Li, J. Tian, and K. Lee. "Neural Trade-Offs between Recognizing and Categorizing Own- and Other-Race Faces." *Cereb Cortex* 25 no. 8 (August 2015): 2191–203. Doi: 10.1093/cercor/bhu025.

López, Lenny, and Sherita Hill Golden. "A New Era in Understanding Diabetes Disparities among U.S. Latinos—All Are Not Equal." *Diabetes Care* 37, no. 8 (August 2014): 2081–83.

Lorde, Audre. *Sister Outsider: Essays and Speeches*. Berkeley, CA: Crossing Press, [1984] 2007.

Lowen, Alexander. *The Language of the Body*. New York: Grune and Stratton, [1958] 2006.

———. *The Betrayal of the Body*. Alachua, FL: Bioenergetics Press, 1967.

———. *The Voice of the Body*. Alachua, FL: Bioenergetics Press, 2005.

Luck, S. J., and M. A. Ford. "On the Role of Selective Attention in Visual Perception." In *Proceedings of the National Academy of Sciences*, 825–30. Washington, DC: National Academy of Science, 1998. PubMed ID: 9448247.

Lynd, Helen. *On Shame and Search for Identity*. Oxon: Routledge, [1958] 1999.

Mack, Arien, and Irvin Rock. *Inattentional Blindness*. Cambridge, MA: MIT Press, 1998.

Magarshack, David. *Stanislavsky: A Life*. London: Faber & Faber, Limited, [1950] 2010.

Mallett, Cassandra. "The Symbolism of Uncle Remus, Brer Rabbit, and Brer Fox in the Uncle Remus Tales." Paper presented at the *Annual Meeting for the National Association of African American Studies*, Scarborough, ME, February 11–16, 2002.

Manalansan IV, Martin F. "Immigrant Lives and the Politics of Olfaction in the Global City." In *The Smell Culture Reader*, edited by Jim Drobnick, 41–52. New York: Berg, 2006.

Mangold, Deborah L., Gary Wand, Martin A. Javors, and Jim Mintz. "Acculturation, Childhood Trauma and the Cortisol Awakening Response in Mexican American Adults." *Hormones and Behavior* 58, no. 4 (2010): 637–46.

Mar, Raymond A., Keith Oatley, and Jordan Peterson. "Exploring the Link between Reading Fiction and Empathy: Ruling Out Individual Differences and Examining Outcomes." *Communications* 34 (2009): 407–28. Doi: 10.1515/COMM.2009.025.

Margolin, Uri. "Cognitive Science, The Thinking Mind, and Literary Narrative." *Narrative Theory and the Cognitive Sciences*, edited by David Herman. Chicago: University of Chicago Press, 2003.

Martin, Michael. *The Submerged Reality: Sophiology and the Turn to a Poetic Metaphysics*. Foreword by Adrian Pabst. Kettering, OH: Angelico Press/Sophia Perennis, 2015.

———. *The Heavenly Country: An Anthology of Primary Sources, Poetry, and Critical Essays on Sophiology*. Kettering, OH: Angelico Press/Sophia Perennis, 2016.

Martinez, Jacqueline M. *Phenomenology of Chicana Experience and Identity: Communication and Transformation in Praxis*. New Critical Theory. Lanham, MD: Rowman & Littlefield Publishers, 2000.

Martín-Rodríguez, Manuel M. *Life in Search of Readers: Reading (in) Chicano/a Literature*. Albuquerque: University of New Mexico Press, 2003.

Mason, David V. "Metatheatre and Consciousness." *Embodied Consciousness: Performance Technologies*, edited by Jade Rosina McCutcheon and Barbara Sellers-Young, 209–18. London: Palgrave, 2013.

Mayer, Emeran. "The Neurobiology of Stress and Gastrointestinal Disease." *Gut* 47 (2000): 861–69. Doi: 10.1136/gut.47.6.861.

McCarroll, Sarah E. "The Historical Body Map: Cultural Pressures on Embodied Cognition." In *Theatre, Performance, and Cognition: Languages, Bodies, and Ecologies*, edited by Rhonda Blair and Amy Cook, 141–58. London and New York: Bloomsbury, 2016.

McConachie, Bruce. *Engaging Audiences: A Cognitive Approach to Spectating in the Theatre*. New York: Palgrave, 2008.

McConnell, Allen R., and Jill Leibold. "Relations among the Implicit Association Test, Discriminatory Behavior, and Explicit Measures of Racial Attitudes." *Journal of Experimental Social Psychology* 37, no. 5 (2001): 435–42. Doi: 10.1006/jesp.2000.1470.

McEwen, Bruce. "Protective and Damaging Effects of Stress Mediators." *The New England Journal of Medicine* 338, no. 1 (1998): 171–79. Doi: 10.1056/NEJM199801153380307.

McNulty, Charles. "An Oracle in a Crowded Room: Octavio Solís' 'Lydia' Insists on Exploring Every Character, Even to the Play's Detriment." *Los Angeles Times*, April 16, 2009. http://articles.latimes.com/2009/apr/16/entertainment/et-lydia16

Mehrabian, Albert. *Nonverbal Communication*. New Brunswick, NJ: Aldine Transaction, 1972.

Menchaca, Martha. *Recovering History, Constructing Race—The Indian, Black, and White Roots of Mexican Americans*. Austin: University of Texas Press, 2010.

Mendes, Wendy Berry. "Emotion and the Autonomic Nervous System." In *Handbook of Emotions*, edited by Lisa Feldman Barrett, Michael Lewis, and Jeannette M. Haviland-Jones, 166–81. 4th ed. New York: The Guilford Press, 2016.

Merleau-Ponty, Maurice. *Phenomenology of Perception*. Foreword by Taylor Carman. Translated by Donald A. Landes. New York: Routledge, [1945] 2014.

Merlin, Bella. "When Consciousness Fragments: A Personal Encounter with Stage Fright in Performance." In *Embodied Consciousness: Performance Technologies*, edited by Jade Rosina McCutcheon and Barbara Sellers-Young, 57–72. London: Palgrave, 2013.

Miles, Lynden K., Louise K. Nind, and Neil C. Macrae. "The Rhythm of Rapport: Interpersonal Synchrony and Social Perception." *Journal of Experimental Social Psychology* 45, no. 3 (2009): 585–89.

Miller, Joshua L. *Accented America: The Cultural Politics of Multilingual Modernism*. London: Oxford University Press, 2011.

Miller, Ian. *A Modern History of the Stomach: Gastric Illness, Medicine and British Society, 1800–1950*. New York: Routledge, [2011] 2016.

———. "Darwin's Disgust." In *Empire of the Senses: The Sensual Culture Reader*, edited by David Howes, 335–36. Oxford: Berg, 2005.

———. *The Anatomy of Disgust*. Cambridge, MA: Harvard University Press, [2011] 2016.

Milosz, Czeslaw. *The Art of Poetry No. 70*. By Robert Faggen. *The Paris Review*, no. 133 (Winter 1994): n.p. https://www.theparisreview.org/interviews/1721/czeslaw-milosz-the-art-of-poetry-no-70-czeslaw-milosz

Minich, Julie Avril. *Accessible Citizenships: Disability, Nation, and the Cultural Politics of Greater Mexico*. Philadelphia, PA: Temple University Press, 2013.

Minor, E. Kyle. "Solís' Poetic Writing Makes Rep's 'Lydia' a Gripping Drama." *New Haven Register News*, February 15, 2009. http://www.nhregister.com/general-news/20090215/solis-poetic-writing-makes-reps-lydia-a-gripping-drama

Montoya, Andrés. *The Ice Worker Sings and Other Poems*. Tempe, AZ: Bilingual Press, [1999] 2017.

———. *A Jury of Trees*. Edited by Daniel Chacón. Introductions by Daniel Chacón and Stephanie Fetta. Tempe, AZ: Bilingual Review Press, 2017.

Mooney, Chris, and Indre Viskontas. "The Science of Your Racist Brain: Neuroscientist David Amodio on Subconscious Racial Prejudice and Why We're Still Responsible for Our Actions." *Mother Jones*, May 9, 2014. Accessed July 13, 2016. http://www.motherjones.com/politics/2014/05/inquiring-minds-david-amodio-your-brain-on-racism/

Moraga, Cherríe. *A Xicana Codex of Changing Consciousness: Writings, 2000–2010*. Durham, NC: Duke University Press, 2011.

Morrison, Andrew P. *Shame, The Underside to Narcissism*. New York: Routledge, 1989.

Morrison, Karl Frederick. *Conversion and Text: The Cases of Augustine of Hippo, Herman-Judah, and Constantie Tsatsos*. Charlottesville: University of Virginia Press, 1992.

Morton, Samuel. *Crania Americana*. Philadelphia, PA: J. Dobson; London: Simpkin, Marshall & Co., 1839.

Mosley, Michael. "The Second Brain in Our Stomachs." *BBC News*, July 11, 2012. http://www.bbc.com/news/health-18779997

Moya, Paula M. L. *The Social Imperative: Race, Close Reading, and Contemporary Literary Criticism*. Stanford, CA: Stanford University Press, 2016.

———, and Ramón Saldívar. "Fictions of the Trans-American Imaginary." *MFS: Modern Fiction Studies* 49 no. 1 (2003): 1–18. Doi:10.1353/mfs.2003.0007.

Moyer, Alene. *Foreign Accent: The Phenomenon of Non-Native Speech*. Cambridge, UK: Cambridge University Press, 2013.

Muñoz, José Esteban. *Disidentifications: Queers of Color and the Performance of Politics*. Minneapolis: University of Minnesota Press, 1999.

———. "Feeling Brown, Feeling Down: Latina Affect, the Performativity of Race, and the Depressive Position." *Signs: Journal of Women in Culture and Society* 31, no. 3 (2006): 678–88. Doi: 10.1086/499080.

———. "'Chico, What Does It Feel Like to Be a Problem?': The Transmission of Brownness." In *A Companion to Latina/o Studies*, edited by Juan Flores and Renato Rosaldo, 441–51. Malden, MA: Blackwell, 2007.

Murray, Xyta Maya. *Locas*. New York: Grove Press, 1997.

Nathansan, Donald L. *The Many Faces of Shame*. New York: Guilford Press, 1987.

———. *Shame and Pride: Affect, Sex, and the Birth of the Self*. New York: W. W. Norton, 1994.

———. *The Psychology of Shame: Theory and Treatment of Shame-Based Syndromes*. New York: Springer, [1989] 2004.

Negrón-Mutaner, Frances. "Looking Good." In *A Companion to Latina/o Studies*, edited by Juan Flores and Renato Rosaldo, 427–40. Malden, MA: Blackwell, 2007a.

———. *None of the Above: Puerto Ricans in the Global Era, and Sovereign Acts*. New Directions in Latino American Cultures. New York: Palgrave Macmillan, 2007b.

Neuliep, James W. *Intercultural Communication: A Contextual Approach*. 6th ed. Thousand Oaks, CA: Sage, 2014.

New International Version Bible. Colorado Springs, CO: Biblica, [1973] 2011.

New Living Testament. Carol Stream, IL: Tyndale House, [1996] 2015.

Ngai, Sianne. *Ugly Feelings*. Cambridge, MA: Harvard University Press, 2005.

Nicolescu, Basarab, *Manifesto of Transdisciplinarity*. New York: State University of New York Press, 2002.

———, ed. *Transdisciplinarity: Theory and Practice*. New York: Hampton Press, 2008.

Noë, Alva. *Action in Perception*. Cambridge, MA: MIT Press, 2006.

Norton, Kevin, and Tim Olds. *Anthropometrica: A Textbook of Body Measurement for Sports and Health Courses*. Australian Sports Commission: UNSW Press, 1996.

Nutton, Vivian. *Ancient Medicine*. 2nd ed. New York: Routledge Press, [2004] 2013.

Obama, Barak. "Commencement, University of Massachusetts at Boston Commencement." *The American Presidency Project*. University of California, Santa Barbara. June 2, 2006. http://

obamaspeeches.com/074-University-of-Massachusetts-at-Boston-Commencement-Address-Obama-Speech.htm

Obasogie, Osagie. *Blinded by Sight: Seeing Race through the Eyes of the Blind*. Stanford, CA: Stanford University Press, 2013.

Okorafor, Nnedi. "Stephen King's Super-Duper Magical Negroes." *Strange Horizons*, October 25, 2004.

Oreopoulos, Philip. "Why Do Skilled Immigrants Struggle in the Labor Market? A Field Experiment with Six Thousand Resumes." NBER Working Paper No. 15036, National Bureau of Economic Research, June 2009.

Orr, Jackie. *Panic Diaries: A Genealogy of Panic Disorder*. Durham, NC: Duke University Press, 2006.

Ortega, Mariana. *In-Between: Latina Feminist Phenomenology, Multiplicity, and the Self*. Albany: SUNY Press, 2016.

Otis, Laura. "The Value of Qualitative Research for Cognitive Literary Studies." In *The Oxford Handbook of Cognitive Literary Studies*, edited by Lisa Sunshine. Oxford, UK: Oxford University Press, 2015.

Paddock, Catharine. "Not Only Does Our Gut Have Brain Cells, It Can Also Grow New Ones." *Medical News Today*, August 5, 2009. Accessed December 26, 2016. http://www.medicalnewstoday.com/articles/159914.php

Padilla, Genaro M. "The Self as Cultural Metaphor in Acosta's *Autobiography of a Brown Buffalo*." *Journal of General Education* 35, no. 4 (1984): 242–58.

Paredes, Américo. *George Washington Gómez: A Mexicotexan Novel*. Houston, TX: Arte Público, 1990.

Parra, Angelo. *Song of the Coquí*. In *Chicano/Latino Literary Prize: An Anthology of Prize-Winning Fiction, Poetry, and Prose*, edited by Stephanie Fetta, 277–84. Houston: Arte Público Press, 2008.

Pattison, Stephen. *Shame: Theory, Therapy, Theology*. Cambridge, MA: Cambridge University Press, 2000.

Pearson, Birger A., ed. *The Coptic Gnostic Library. A Complete Edition of the Nag Hammadi Codices*. Vol. 5. Leiden, Netherlands: E. J. Brill, 2000.

Phelps, Elizabeth, Kevin O'Connor, William A. Cunningham, Sumie E. Funayama, Christopher Gatenby, John Gore, and Mahzarin R. Banaji. "Performance on Indirect Measures of Race Evaluation Predicts Amygdala Activation." *Journal of Cognitive Neuroscience* 12, no. 5 (2000): 729–38. Doi: 10.1162/089892900562552.

Porter, Roy. *Blood and Guts: A Short History of Medicine*. New York: W. W. Norton, [2002] 2003.

——. *Flesh in the Age of Reason: The Modern Foundations of Body and Soul*. First American ed. New York: W. W. Norton, 2004.

Probyn, Elspeth. *Blush: Faces of Shame*. Minneapolis: University of Minnesota Press, 2005.

Pugh, S. D., M. Groth, and T. Hennig-Thurau. "Willing and Able to Fake Emotions: A Closer Examination of the Link between Emotional Dissonance and Employee Well-Being. *Journal of Applied Psychology* 96, no. 2 (2011): 377–90. Doi: 10.1037/a0021395.

Purnis, Jan. "The Stomach and Early Modern Emotion." *University of Toronto Quarterly* 79, no. 2 (2010): 800–818. Accessed January 4, 2013. http://www.utpjournals.press/doi/full/10.3138/utq.79.2.800

Rabinowitz, Peter J. "Towards a Narratology of Cognitive Flavor." In *The Oxford Handbook of Cognitive Literary Studies,* edited by Lisa Zunshine, 85–103. Oxford and New York: Oxford University Press, 2015.

Ramazani, Vaheed. *Writing in Pain: Literature, History, and the Culture of Denial.* New York: Palgrave, 2007.

Reagan, Ronald. "Election Eve Address: A Vision for America." *The American Presidency Project,* November 3, 1980. University of California, Santa Barbara. Accessed January 5, 2014. http://www.presidency.ucsb.edu/ws/?pid=85199

———. "Farewell Address to the Nation." *The American Presidency Project.* January 11, 1989. University of California, Santa Barbara. Accessed January 5, 2014. http://www.presidency.ucsb.edu/ws/index.php?pid=29650

Reinarz, Johnathan. *Past Scents: Historical Perspectives on Smell.* Champaign: University of Illinois Press, 2014.

Richeson, Jennifer A., Abigail Baird, H. L. Gordon, Todd Heatherton, Carrie Wyland, Sophie Trawalter, and Nicole Shelton. "An fMRI Investigation of the Impact of Interracial Contact on Executive Function." *Nature Neuroscience* 6, no. 12 (2003): 1323–28. Doi: 10.1038/nn1156.

Riley, Patrick. *Character and Conversion in Autobiography: Augustine, Montaigne, Descartes, Rousseau, and Sartre.* Charlottesville: University of Virginia Press, 2004.

Rivett, Sarah. *The Science of the Soul in Colonial New England.* Chapel Hill: The University of North Carolina Press, 2011.

Robinson, Douglas. *Estrangement and the Somatics of Literature: Tolstoy, Shklovsky, Brecht.* Baltimore, MD: The Johns Hopkins University Press, 2008.

Rodriguez, Richard. *Brown: The Last Discovery of America.* New York: Penguin, 2003.

Roediger, David R. *Wages of Whiteness: Race and the Making of the American Working Class.* Rev. ed. Brooklyn, NY: Verso Books, [1999] 2003.

Romero, Mary. *Maid in the U. S. A.* New York: Routledge, [1995] 2016.

Rosario, Nelly. *Song of the Water Saints.* New York: Pantheon, 2002.

Rosson, Doug. "Re-Examining Heidegger to Uncover Creativity in the Iteratively Bound Performer." In *Embodied Consciousness: Performance Technologies,* edited by Jade Rosina McCutcheon and Barbara Sellers-Young, 179–94. London: Palgrave, 2013.

Rothman, Joshua. "The Lives of Poor White People." *The New Yorker,* September 12, 2016. http://www.newyorker.com/culture/cultural-comment/the-lives-of-poor-white-people

Rousseau, Jean-Jacques. *Confessions.* Charleston, NC: Nabu Press, [1781] 2010.

The Royal College of Physicians. *The Vegetative State: Guidance on Diagnosis and Management.* London: The Royal College of Physicians, 2003.

Russell, Emily. *Reading Embodied Citizenship: Disability, Narrative, and the Body Politic.* New Brunswick, NJ: Rutgers University Press, 2011.

Saldívar, José David. *Trans-Americanity: Subaltern Modernities, Global Coloniality, and the Cultures of Greater Mexico.* Durham, NC: Duke University Press, 2012.

Saldívar, Ramón. *Chicano Narrative: Dialectics of Difference.* Madison: University of Wisconsin Press, 1990.

———. *The Borderlands of Culture: Américo Paredes and the Transnational Imaginary.* Durham, NC: Duke University Press, 2006.

Saldívar-Hull, Sonia. *Feminism on the Border: Chicana Gender Politics and Literature.* Berkeley: University of California Press, 2000.

Sanchez-Hucles, Janis, and Alex Dryden. "Race-Based Traumatic Stress." In *Encyclopedia of Trauma: An Interdisciplinary Guide,* edited by Charles R. Figley, 511–13. Thousand Oaks, CA: Sage, 2012. Doi: 10.4135/9781452218595.n172.

Sanchez-Scott, Milcha. *Latina.* In *The Collected Plays of Milcha Sanchez-Scott,* 1–90. Charleston, SC: CreateSpace, 2018.

Sartre, Jean-Paul. *Nausea.* New York: New Directions Publishing, [1937] 2013.

———. *The Emotions.* New York: Philosophical Library, 1948.

"sarx." Accessed February 3, 2015. https://www.biblestudytools.com/lexicons/greek/nas/sarx.html

Scarry, Elaine. *On Beauty and Being Just.* Princeton, NJ: Princeton University Press, 2001.

Scheff, Thomas J. *Bloody Revenge: Emotions, Nationalism, and War.* Lincoln, NE: iUniverse.Com, Inc., [1994] 2000.

———. "Shame and Self in Society." *Symbolic Interaction* 26, no. 2 (2003): 239–62. Doi: 10.1525/si.2003.26.2.23.

———. "The Emotional/Relational World: Shame and the Social Bond." In *Handbook of Sociological Theory,* edited by Jonathan H. Turner, 255–68. New York: Springer, 2006. http://www.soc.ucsb.edu/faculty/scheff/2.html

Schipflinger, Thomas. *Sophia-Maria: A Holistic Vision of Creation.* Translated by James Morgante. York Beach, ME: Samuel Weiser Press, 1998.

Schweik, Susan M. *The Ugly Laws: Disability in Public.* New York: New York University Press, 2009.

Sellers-Young, Barbara. "Breath, Perception, and Action: The Body and Critical Thinking." *Consciousness, Literature, and the Arts* 3, no. 2 (2002): 1–15.

Selye, Hans. "Stress and the General Adaptation Syndrome." *British Medical Journal* 1, no. 4667 (1950): 1383–92.

Serres, Michel. *The Five Senses: A Philosophy of Mingled Bodies.* Translated by Margaret Sankey and Peter Crowley. New York: Continuum International Publishing Group, [1985] 2016.

Shakespeare, Tom. "The Social Model of Disability." *The Disability Studies Reader,* edited by Lennard J. Davis, 197–204. 3rd ed. New York: Routledge, 2010.

Shapiro, Lisa. Introduction to *The Correspondence Between Princess Elisabeth of Bohemia and René Descartes.* Chicago: University of Chicago Press, 2007.

Sheldon, William Herbert, and Stanley Smith Stevens. *The Varieties of Temperament: A Psychology of Constitutional Differences.* New York: Harper Brothers Press, 1942.

Shepherd, Simon. *Theater, Body and Pleasure.* New York: Routledge, 2006.

Shusterman, Richard. *Thinking through the Body: Essays in Somaesthetics.* London: Cambridge University Press, 2012.

Simmel, Georg. "Fashion." *The American Journal of Sociology* 62, no. 6 (1957): 541–58.

Smith, Sidonie, and Julia Watson. *Reading Autobiography: A Guide for Interpreting Life Narratives.* Minneapolis: University of Minnesota Press, [2001] 2010.

Solís, Octavio. *Lydia.* New York: Samuel French, 2010.

Soltero, Carlos R. *Latinos and American Law: Landmark Supreme Court Cases.* Austin: University of Texas Press, 2006.

"soma." Accessed March 1, 2015. https://www.biblestudytools.com/lexicons/greek/nas/soma.html

Somerville, Margaret A., and David J. Rapport. *Transdisciplinarity: Creating Integrated Knowledge*. 1st ed. Montreal, QC: McGill-Queen's University Press, 2002.

Sorisio, Carolyn. *Fleshing Out America: Race, Gender, and the Politics of the Body in American Literature, 1833–1879*. Athens: University of Georgia Press, 2002.

Sproul, R. C. *What We Believe: Understanding and Confessing the Apostles' Creed*. Grand Rapids, MI: Baker, [1973] 2015.

Stamm, R., L. M. A. Akkermans, and V. M. Wiegant. "Trauma and the Gut: Interactions Between Stressful Experience and Intestinal Function." *Gut* 40 (1997): 704–9.

Stavans, Ilan. *The Hispanic Condition: Reflections on Culture and Identity in America*. 2nd ed. New York: HarperCollins, [1995] 2001.

———. *Bandido: The Death and Resurrection of Oscar "Zeta" Acosta*. Evanston, IL: Northwestern University Press, [1995] 2003.

———. *Oscar "Zeta" Acosta: The Uncollected Works*. Houston, TX: Arte Público, 1996.

Stoddart, Michael. *The Scented Ape: The Biology and Culture of Human Odor*. London: Cambridge University Press, 1990.

Stowe, Harriet Beecher. *Uncle Tom's Cabin*. Minneola, NY: Dover Publications, [1852] 2005.

Streeck, Juergen, Charles Goodwin, and Curtis LeBaron. *Embodied Interaction in the Material World: An Introduction*. Cambridge, UK: Cambridge University Press, 2011.

Sullivan, Shannon. *Living across and through Skins: Transactional Bodies, Pragmatism, and Feminism*. Bloomington: Indiana University Press, 2001.

———. *The Physiology of Sexist and Racist Oppression*. Oxford: Oxford University Press, 2015.

Thalburg, Irving. "Visceral Racism." *The Monist* 56, no. 1 (1972): 43–63.

Thomas, Piri. *Down These Mean Streets*. New York: Vintage, [1967] 1997.

Tomkins, Silvan. *Affect Imagery Consciousness: The Complete Edition*. 4 vols. New York: Springer, [1962–92] 2008.

Torres, Hector Avalos. *Conversations with Contemporary Chicana and Chicano Writers*. Albuquerque: University of New Mexico Press, 2007.

Trotter, Thomas. *A View of the Nervous Temperament: Being a Practical Inquiry into the Increasing Prevalence, Prevention, and Treatment of Those Diseases, Commonly Called Nervous, Bilious, Stomach & Liver Complaints, Indigestion, Low Spirits, Gout, &c*. Troy, NY: Wright, Goodenow, & Stockwell, 1808.

Trump, Donald. Acceptance Speech for Republican Presidential Candidate. June 16, 2015. Accessed September 2, 2015. https://www.washingtonpost.com/news/post-politics/wp/2015/06/16/full-text-donald-trump-announces-a-presidential-bid/?noredirect=on&utm_term=.faf634179962

Utsey, Shawn O., N. Giesbrecht, J. Hook, and P. M. Stanard. "Cultural, Sociofamilial, and Psychosocial Resources That Inhibit Psychological Distress in African Americans Exposed to Stressful Life Events and Race-Related Stress." *Journal of Counseling Psychology* 55 (2008): 49–62.

Vacharkulksemsuk, Tanya, and Barbara Fredrickson. "Strangers in Sync: Achieving Embodied Rapport through Shared Movements." *Journal of Experimental Social Psychology* 48, no. 1 (2012): 399–402. Doi: 10.1016/j.jesp.2011.07.015.

Valdez, Luis. *No saco nada de la escuela*. In *Early Works: Actos, Bernabé and Pensamiento Serpentino*, 66–90. Houston: Arte Público Press, [1971] 1990.

Vance, J. D. *Hillbilly Elegy: A Memoir of a Family and a Culture in Crisis*. New York: Harper, 2016.

Van den Stock, Jan, Ruthger Righart, and Beatrice de Gelder. "Bodily Expressions Influence Recognition of Emotions in the Face and Voice." *Emotion* 7, no. 3 (2007): 487–94. Doi: 10.1037/1528-3542.7.3.487.

Vila, Anne C. "The Philosophe's Stomach." In *Cultures of the Abdomen: Diet, Digestion, and Fat in the Modern World*, edited by C. Forth and A. Carden-Coyne, 89–104. New York: Palgrave, 2005.

Viswanathan, Gauri. *Outside the Fold: Conversion, Modernity, and Belief*. Princeton, NJ: Princeton University Press, 1998.

Waterman, Bryan. *Republic of Intellect: The Friendly Club of New York City and the Making of American Literature*. Baltimore, MD: Johns Hopkins University Press, 2007.

Weber, Jean-Jacques. *Language Racism*. New York: Palgrave Macmillan, 2015.

Weber, Max. *The Protestant Ethic and the Spirit of Capitalism*. Translated by Talcott Parsons. Foreword by R. H. Tawney. New York: Dover, [1958] 2003.

Wei, Meifen, Kenneth T. Wang, Puncky Paul Heppner, and Yi Du. "Ethnic and Mainstream Social Connectedness, Perceived Racial Discrimination, and Posttraumatic Stress Symptoms." *Journal of Counseling Psychology* 59, no. 3 (2012): 486–93.

Wolpert, Daniel M., Kenji Doya, and Mitsuo Kawato. "A Unifying Computational Framework for Motor Control and Social Interaction." *Decoding, Imitating, and Influencing the Actions of Others: Mechanisms of Social Interaction*. Series Philosophical Transactions of the Royal Society of London. Series B Biological Sciences, 358, no. 1431 (2003): 593–602.

Wurmser, Léon. *The Mask of Shame*. Baltimore, MD: Johns Hopkins Press, 1981.

———. "Shame: The Veiled Companion of Narcissism." In *The Many Faces of Shame*, edited by Donald Nathansan, 64–92. New York: Guilford Press, 1987.

Zahavi, Dan. *Self and the Other: Exploring Subjectivity, Empathy, and Shame*. Oxford: Oxford University Press, 2014.

Zaidel, Dahlia W. "Consciousness and the Brain: A Window to the Mind." In *Embodied Consciousness: Performance Technologies*, edited by Jade Rosina McCutcheon and Barbara Sellers-Young, 12–27. London: Palgrave, 2013.

Zunshine, Lisa. *Why We Read Fiction: Theory of Mind and the Novel*. Columbus: Ohio State University Press, 2006.

———. "Lying Bodies of the Enlightenment: Theory of Mind and Cultural Historicism." In *Introduction to Cognitive Cultural Studies*, edited by Lisa Zunshine. 115–33. Baltimore, MD: The Johns Hopkins University Press, 2010.

INDEX

Accented America: The Cultural Politics of Multilingual Modernism (Miller), 56
accents, 56–59, 61, 63, 113, 173nn21–22
Acosta, Oscar "Zeta": experiences of intraracialization, 80–82; as Gonzo alter ego, 174n2; as intellectual and writer, 86–88, 174n9; involvement in Chicano Movement, 76–77; literary style of, 66, 69, 76, 77–78, 84, 174–75n13. See also Autobiography of a Brown Buffalo
acting: acting methods, 95–98; portrayal of characters, 64, 91, 93–99, 108, 111–12, 122, 176n4, 177n10; racialized archetypes, 116; theatrical speech, 177n8; use of vocalizations, 102–3
affects, 21, 29, 45, 164, 167n1. See also anger; disgust; dissmell; fear; humiliation; self-loathing; shame and shaming; startle
Ahmed, Sara, 85
Alarcón, Norma, 8
Alcoff, Linda Martín, xvii, 169n14, 174n12
Aldama, Frederick Luis, 23, 78, 111–12, 181n10
Americans with Disabilities Act, 106
anger, 12–14, 85, 171n27. See also affects
Aparicio, Frances, 162
Arai, Mahmood, 172n12

archetypes of racialization, 26, 110–17, 179n30
Arnold, Gottfried, 180n1
art as medium for theology, 124, 126
auditory modality, 39–40, 48–49, 56–65, 97, 107–8, 135, 143–44. See also Song of the Coquí
Augustine of Hippo (saint), 131–32, 151, 181n12
Autobiography of a Brown Buffalo, The (Acosta), 66–89; bathroom scene in, 69–71; erudition and bad stomachs, 86–88; internalized racialization, 75–82, 175n14; mind/body understanding of digestion, 72–74; overview of, 66–69, 174n4, 174n11; race and unrequited childhood love, 82–86

Baartman, Sarah, 181n10
Beats, the, 78, 174n12
Beckett, Samuel, 178n27
Benedict, Ruth, 10–11
Bible: biblical soma, 146–49; fire and brimstone, 127–28; genealogy of gutterals, 102; sarx and somatic states, 147; Sophia, 137; structure of conversion narrative, 181n13; texts on shame, 9; transcendence, 126

202 • INDEX

bilingualism, 58–59
bioenergetic analysis, 45–46
Blair, Rhonda, 96–97, 177n8
Bland, Sandra, 13–14, 170n18, 179n33
blood motif, 149–51, 153, 155
body image and body language, 33–34, 60, 84, 172n8, 172n10
body image management, 95–98, 100, 110–11, 113–14, 121, 176–77n7, 177n9, 179n34
body posture: communication through, xiv, xv, 167n1; and *latinidad*, 5; mirroring, 15; oral character, 14; in psychotherapy, 45; reading comprehension, 31; self-exclusion revealed by, 9; Uncle Remus, 110
body types, 37–38
Boehme, Jacob, 180n1
Bohara, Alok K., 63
Bonilla-Silva, Eduardo, 82
boricua, 5, 168n6
Bost, Suzanne, 5, 99
Brecht, Bertolt, 96
"brittle green teeth" (Montoya), 152
Brown, Claude, 88
Brown, Michael, 145
Brown, terms for, 8, 10
Browning of America, 143–46, 164, 169n9, 182n20
Brownness: Brown Power, 168n2; as capitalist ethic, 11; coercion of, xvii; hearing through accents, 56–57; hypervisibility of, 168n5; self-knowledge of, 162; as shameful form of being, 4, 10, 18
Bruce-Novoa, Juan, 174n4
Bultmann, Rudolf, 147
Bush, George W., 128

Calderón, Héctor, 78, 81, 174nn9, 174nn13
Candelario, Ginetta, 4–5
Carden-Coyne, Ana, 74
Carlin-Metz, Elizabeth, 95
Caroline, or Change (Kushner), 178n28
Carrasquillo, Marci L., 77
Carter, Robert T., 68
Cartesian self, xviii, 76, 78, 86, 138, 169n7. *See also* mind/body linkage
Cervantes, Lorna Dee, 28
Chacón, Daniel, 180n8

Chicano Movement and Chicano Moratorium, 76–77, 132, 135, 176n23
Chican@/x: cultural nationalism, 156, 158; plays featuring domestic workers, 180n35; as term, 167n2, 168n1; texts, 42, 99, 124–25. *See also* identity
Chiu, Monica, 162
Clarissa (Richardson), 172n10
Clark, Van Tilburg, 88
Clinton, Bill, 140–42, 181n17
clothing as source of shaming, 21–22
Coates, Ta-Nehisi, 83–84
Cobas, José A, 4
cognition, xvi, 32–37. *See also* deanimation
Cohen, Charles Lloyd, 139
colonialism, 5, 38, 51, 56
confessions, 151–52
confirmation: in assessing phenotypes, 30, 31; in conversion narrative, 133; description of, 15, 17–18; in Latin@/x texts, 49, 52, 64; use of accents and bilingualism, 57, 58
Connor, Steven, 102, 178n20
contempt, 17, 31, 63
conversion narratives: by colonized peoples, 142–43; Montoya's stages, 131–33; public confessions, 139–43; to revalorize community struggles, 129; somatic portrayals in, 133; structure of, 181n13; unvoiced shame in, 151–56
Cook, Amy, 96–97, 177n8
Cotton, John, 131
Couple in the Cage, The (Gómez-Peña and Fusco), 98–99
Crania Americana (Morton), 38
Cruz, Migdalia, 91
culture, identity, and racism, 37, 68, 89, 99, 117, 144–45

Dale, Thomas, 142
Damasio, Antonio, 95, 176n7
Daubenmire, M. Jean, 120
Davie, Fred, 141
Dávila, Alberto E., 63
deanimation: in assessing phenotypes, 30, 31; description of, 15, 16–17; in Latin@/x texts, 49, 52, 53, 64, 70, 71; use of accents and bilingualism, 57, 58
Deleuze, Gilles, 47

Delgado, Richard, 7, 22
"denial" (Montoya), 159
Descartes, René, 28, 166, 171n2
Dettering, Richard, 88
digestive system, 72–74, 87, 102, 175n18, 177–78n18. See also *Autobiography of a Brown Buffalo*
disability, 90–91, 92, 100, 106, 178n24, 178n27. See also ugly soma
disability studies, 99, 105, 177n13
disabled individuals, 25–26, 30, 92–95, 108, 171n3
disgust, 17–18, 21, 133. See also confirmation
dissmell, 13, 17, 51, 83, 170n17, 175n15
Dollard, John, 52
domestic workers: archetypes of, 26, 109–17, 120; in Chicano plays, 180n35; lived experience of, 122; racialized, 98, 178n28, 180n35; resistance of, 115–16; social invisibility of, 48; work expectations, 119, 121. See also *Lydia*; ugly soma
doppelgangers, 26, 117–23, 180n36
Dowdy, Michale, 182n19
Down These Mean Streets (Thomas), 1–3, 6, 19–21, 36, 81, 168n2
Duany, Jorge, 4
Dunbar, Paul Laurence, 106
dyadic relationships, 120, 180n37

Ekman, Paul, 45, 171n6
Elias, Norbert, 170n26
Elisabeth of Bohemia, xvi, 167n3
Emerson, Ralph Waldo, 88
Emmerich, Anne Catherine, 180n1
emotions *versus* feelings, 170n16
empathy. *See* reading as corporeal process; somatic mirroring; somatic resonance
exceptionalism, 48, 125, 128

Fabian, Ann, 38
Facio, Elisa, 5
Feagin, Joe R., 4, 7
fear, xv, 4, 12, 36, 45, 54, 169n14. See also specific Latin@/x texts
Fear and Loathing in Las Vegas: A Savage Journey to the Heart of the American Dream (Thompson), 77
Ferrus, Diana, 181n10
Fishburn, Katherine, 165

Flesh in the Age of Reason, The (Porter), 104
Fleshing the Spirit: Spirituality and Activism in Chicana, Latina, and Indigenous Women's Lives (Facio and Lara, eds.), 5
foreclosure: in conversion narratives, 134; description of, 15, 18–20, 30, 32; in institutional racism, 81; in Latin@/x texts, 49, 52, 53, 55, 61, 64–65, 70, 80, 84, 91, 115, 122; use of accents and bilingualism, 57, 59
Forth, Christopher E., 74
Foucault, Michel, 105
Freemen's Oath, 139
"fresno night" (Montoya), 158–59
Freud, Sigmund, 54
Fusco, Coco, 98, 177n12

Galen of Pergamum, 72
Galton, Francis, 37
García Lorca, Federico, 88
Garfinkel, Harold, 169n8
Gargantua and Pantagruel (Rabelais), 174n11
Gelder, Beatrice de, 45
George Washington Gómez (Paredes), 42–43
Gichtel, Johann Georg, 180n1
Gilroy, Paul, 21–22
Ginsberg, Allan, 77, 87
Goffman, Erving, 11–12, 169n15, 170n26
Gold, Herb, 88
Gómez-Peña, Guillermo, 98
González, Rigoberto, 130
Gonzo journalistic style, 77–78, 174n2, 174n4, 174n9, 174n13
Grosz, Elizabeth, 169n7
guilt, 10–11, 140, 150, 151, 152
gutteral vocalizations, 102–3, 178n20

Halperin, Laura, 5, 99
Hames-García, Michael, 77, 174n11
Harcup, Tony, 77
Harris, Joel Chandler, 110, 178n28
Harris, Mark, 88
Hart, Allen J., 17
hate speech, 7
Hayakawa, S. I., 88
Haywood, Eliza, 172n10
health and wellness: caregivers and patients, 119–20; digestive system as center of,

72–74; health practitioners, 67; notions of, 37, 72, 73, 74; role of shaming in, 25, 163; society's role in, 85
hearing. *See* auditory modality
Heath-Carter formula, 38
Helms, Dieter, 78
Help, The (film), 178n28
Hernandez v. New York, 58–59
Hildegard of Bingen (saint), 180n1
Hinojosa-Smith, Rolando, 175n21
Hispanic, as term, 10, 169n10
Hongo, Garrett, 130
hooks, bell, 48
Hottentot Venus, 181n10
Houck, Harry, 13–14
human senses and the soma, 28–65; auditory modality, 56–65; deciphering the soma, 44–46; historical practices, 37–39; olfaction, 50–56; sense perception in cognition, 32–37; sight, 46–50; and social intelligence, 29–32; somatic analysis and shaming, 39–44
humiliation, 10, 133, 148, 150
Husserl, Edmund, 34, 171n2

I Don't Have to Show You No Stinking Badges! (Valdez), 180n35
"ice worker considers mercy and grace, the" (Montoya), 151–52, 156
"ice worker in love, the" (Montoya), 136–38, 158
"ice worker sings, the" (Montoya), 135–36
Ice Worker Sings and Other Poems, The (Montoya), 124–60; Biblical soma, 146–49; blood motif in, 149–51; Browning of America, 143–46, 182n20; confession and performative shame, 151–56; critical assessment of, 129–30; love, sex, and spirituality, 137–39; overview of, 132–33; public shaming and US culture, 139–43; racial shame and spiritual signs, 134–37; shaming into silence, 156–59; Sophia and religious conversion, 124–29; US social shaming, 131–34. *See also specific poems*
"ice worker sings of mercy and grace, the" (Montoya), 152–54
identity, xiv, 8, 73–74, 119, 162, 164, 167n2, 168n1. *See also* Brownness
immigrants, 7, 25–26, 52, 60, 98, 109, 110, 172–73n12
"in brown america" (Montoya), 143–46

"in love" (Montoya), 136–37, 144
"in search of aztlán" (Montoya), 134–35, 156
intelligence, as centered in the gut, 72–73, 86–88
intersectional intraracialization: Acosta's experiences of, 81; actors use of somatic expression to elaborate, 92–93, 98; dependence on the soma, 65; of domestic workers, 116; nature of, 90; as subject of *Lydia*, 93, 109. *See also Down These Mean Streets*; *Locas*; *Lydia*; *Song of the Coquí*
intersectional racialization, 78, 98–99, 105–6; concept of, 5; cumulative effect of, 7, 128; four steps of, 90, 135 (*See also* scenes of racialization); in Latin@/x literature, 161; and social equity, 68; and the Sophiatic soma, 129, 137; through the senses (*See* human senses and the soma); through the soma, xiii–xix, 3, 13; as universal practice, 11. *See also Autobiography of a Brown Buffalo*; "in brown america"; intraracialization; "locura"; *Lydia*; shame and shaming
intraracialization: concept of, 90; in Latin@/x texts, 59, 90; steps in, 48–49, 65. *See also* intersectional intraracialization; *Lydia*
"I've Come to Take You Home" (Ferrus), 181n10

Jaggar, Alison M, 12–13
Jiménez Román, Miriam, 1, 3, 168n2
job interview, 33–34
Johnson, Erica, 10

Kahan, Dan M., 142
Kalin, Rudolf, 63
Kaufman, Gershen, 9
Kennedy, John F., 128
Kerouac, Jack, 77
Khimm, Suzy, 142
King, Rodney, 144–45
Knowlton, Brian, 141
Krieger, Nancy, 19
Kushner, Tony, 178n28

La Fountain-Stokes, Larry, 21–22
language. *See* accents; bilingualism; Spanish language
Lara, Irene, 5
Latina (Sanchez-Scott), 180n35

Latina/o, Latin@, Latinx, and Latin@/x as terms of Brownness, xvii, 10, 167n2, 168n1, 168n3. *See also* identity

latinidad, xvii, 5, 10, 99

Latin@/x texts: exceptionalism in, 48; hegemonic thinking about, xvii; as illustrative of racial shaming, 6, 7–8; methodology to study, 22–24; racialization of Latin Americans, 1; scenes of racialization in, xv–xvi; somatic understanding of intersectional racism, 161–62; in US publishing industry, 8; as vibrant, 166. *See also specific texts*

Lead, Lady Jane, 180n1

Leary, Timothy, 77

LeDoux, Joseph E., 36

Lee, Spike, 179n30

"letter to kb, a" (Montoya), 154–56

Lewinsky, Monica, 181n17

Lewis, Helen Block, 170n21, 170n25, 171n27

Lippi-Green, Rosina, 61–63

literary studies, xviii, 29, 35, 65

lived body, the, 28–29, 127, 171n2

Locas (Murray), 46–50

"locura" (Montoya), 156–57

love, sex, and spirituality, 136–39. *See also* sexual love

Love in Excess (Haywood), 172n10

Lowen, Alexander, 9–10, 14–15, 36, 45–46, 164, 173n14

"luciana: this is how i see you" (Montoya), 129–30

Lydia (Solís), 90–123; acting style in, 93–99, 176n4; Ceci's soliloquies, 94, 107–8; Ceci-the-body, 92, 99–103; domestic worker archetypes in, 109–17; doppelgangers, 117–23, 180n36; legacy of the Ugly laws, 103–7; and other plays on disability, 178n27

Lynd, Helen, 170n25

magical Negro, 179n30

magic*o* nanny, 111, 113, 119, 120

magicorealism, 110, 111–12

Mallett, Cassandra, 179n29

Manalansan, Martin F., IV, 51–52

Many Costs of Racism, The (Feagin and McKinney), 7

Martin, Michael, 124–25

Martin, Trayvon, 145

Martín-Rodríguez, Manuel M., 8

Mason, David V., 96, 176n7

Mather, Cotton, 131

Mather, Increase, 131

Mather, Richard, 131

McCarroll, Sarah E., 93

McKinney, Karyn D., 7

Mehrabian, Albert, 172n8

Mendes, Wendy Berry, 101

Méndez, Miguel, 175n21

mental and physical health, 67–68, 104–5. *See also* health and wellness; Ugly Laws

mental schemas, 34–35

"mercy and grace" (Montoya), 156

Merleau-Ponty, Maurice, 28–29, 34, 171n2

Merton, Thomas, 126

Method acting, 95–96, 176n4, 176n5

Mexicans *(mexicanos),* 35, 84, 134, 145–46, 158, 182n19. See also *Lydia*

Mexico, Greater, 134, 158

Miller, Arthur, 91

Miller, Ian, 73, 174n8

Miller, Joshua, 43

Miller, William Ian, 50–51, 56–57

mind/body linkage: historical practice, 37–39, 72, 166, 167n3, 169n7; metaphor of, 169n7; as new line of inquiry, 68; stomach and intelligence, 86–88, 175n20; in Western tradition, 166

Minich, Julie Avril, 99

mirroring. *See* somatic mirroring

Modern History of the Stomach, A (Miller), 73

Montoya, Andrés: artistic agenda, 130, 181n10; education, 125, 180n3; introduction of *brown,* 182n20; legacy, 181nn7–9; placement of poems in *Ice Worker Sings,* 146; uniting poetry with spirituality, 125; use of conversion narrative, 26, 129, 160. *See also The Ice Worker Sings and Other Poems*

Moraga, Cherríe, 91

moral shame, 128, 129, 150, 159–60

Morales, Alejandro, 175n21

Moran, Patricia, 10

Morton, Samuel, 38

Moya, Paula M. L., 29, 34–35

Muñoz, José Esteban, 8, 11, 85, 99

Murray, Xyta Maya, 46–50

Muslims as Mooslims, 10, 11, 32, 146, 171n4

Negrón-Muntaner, Frances, 4–5
"1981" (Montoya), 149–51
No saco nada de la escuela (Valdez), 40–42, 173n13
nonverbal communication, 34, 54, 92–93, 172n8
Nussbaum, Martha, 142

Obama administration, 35
Obama, Barack, 128
olfaction, 50–56, 67. See also dissmell; stink
O'Neill, Eugene, 91
oral character, 14. See also Lowen, Alexander
ordo salutis, 131–32, 133–34, 152, 156, 158, 181nn13–14
Orr, Jackie, 85–86
Other *versus* other, 167n2, 168n1
"out of sight" (Montoya), 134

Padilla, Genaro, 76
pain: physical, 4, 16, 83, 149, 152; psychological and psychosocial, 2, 71; of racialization, 4, 144; of shame, 9–15, 103. See also stress; violence
Paredes, Américo, 42–43
Parra, Angelo, 59–65
Pasricha, Jay, 174n7
persistent vegetative state (PVS), 93, 98, 99–103, 100, 176n2, 177nn14–15
phenomenological theories, 16–17, 34. See also *lived body, the*
phenotypes, 3, 15, 25, 30, 43–44, 47, 60
philosophy of mind (PoM), 35–36
phrenology, 37, 39
Polemon's notions on physiognomy, 87
police, encounters with, 2–4, 13–14, 135, 168n4, 170n18, 179n33
Porter, Roy, 104
prejudice, 6, 43, 47, 63, 89, 108
Problem of Embodiment in Early African American Narrative, The (Fishburn), 165
proper names and naming in racialization, 39–44, 172–73n12
public shaming, 128, 139–43, 182n18

Puritan conversion narrative, 26; and civic participation, 125, 139; confessing sin publicly, 140–41; didactic intent, 131, 133; public confession, 148; and somatic patterns of oppression, 134; use by Montoya, 125–26, 129, 160
Puritanism and American racial shaming, 128, 158

Quarles, Francis, 90, 92, 104

Rabelais, Francois, 174n11
race: historical antecedents of, 38; inferred through the senses, 29, 39; notion of, xvii, 3, 7, 28, 32, 161, 172n10; shame of, 4–5, 170n24; as social construct, 30–31, 44; transacting through somatic expression, xv–xvi. See also intersectional intraracialization; intersectional racialization; intraracialization; racial shaming; scenes of racialization
racial shaming: in Acosta's experience, 83–84; as bidirectional, 55, 56, 113–14; defenses to, 13–14; as enforcer of marginalization, 6–7, 11–12, 26–27; gendered shaming, 48–50, 51–56; intraracial shame, 92; legacy of Puritanism, 128, 134; pain of, xiv–xv; paradigm of and conversion narratives, 133; physical, psychological, and social experience of, 9–10; role of soma in, xvi, 3–7; as shaming into race, 170n24; terminologies of, xvii; through pronunciation, 32, 40–44 (See also accents); through smell, 83; triggers for, 10; as unconscious practice, 12. See also shame
racialization: and disease, 74; historical legitimation of, 38–39; physical ambiguity of, 146; as process, xix, 22; through sense perception, 65 (See also human senses and the soma); use of term, 10. See also intersectional racialization; intraracialization
racism: centrality of in US social relations, 6; colorblind, 82; complicity in, 63; intersectional, xiv, 1, 68, 107, 143–45, 157; use of term, 3; visceral, 12, 51. See also racial shaming
Ramazani, Vaheed, 170n20
Raphael, Lev, 9
rapport, withdrawal of: in assessing phenotypes, 30–31; in conversion narrative,

133; description of, 15–16, 18; in Latin@/x texts, 60, 61, 70; and use of accented English, 57
Rayko, Donald S., 63
reading as corporeal process, 8, 16, 36, 163
Reagan, Ronald, 128
redemption, 26, 126, 132, 138, 148, 151, 154
Reich, Wilhelm, 45
Republic of Intellect: The Friendly Club of New York City and the Making of American Literature (Waterman), 87
Revolt of the Cockroach People, The (Acosta), 77, 176n23
Rice, Kathleen, 142
Righart, Ruthger, 45
Riley, Patrick, 151
Rivera, José, 91
Robinson, Douglas, 96, 176n7, 177n10
Rodriguez, Richard, 10, 18, 145–46, 163–64, 169n9, 173n17
Rosario, Nelly, 51–56
Rosson, Doug, 176n7
Rothman, Joshua, 169n13
Rousseau, Jean-Jacques, 151

Saenz, Rogelio, 63
Saint Martin, Louis-Claude, 180n1
Salazar, Rubén, 51
Saldívar, Ramón, 6, 43, 78
salvation, order of. See *ordo salutis*
Sanchez-Scott, Milcha, 180n35
Sandra Bland Bill, 170n18
Sartre, Jean-Paul, 34, 149–50
sarx, 146–47
Scarlet Letter, The (Hawthorne), 170n19
Scarry, Elaine, 178n22
scenes of racialization: cultural extension of shaming, 169n8; human senses as key to, 24–25, 65; interpretation of, 162; in Latin@/x texts, 7–8; in public policies, 32; soma as strategy in, 21–22; steps in, 15–21, 30–32, 133; theoretical concept of, xv–xvi. See also confirmation; deanimation; foreclosure; rapport, withdrawal of
Scheff, Thomas J., 18, 22, 170n25
Scheler, Max, 16
Schweik, Susan, 104–6, 178n23

scientific studies and theories, 23–24, 35, 161
Searles, Sharon, 120
self-loathing, 75–82, 133, 148, 154, 160
self-marginalization, 47–48, 49, 64
Sellers-Young, Barbara, 177n10
sense making, xvii–xviii, 3, 163, 166
sense perception, 29–32, 30, 32–37, 44, 145–46. See also auditory modality; human senses and the soma; olfaction; sight and the visual
Serres, Michel, 29, 37, 42, 102
sexual love and desire: and domestic workers, 117; and human connection, 147; in *Lydia*, 103, 108, 118–21; and Sophia, 127, 136–39, 147. See also *Autobiography of a Brown Buffalo, The*; *Song of the Coquí*; *Song of Water Saints*
sexuality, 78–80
shame and shaming: as anger, 171n27; as endemic to Brownness, 18; feeling through vocalizations, 103; *versus* guilt, 11; in-group shaming, 169n13; internalization of social defectiveness, 150; and Monica Lewinsky, 181n17; Montoya's use of term, 154–55; as moral deterrent, 142; pain of, 9–15, 22; in Puritan conversion narrative, 26, 128; social logic of, 131–34; societal expectation, 170n19; sociological studies of, 170n25; through somatic racialization, 22; unvoiced, 152. See also public shaming; racial shaming
shame of race, studies of, 4–5
Sheldon, William Herbert, 37–38
Shepard, Sam, 91
"sight" (Montoya), 135, 156
sight and the visual, 30, 39, 46–50, 67
"silence" (Montoya), 156–58
Silverman-Chavez, Susana, 162
Simmel, Georg, 170n26
smell. See dissmell; olfaction; stink
social intelligence, 29–32
"sofía" (Montoya), 136–37
Solís, Octavio. See *Lydia*
Soltero, Carlos R., 58
soma: Biblical, 146–49; as communicator of deep feelings and truth, 33, 85, 92–93, 172n7; concept of, xiii, xv, 28, 66; deciphering, 44–46; intentionality of, 172n10; and Latin@/x hyperphysical-

ity, 163; and Method acting, 95–99; as site of subjectivity, xvi, xvii, xviii, 2, 23; Sophiatic, 127–29, 154–55; as strategy, 21–22; suppression of, 25–26, 113–14, 115, 179n34; as whole body knowledge, 180n2. *See also* human senses and the soma; ugly soma

soma's role in racialization: in *Down These Mean Streets*, 1–2, 4, 5, 16, 17, 19–21; in literary scenes of racialization, 7–8, 15–22; methodology for study, 22–24; overview of chapters, 24–27; pain of shame, 9–15; police beating video, 2–4; role of shaming in, 3–7

somatic analysis, xvii, 8, 27, 28–29, 39–44, 166

somatic dissonance, 16, 48, 60, 133. *See also* rapport, withdrawal of

somatic expression: author's childhood experience, xv; of bodily affect, 102, 178n19; of cadavers, 154–55, 157–58; in Clinton's address, 140–41; in the digestive system, 71 (see also *Autobiography of a Brown Buffalo, The*); of Donald Trump, 32; as embodied in cultural paradigms and customs, 37; as ephemeral, xvi; of fear, 36; masochism and oral character, 14–15; scholarly study of, xvii–xviii; of singing, 135; Sophiatic *versus* Puritan, 127–28; of threat, 2. *See also* contempt; disgust; redemption

somatic mirroring, 15–16, 18, 31, 163, 170n21

somatic portrayal, 95–103, 112

somatic resonance, 8, 16, 19, 31, 57

somatotypes, 37–38

Song of Songs, 126, 180n4

Song of the Coquí (Parra), 59–65

Song of Water Saints (Rosario), 51–56

Sophia: as bridge between sinner and redeemer, 154–55; as figure in Christianity, 26, 125, 126, 160, 180n6; intercession between sarx and Biblical soma, 147; love, sex, and spirituality, 135–39; as Sofía, racialized Chicana, 137–38

Sophiatic soma, 154–55

Sophiology, 126, 127, 180n1

Spanish language, 58, 80–81. *See also Song of the Coquí*

spirituality, 124

Stanislavski, Konstantin, 95

startle, 3, 13, 30–31, 45, 81, 100

Stavans, Ilan, 81, 88

Stefancic, Jean, 7, 22

Stevens, John Paul, 58

stink, 50, 55–56, 67, 83, 175n15

stomach. *See* digestive system

Stowe, Harriet Beecher, 179n29

stress, 34, 74, 85–86, 174n3, 175n16, 175n18. *See also* digestive system; trauma

subaltern realist style, 67–71, 78

subjectivity: and human communication, 161; in the physical body, 73–74, 77–78; of a PVS sufferer, 121–22; reciprocity of, 119; soma as site of, xiii, xvi, xvii, xviii, 2, 23, 33; and somatic analysis, xvii

Sullivan, Shannon, 101

talk shows (television), 141

Taylor, Diana, 177n12

Taylor, Tate, 178n28

Teatro Campesino, 175n21

telepathy, 118–19, 180n37

Thalburg, Irving, 12

theology, 124, 126, 138–39

theories of mind (ToM), 35–36

Thomas, Piri: about, 1–2; nondeferential somatic expression of, 13; pain of racialization, 4, 6; withdrawal of rapport, 16, 36, 81, 88, 168n2, 173n17. *See also Down These Mean Streets*; intersectional intraracialization

Thompson, Hunter S., 67, 77, 174n2

Thomson, Rosemarie Garland, 105, 177n13

Thoreau, Henry David, 88

Thoursie, Peter Skogman, 172n12

Tomkins's theory of affects: body semiotics, 9–10, 164; contempt, disgust, and dissmell, 17, 51, 164, 170n17, 175n15; contribution to psychotherapy, 44, 45; humiliation, 150; range of affects, 173nn14–15; semiotics of racial shaming, 15; universality of feelings, 167n1, 170n16

Torres, Gerald, xviii

Torres, Hector A., 163

transcendence, 126, 129, 130, 147

transdisciplinary analysis, 22–24, 161–66, 168n5, 171nn28–29

trauma, 14–15, 46, 68–69, 85–86, 170n20, 173n14, 174n3, 178n19

Treaty of Guadalupe de Hidalgo, 158

tropicalization of texts, 162

Trotter, Thomas, 87

Trump, Donald, 32, 35
Tuke, William, 105

Ugly Betty (television program), 178n26
Ugly Laws, 103–7, 178n23, 178n26
ugly soma, 90, 98–99, 103, 106, 122, 178n23, 178n25. See also *Lydia*
Uncle Remus, 110–11, 178–79n28, 179nn29–30
Uncle Tom's Cabin (Stowe), 111, 179n29
US culture, role of shaming in, 11, 139–43. *See also* Puritan conversion narrative; shame and shaming: *versus* guilt

Valdez, Luis, 40–42, 173n13, 175n21, 180n35
Van den Stock, Jan, 45
Vance, J. D., 169n13
Ventura, Melissa, 145
View of the Nervous Temperament, A (Trotter), 87

Villanueva, Pedro, 145
violence, 38, 149–51, 153–54, 156–59
vision. *See* sight and the visual
Voltaire, 175n20

Waterman, Bryan, 87
Weber, Max, 124
Weiskopf, Dan A., 172n11
Whitman, Walt, 88
Williams, Tennessee, 91, 178n27
Wirz, Johann Jacob, 180n1
Wolfe, Gregory, 138
Wright, Richard, 88

Zahavi, Dan, 16–17
Zaidel, D. W., 96
Zunshine, Lisa, 172n10

COGNITIVE APPROACHES TO CULTURE
FREDERICK LUIS ALDAMA, PATRICK COLM HOGAN,
LALITA PANDIT HOGAN, AND SUE J. KIM, SERIES EDITORS

This series takes up cutting edge research in a broad range of cognitive sciences insofar as this research bears on and illuminates cultural phenomena such as literature, film, drama, music, dance, visual art, digital media, and comics, among others. For the purpose of the series, "cognitive science" is construed broadly to encompass work derived from cognitive and social psychology, neuroscience, cognitive and generative linguistics, affective science, and related areas in anthropology, philosophy, computer science, and elsewhere. Though open to all forms of cognitive analysis, the series is particularly interested in works that explore the social and political consequences of cognitive cultural study.

Shaming into Brown: Somatic Transactions of Race in Latina/o Literature
STEPHANIE FETTA

Resilient Memories: Amerindian Cognitive Schemas in Latin American Art
ARIJ OUWENEEL

Permissible Narratives: The Promise of Latino/a Literature
CHRISTOPHER GONZÁLEZ

Literatures of Liberation: Non-European Universalisms and Democratic Progress
MUKTI LAKHI MANGHARAM

Affective Ecologies: Empathy, Emotion, and Environmental Narrative
ALEXA WEIK VON MOSSNER

A Passion for Specificity: Confronting Inner Experience in Literature and Science
MARCO CARACCIOLO AND RUSSELL T. HURLBURT

www.ingramcontent.com/pod-product-compliance
Lightning Source LLC
Chambersburg PA
CBHW030136240426
43672CB00005B/152